AI-Powered Insurance

Exploring New Frontiers

Editors

Gulbir Singh

Department of Computer Science and Engineering
Graphic Era Hill University, Haldwani Campus
Nainital, Uttarakhand, India

Om Prakash Dubey

Department of Mathematics, J. J. College
Veer Kunwar Singh University
Ara, Bhojpur, Bihar, India

Efrén Mezura-Montes

Artificial Intelligence Research Institute
University of Veracruz
Veracruz, Mexico

CRC Press
Taylor & Francis Group
Boca Raton London New York

CRC Press is an imprint of the
Taylor & Francis Group, an **informa** business
A SCIENCE PUBLISHERS BOOK

Cover credit: Editors generated the image using ChatGPT.

First edition published 2027
by CRC Press
2385 NW Executive Center Drive, Suite 320, Boca Raton FL 33431

and by CRC Press
4 Park Square, Milton Park, Abingdon, Oxon, OX14 4RN

CRC Press is an imprint of Taylor & Francis Group, LLC

Library of Congress Cataloging-in-Publication Data (applied for)

ISBN: 978-1-041-04239-6 (hbk)
ISBN: 978-1-041-06834-1 (pbk)
ISBN: 978-1-003-63730-1 (ebk)

DOI: 10.1201/9781003637301

Typeset in Palatino Linotype
by Prime Publishing Services

Foreword

In an era defined by rapid technological progress and data-centric decision-making, the insurance industry stands on the threshold of a profound transformation. Artificial Intelligence (AI)—once a distant concept confined to the realm of theoretical computer science—has now emerged as a powerful catalyst, reshaping the very foundations of how risk is assessed, policies are designed, and customer relationships are nurtured. This volume, *AI-Powered Insurance: Exploring New Frontiers*, offers a comprehensive, critical, and forward-looking examination of the ways in which AI is redefining the insurance ecosystem and, in doing so, shaping the future of financial security and risk management.

The significance of this work lies in its interdisciplinary breadth and analytical depth. The chapters collectively illuminate how AI and its allied technologies—including machine learning, natural language processing, predictive analytics, blockchain, and the Internet of Things—are revolutionizing every aspect of insurance operations. From underwriting and claims management to fraud detection, personalized policy design, and customer engagement, AI is enabling insurers to transition from a reactive "detect and repair" model to a proactive "predict and prevent" paradigm. This shift represents more than a technological upgrade; it signifies a fundamental reimagining of the insurance value chain and its role in a rapidly digitizing global economy.

Equally noteworthy is the authors' commitment in engaging with the broader implications of this transformation. Beyond the technical and operational dimensions, this book explores the ethical, regulatory, and socio-economic challenges that accompany AI integration. Issues such as data privacy, algorithmic bias, explainability, and regulatory compliance are addressed not as peripheral concerns but as central pillars of a sustainable and equitable AI-driven insurance landscape. The emphasis on responsible innovation—one that balances technological advancement with transparency, accountability, and fairness—enriches the discourse and underscores the importance of human-centric governance in the age of intelligent systems.

Moreover, this volume situates its analyses within a global context, drawing on empirical evidence, case studies, and theoretical frameworks to demonstrate how AI is being applied across diverse insurance markets and demographic segments. The insights offered here are not only academically rigorous but also practically relevant, making the text a valuable resource for scholars, practitioners, policymakers, and students seeking to understand and shape the future trajectory of the insurance sector.

As we move deeper into the fourth industrial revolution, it is increasingly clear that the convergence of data, computation, and intelligent algorithms will continue to redefine industries and institutions. Insurance, with its unique mandate to manage uncertainty and safeguard societal resilience, will be at the forefront of this transformation. *AI-Powered Insurance: Exploring New Frontiers* provides both a scholarly foundation and a visionary outlook for navigating this evolving landscape. It challenges readers to think critically, act responsibly, and innovate boldly as they engage with the opportunities and complexities of AI in the insurance domain.

I commend the authors for their thoughtful and comprehensive contribution to the literature and am confident that this book will serve as an essential reference for those committed to advancing research, policy, and practice in this rapidly evolving field.

Gulbir Singh
Om Prakash Dubey
Efrén Mezura-Montes

Preface

The insurance industry has long been regarded as a cornerstone of financial stability, a system designed to safeguard individuals, businesses, and societies against uncertainty. Yet, in the 21st century, the industry is undergoing a transformation more profound than any it has experienced in its centuries-long history. At the heart of this transformation lies Artificial Intelligence (AI)—a technological force that is redefining how risks are assessed, policies are designed, claims are processed, and customers are engaged. It is against this backdrop that *AI-Powered Insurance: Exploring New Frontiers* was conceived—to examine, explain, and envision the ways in which AI is reshaping the insurance landscape.

This book is the culmination of an effort to bridge the gap between technological innovation and its practical implications for the insurance ecosystem. While numerous studies have explored the potential of AI in sectors such as healthcare, finance, and manufacturing, its applications in insurance remain comparatively underexplored in academic literature. This volume aims to fill that gap by providing a comprehensive, interdisciplinary perspective that combines theoretical foundations, technological advancements, practical implementations, and future possibilities.

At its core, the book is organized around the transformative capabilities of AI across the insurance value chain. It explores how technologies such as machine learning, natural language processing, predictive analytics, computer vision, and blockchain are enabling insurers to transition from a reactive "detect and compensate" model to a proactive "predict and prevent" paradigm. Through detailed discussions, empirical analyses, and real-world case studies, it illustrates how AI is being used to personalize policies, automate claims, detect fraud, improve underwriting accuracy, enhance customer engagement, and optimize operational efficiency.

However, this transformation is not without its complexities. The adoption of AI in insurance raises critical questions around data privacy, ethical governance, algorithmic bias, and regulatory compliance. These issues are explored throughout the book, emphasizing that the future of AI-powered insurance must balance technological advancement with accountability, fairness, and trust. Moreover, as the industry evolves, it must also address challenges related to workforce transformation, customer transparency, and the social implications of increasingly data-driven decision-making.

This book is intended for a diverse readership—scholars and researchers seeking to deepen their understanding of AI's role in financial services; policymakers and regulators striving to develop frameworks that ensure responsible innovation; practitioners and industry leaders aiming to implement AI-driven solutions; and students aspiring to enter a rapidly evolving field at the intersection of technology and risk management.

Writing this book has been an intellectually rewarding journey, made possible through extensive research, collaboration, and the generous sharing of insights by industry experts and academic peers. It is our hope that *AI-Powered Insurance: Exploring New Frontiers* will serve as both a foundational text and a forward-looking guide—one that informs, inspires, and empowers readers to actively shape the future of insurance in the age of intelligent systems.

We believe that the convergence of AI and insurance represents not merely a technological shift but a paradigm change—one that will redefine how societies understand and manage risk in the decades to come. As we stand on the cusp of this new era, this book invites readers to explore the opportunities, challenges, and innovations that will shape the next chapter of insurance.

Gulbir Singh
Om Prakash Dubey
Efrén Mezura-Montes

Content

Chapter 1

Introduction to AI in Insurance & Transforming Insurance

Kirti Vasdev,[1] *Tejinder Kaur,*[2,*] *Vivek Bhatnagar,*[2] *Anima Bag,*[3]
Manmeet Singh[4] and *Jaya Sharma*[5]

Introduction to AI in Insurance

Knowing about AI

Artificial Intelligence (AI) is defined as the simulation of human intelligence in machines that are organized to learn, think, and perform tasks normally that requires human intelligence (Alt et al., 2020). These comprises of various modes for solving problems, decision-making, judgment-calls, comprehension of spoken language, and pattern recognition. AI covers range of technologies such as machine learning, computer vision, NLP (Natural Language Processing), and robotics, that make machines operate independently and logically (Alt et al., 2020).

[1] Distinguished Engineer, Network Engineering, Verizon Data Services, Tampa, FL 33637. Email: kirtivasdev12@gmail.com

[2] Department of MMICTBM, Maharishi Markaneshwar (Deemed to be University), Mullana, Ambala, Haryana, India. Email: bhatnagar.78@gmail.com

[3] Department of Statistics Rama Devi Women's University, Bhubaneswar, Odisha, India. Email: animabag2025@gmail.com

[4] Mechanical Engineering department, Maharshi markandeshwar (Deemed to be University, Mullana, Ambala, Haryana, India. Email: manmeetynr@gmail.com

[5] Department of Management (MMIM), Maharishi Markandeshwar Deemed to be University, Mullana, Ambala, Haryana, India. Email: jaya.sharma@mmumullana.org

* Corresponding author: teji7890@gmail.com

DOI: 10.1201/9781003637301-1

Overview of the Insurance Industry

The insurance industry is one of the critical sectors in the global economy, offering risk management solutions and financial protection to humans, associations and governments (Corcoles et al., 2019). By giving coverage for a wide range of risks, such as accidents, natural disasters, health issues, and business interruptions, it helps in diminishing the impression of unpredictable incidents. The industry can be broadly categorized into several types of insurance such as Life insurance, health insurance, Reinsurance, etc. Claim management, risk management, underwriting, and customer service are considered as the various essential roles of the insurance industry. This sector is dynamic, continually adjusting to new risks, technological advancements, as well as changes in the expectations of customers. Its coming time is being shaped in great part by Artificial Intelligence (AI) and digital transformation, which are polishing up customer satisfaction, efficiency, and accuracy (Dietzmann et al., 2020).

Importance of AI in Modern Insurance

Artificial Intelligence (AI) has greatly put its impact on the insurance industry by modifying traditional processes, enhancing customer experiences, and improving risk management. AI is indispensable in modern insurance because it constringe the accuracy, efficiency, along with customer satisfaction. As it provides improved underwriting and risk assessment, operational efficiency, streamlined claim processing, and many more, it is regarded as an essential part of modern insurance. By utilizing AI, insurance companies can quickly remain competitive, innovate their product offerings, and manage risks more effectively (Faraj et al., 2018).

History and Evolution of AI in Insurance

Early Uses of AI

Over time, the integration of Artificial Intelligence (AI) in the insurance industry has evolved with early applications laying the foundation for today's advanced uses are being seen. Below we are going to discuss some of the pioneering applications of AI in the insurance sector (Hukal et al., 2020).

Expert Systems: Expert systems that are an early form of AI were integrated to emulate the abilities of decision-making of people underwriters.

Pattern Recognition: Artificial Intelligence was in employment to test past claims data and spots patterns with fraud activities.

Virtual Assistants and Chat bots: Development of basic AI-driven chat bots to handle queries of common customers, assists with simple exchanges, and gives guidance about policies.

Data Mining: To uncover insights from large datasets, insurers have found a way of utilizing AI for data mining (Kannan and Bernoff, 2019).

Prediction of Health Analytics: Based on past medical data, early AI applications in health insurance are involved in diagnosing health risks and outcomes.

Analysis of Document: AI technologies like optical character recognition (OCR) were helping in reducing the time and effort linked with manual data entry by automating the process of information extraction from paper-based claims forms and other documents. These early applications of AI in insurance were involved in flaunting AI's ability to enhance efficiency, correctness, and services to customer. They set the way for more complex AI technologies and unconventional analytics that are still transfiguring the insurance industry in today's era (Kraus et al., 2020).

Technological Milestones

The application of Artificial Intelligence (AI) in the insurance industry has been noticeable by numerous significant technological milestones. These advancements have had a great impact by improving the capabilities of insurers, transformed traditional processes and driven innovation. Here we are going to discuss some of the notable milestones:

Expert Systems (1980s–1990s): Rule-Based Automation: Early AI systems using predefined rules to automate underwriting and risk assessment.

Machine learning (1990s–2000s): Frauds Detecting Algorithms used to analyze data and identify patterns of different fraud activities.

Natural Language Processing (NLP) (2000s): Chat bots and virtual assistants were developed for improved interaction between customers.

Predictive Analytics (2000s): Utilization of historical data and models to forecast risks and optimize pricing (Mikalef et al., 2020).

Telemetric and IOT (2010s): Real-time monitoring of driving behavior for personalized premiums.

Computer Vision (2010s): Analysis of images and videos for automated damage assessment.

Deep Learning (2010s–2020s): Enhancement in accuracy in fraud detection and risk assessment.

Advanced NLP: Better understanding and generation of human language for customer service.

AI-Driven Personalization (2020s): Reshaped insurance products based on customer data analysis (Park et al., 2021).

Current Trends and Innovations

AI is the biggest catalyst in reshaping this industry, and now there are trends & innovations which are responsible for transforming insurance sector. Digital transformation easily connects and manages customer relationships in addition to becoming more efficient through e-commerce or online operations. The personalization driven by AI has played a great role in enabling customized policies and targeted marketing, while Insure tech integration allows innovation via collaborations with technology startups .It leverages predictive analytics and enhanced detection of fraud activities for improved security and better risk prediction, all credit goes to powerful algorithms combined with real-time monitoring. AI chatbots and virtual assistants have played a great role in achieving enhanced customer service, providing 24/7 support. The use of telematics and IOT supports continuous risk monitoring and usage-based insurance. In addition to this, automated compliance ensures regulatory adherence and transparency. Emphasizing sustainability, insurers are integrating environmental, social, and governance (ESG) criteria into their strategies and developing green insurance products. These trends focus on the essential role of AI in upgrading efficiency, customer satisfaction, and competitiveness in the insurance sector (Park et al., 2021).

Key AI Technologies Used in Insurance

The insurance field has been revolutionized by different AI technologies as it enhances efficiency, improves customer experience, and enables better risk assessment. Here are some key AI technologies which are used in insurance sector.

Machine Learning Detection of Frauds

Algorithms of machine learning analyze large datasets for recognizing anomalies and patterns that indicates different scams (Zarifis and Cheng, 2021).

Underwriting: Analyzing various data points, helping underwriters to make more informed decisions, also helping ML models to assess risk.

Natural Language Processing (NLP)

Customer Service: Use of NLP by chatbots and virtual assistants to interact with customers, answer queries, and process claims, providing all time support and decreasing response times.

Processing of Document: Natural Language Processing helps in retrieving and processing information from policy documents, claim forms, and other text-heavy documents, streamlining administrative tasks.

Computer Vision

Claims Processing: For claims such as property damage or auto accidents, image and Video analysis offer faster and more accurate claim statements.

Risk Assessment: Assessing risks in property by looking over satellite images or drone Footages.

Predictive Analytics Risk Management

With the help of predictive models, insurers are easily forecasting potential risks and losses for pricing policies more accurately and managing their risk portfolios effectively.

Customer Retention: Examining behavior of customer to predict churn and invent methods for retention, like targeted communication and personalized offers (Zarifis and Cheng, 2021).

Robotic Process Automation (RPA) Claims Handling: Automating repetitive tasks such as data entry, verification, and routing in claims processing helps in speeding up the claims lifecycle and cut operational expenses.

Policy Management: Streamlining policy administration tasks such as renewals, endorsements and cancellations, improving operational effectiveness.

Block chain Smart Contracts: Automating the execution of insurance contracts when predefined conditions are satisfied, decreasing the requirement for intermediaries and speeding up claims processing.

Preventing Frauds: Offering a secure, transparent ledger for verifying claims and putting a stop on fraud by guaranteeing data integrity and detectability.

AI-Driven Insights Customer Insights: Enhancing product offerings, marketing strategies, and customer service via analyzing customer data to gain insights into preferences and behaviors.

Risk Insights: With the use of AI for analyzing trends and external factors affecting risk, like climate change or economic shifts that are helping insurers to adjust their risk models and strategies.

Telemetric and IOT Usage-Based Insurance: Gathering real-time data from IOT devices, such as car telemetric, to provide personalized insurance based on actual usage, driving behavior, and mileage.

Health Monitoring: Using wearable devices to monitor health measurements, influencing health and life insurance policies by offering data-driven insights into policyholders' health.

Applications of AI in Insurance

Underwriting

AI algorithms analyze data from various sources (e.g., medical records, financial history) for assessing risk and determining premiums. Machine learning models predict potential risks and future claims based on past data, helping insurers in making more informed decisions.

Claims Processing

AI systems offering help in encounter in gun usual patterns and flag potentially false claims by analyzing large datasets in real time. AI-powered chat bots and virtual assistants streamline the claims process, reducing the time taken to process claims and improving customer satisfaction.

Fraud Detection and Prevention

In the insurance industry, fraud detection and prevention are critical areas where AI can provide fundamental benefits. Deep learning models can detect complex patterns and correlations in data that might be missing in the case of traditional methods. AI uses biometric data (e.g., facial recognition, fingerprint scanning) for verifying the identity of claimants and policyholders, reducing identity fraud. Continuous monitoring of transactions and activities provide help to detect potential fraud early and prevent it before it rises.

Customer Service and Support

AI powered chat bots handle routine inquiries, provide policy information, and guide customers through claim submissions; enhancing customer experience. AI analyzes customer data to provide personalized policy recommendations and offers, improving engagement of customers and retention.

Risk Assessment and Management

AI for property and casualty insurance; AI predicts potential maintenance issues, reducing the likelihood of claims AI models predict the impact of natural disasters, allowing insurers to better manage their risk exposure and prepare for potential claims (Zarifis et al., 2021).

Benefits of AI in Insurance

Insurance industry has been gaining a numerous benefit with the use of AI technologies, transforming various aspects of the business to improve efficiency, customer satisfaction, and overall performance. Here are some of the key benefits:

Efficiency and Cost Reduction

Robotic Process Automation (RPA) handles repetitive tasks such as data entry and document processing, reducing operational costs and human error. AI tools manage and analyze large sets of data, providing actionable insights and supporting better decision-making. By automating routine processes and improving accuracy, insurers are getting AI help in reducing operational costs.

Improved Accuracy and Decision Making

AI significantly enhances accuracy and decision-making in the insurance industry, leading to better risk management, improved customer service, and greater operational efficiency. At the end, these improvements ultimately contribute to the overall successfulness and competitiveness of insurance companies.

Enhanced Customer Experience AI chat bots provide round-the-clock customer services, handling questions, and updating policies efficiently. AI analyzes customer data to offer personalized recommendations and tailored solutions, improving customer engagement and loyalty. To quickly analyze and respond to customer queries, AI is considered essential, helping in reducing wait times and enhancing service quality (Zarifis et al., 2021).

Better Risk Management AI plays a great role in significant advancement of risk management in the insurance industry by enhancing risk assessment, prediction, and mitigation capabilities. These developments lead to added effective and proactive risk management plans, ultimately contributing to the insurer's financial stability and competitiveness.

Challenges and Limitations

The potential of AI has led to the significant transformations in the insurance industry, providing advantages like enhanced efficiency, personalized services, and improved risk assessment. However, there are so many challenges and limitations that needs to be kept in mind to realize its full potential:

Data Security and Privacy

In the insurance industry, these data security and privacy challenges are mandatory for the successful and ethical deployment of AI that needs to be handled carefully. There are some demanding regulations for data privacy such as GDPR in Europe and CCPA in California, with which insurance companies must comply. These laws can be used for mandating the handling strictly, processing, and storing the personal data, limiting the use of sensitive customer information for AI training and making decisions. The use of AI in insurance comprises of storing and processing large volumes of sensitive information, that will be regarded as a prime target for hacks. It is essential to have strong cyber security safeguards in place to prevent data breaches. Making the use of safe methods for data storage and transmission is necessary to secure sensitive information from unauthorized access during the AI processing stages (Zarifis et al., 2021; Singh et al., 2024).

Ethical and Regulatory Concerns

Focusing on these ethical and regulatory concerns are important for the deployment of AI responsibly in the insurance industry, ensuring that it is satisfying both companies and customers while preserving trust and compliance. AI systems can lead to unfair treatment of certain groups because of in meriting biases from their training data There raise ethical questions due to the extent to which AI should be allowed to make autonomous decisions, particularly in critical areas. Establishing and maintaining trust with customers is very important. Misuse or perceived misuse of AI can destroy trust and put a question mark on the reputation of insurance companies. The insurance industry is heavily regulated, and AI applications need to abide with existing regulations. This consists of adherence to regulations that are industry specific, as well as privacy laws such as GDPR and CCPA. To develop and implement standardized methods for AI in insurance, it is necessary to provide guarantee regarding consistency and reliability. Governance frameworks must be established by the Regulatory bodies to inspect the deployment and utilization of Artificial Intelligence. To monitor and audit AI systems continuosly is needed, to ensure they run within legal and ethical boundaries. The regulators need to enforce routine supervision and evaluation.

Implementation Costs and Complexity

There is a requirement of a significant initial investment in technology, software, and hardware for implementing AI solutions in insurance. This consists of the cost of AI platforms, data storage solutions, and high-performance computing resources. Hiring skilled professionals with expertise in AI, data science, and insurance is expensive. Due to the high demand for these skills, it has lead to competitive salaries and difficulties in recruitment challenges. To ensure to keep the existing staff up and running effectively with AI technologies, regular training and development programs are necessary. Strengthening the skills of employees in data management, AI ethics, and new operational processes all are a part of this. There are so many insurance firms that operate on legacy systems, may not be aligned with the latest technologies of Artificial Intelligence. This task of infiltrating AI into these systems can be challenging and time-consuming, requiring various overhauls and tweaks. High-quality and well-organized data is the basic requirement of effective AI implementation. Introducing AI within an organization consists of significant modifications to existing workflows, processes, and culture. To handle resistance from employees and ensure a smooth transition, effective change in management strategies are essential.

Resistance to Change within Organizations

For the implementation of AI in insurance, companies often face number of factors that make doing so challenging When it comes to insurance companies using AI, there are several factors that make doing so challenging and many different points within the organization push back against such implementation. There may be some employees who fear job loss or are unconvinced about the security and rightness of AI systems, leading to unwillingness in favoring upcoming technologies. In addition to this, there can be a lack of awareness regarding the benefits and functionality of AI that results in reluctance to move away from traditional processes and adaptation of new ones. Organizational cultures may get hampered with the adoption of AI that value customs and traditions. To get a control over this resistance and promote an innovative culture, it is imperative to implement effective change management strategies, such as education, employee involvement in the transition process, and understandable communication.

Case Studies and Real-World Examples

These case studies tell how AI can alter various aspects of the insurance industry, from customer service and personalized pricing to detection of frauds and processing of claims. By applying AI facts, insurance companies can enhance efficiency, reduce costs, and offer improved services to their customers.

Lemonade Insurance

Overview: Lemonade is one of the digital insurance companies which leverage AI and behavioral economics to offer homeowner's and renter's insurance.

AI Application: AI chat bots are used by Lemonade for tackling customer interactions, from on boarding to claims processing. Their AI, named "Maya," can approve claims by taking a very less time.

Impact: Lemonade has significantly decreased operating costs and increased customer satisfaction with quick, effective service by automating claims processing and underwriting.

Zurich Insurance's Fraud Detection

Overview: Zurich Insurance has integrated AI to confront with various scams that has been occurring.

AI Application: Zurich analyzes claims data using AI to mark the trends that point to possible crimes. The system looks at a lot of variables and marks claims that are found to be suspicious so that they can be investigated more.

Impact: Zurich's-powered fraud detection system can pick out and block the various fault activities lessening financial losses and enhancing the integrity of their claims process.

"Ask Emma"- AXA's Virtual Assistant (Zarifis et al., 2021).

Overview: For upgrading the services provided to clients, a global insurance company - AXA, a virtual assistant has been developed called as "Ask Emma".

AI Application: Ask Emma makes the use of natural language processing (NLP) to understand and reply to customer queries in real-time. It helps with policy information, claim status, and other common inquiries of customer.

Impact: By giving prompt, accurate responses, it is decreasing the strain on human customer support representatives, and gaining the overall customer satisfaction, along with improved customer engagement by virtual assistant.

Future Trends and Predictions

Emerging AI Technologies Natural Language Processing (NLP) and Conversational AI

NLP is enabling AI systems for understanding, interpreting, and giving responses to human language, magnifying customer connections with each other and automating textual data inspection. Virtual assistants, automated claims processing, policy queries, sentiment analysis, and chat bots are used for providing services to clients. Chatbots that are driven by NLP are in use by businesses such as AXA and Lemonade to handle customer enquiries and claims, along with giving prompt and error-free answers to their queries.

Deep Learning and Machine Learning (ML)

AI systems can learn from past data and with time it will get superior in making decisions and predictions, all credit goes to machine learning and deep learning. 'Allstate' increases the precision and speed of processing claims by coming in touch with ML models to predict repair costs from vehicle damage photos.

Computer Vision

By using computer vision to interpret and analyze visual data from photos and videos, Artificial intelligence (AI) can automatically evaluate visual information. Progressive's Snapshot program makes the use of computer vision and cameras and sensors to assess behavior of driver and usage of vehicle.

Voice Recognition and Assistants

AI is providing the benefit of comprehending and reacting to spoken language, credit goes to voice recognition technology, allowing communication that will be totally hand free. "Ask Emma," AXA's virtual assistant, consults with consumers through voice recognition technology and offers rapid answers to their queries.

Telemetric and Internet of Things (IOT)

Telemetric and Internet of Things-connected devices are utilized to gather and transmit real-time data on driving habits, vehicle usage, and environmental conditions. With the help of telematics, Progressive's Snapshot program has provided personalized insurance quotes based on driving patterns.

Block chain Technology

Block chain improves trust and transparency by supplying a secure, decentralized ledger for data management and storage of transactions. Block chain technology can create protected records of insurance agreements and claims, lessening fraud and boosting mutual confidence. These emerging AI technologies are transforming the insurance industry by automating processes, enhancing customer experiences, and improving risk assessment and fraud detection. As there will be advancements in these technologies, they will continue to drive innovation and efficiency, offering new chances for insurers to better serve their customers and streamline operations.

Evolving Expectations from Customers

As the expectations of customers for AI in insurance are evolving; they are rapidly seeking customized, systematic, and crystal-clear interactions. In the current era, they are demanding tailored insurance products, rapid and logical claims processing, and accessible support services that will be available 24/7. Customers also think about dynamic engagement, competitive costs, and powerful data security. AI technologies enable insurers to meet these expectations by providing immediate customized services, improving risk assessment, and enhancing overall customer experience, and hence, promoting greater satisfaction and trust.

Getting Started with AI in Insurance

Procedure for Execution

To get started with AI, insurance companies must get involved in assessing business needs, setting clear objectives, investing in data infrastructure, and getting in touch with appropriate technologies. Building expertise, developing and integrating AI models, and addressing ethical and regulatory concerns are also crucial. In accordance to these steps, insurers can successfully leverage AI to enhance operations, improve customer experiences, and boost growth of their businesses.

Determine Business Needs and Goals

Identify specific applications where AI can add value, such as boosting customer service, automatic processing of claims, or improving risk assessment.

A detailed assessment of running processes and challenges is performed to determine the most significant AI applications.

Establishment of Specific Goals

Define clear, measurable objectives for implementation of Artificial Intelligence, like reducing claim processing times or enlarging customer satisfaction. Apply easy to understand goals and performance metrics for directing the adoption of AI process and measure its effectiveness.

Invest in Infrastructure for Data

AI relies on high-grade information. Make sure that your data infrastructure is has the potential of handling, storing, and processing large volumes of appropriate data securely. Robust data management practices, including data cleaning, integration, and security measures will be put on practice.

Select Appropriate AI Technologies

Choose AI technologies that are in line with your business requirements, like natural language processing for customer service or machine learning for risk assessment. Assess various tools and platforms of AI that best fit for your use case.

Build or Partner with AI Expertise

AI projects require specialized knowledge. Consider building an internal team of data scientists and AI experts or partnering with external vendors. Invest in hiring or training staff with AI expertise or collaborate with AI technology providers and consultants.

Create and Test Models of AI

Develop and test AI models using data of past to ensure they perform good and reach your objectives. Begin with pilot projects to verify the effectiveness of models based on AI and make the adjustments as according to the test results.

Integrate AI into Existing Systems

Make sure that AI solutions are smoothly integrated with your current infrastructure of IT and workflows. Decide and execute integration with a care so that there will be no disruptions and ensure smooth operation.

Monitor and Evaluate Performance

Tracking of AI systems on the continuous basis so that they meet performance objectives and adjust as required. Implement regular updates and evaluations based on performance criteria and feedback by user.

Address Ethical and Regulatory Considerations

Verify that AI applications adhere to moral and legal requirements, such as protecting personal information and avoiding bias. Develop policies and practices to address regulatory requirements and ethical concerns related to AI use.

Elevate Change Management and Training

Effective AI adoption requires managing organizational change and training employees to work with new technologies. Explain the benefits of AI to staff members, give training, and support employees through the transition.

Conclusion

The Future of AI in Insurance

The coming time of AI in insurance is expected to lead a way for transformative modifications, with evolutions in technology bringing unparalleled levels of efficiency, personalization, and innovation. AI technologies led to the enabling of insurers to provide streamline operations through automation, make the risk management better with predictive analytics, and offering real-time personalized products. Through more intuitive and responsive systems, there will be great improvement in interaction between customers, all thanks to AI technologies that are continuing to evolve, and facilitating more correct and proactive making of decisions. In addition to this, the integration of AI with coming up technologies like IOT and block chain will further revolutionize the industry, enhancing transparency, reliability, and real-time data utilization.

References

Alt, R., Leimeister, J. M., Priemuth, T., Sachse, S., Urbach, N., and Wunderlich, N. 2020. Software-defined business: Implications for IT management. Business & Information Systems Engineering 62(6): 609–21. https://doi.org/10.1007/s12599-020-00669-6.

Corcoles, A. D., Kandala, A., Javadi-Abhari, A., McClure, D. T., Cross, A. W., Temme, K. et al. 2019. Challenges and opportunities of near-term quantum computing systems. https://doi.org/10.1109/JPROC.2019.2954005.

Dietzmann, C., Heines, R., and Alt, R. 2020. The convergence of distributed ledger technology and artificial intelligence: An end-to-end reference lending process for financial services competence center ecosystems. In Proceedings of the Twenty-Eighth European Conference on Information Systems (ECIS2020). Association for Information Systems. https://www.researchgate.net/publication/342039353.

Faraj, S., Pachidi, S., and Sayegh, K. 2018. Working and Organizing in the Age of the Learning Algorithm. Information and Organization 28(1): 62–70. https://doi.org/10.1016/j.infoandorg.2018.02.005.

Hukal, P., Henfridsson, O., Shaikh, M., and Parker, G. 2020. Platform signaling for generating platform content. MIS Quarterly 44(3): 1177–1205. https://doi.org/10.25300/MISQ/2020/15190.

Kannan, P. V., and Bernoff, J. 2019. Four challenges to overcome for AI-driven customer experience. MIT Sloan Management Frontiers 16: 1–5. https://sloanreview.mit.edu/article/four-challenges-to-overcome-for-ai-driven-customer-experience/.

Kraus, M., Feuerriegel, S., and Oztekin, A. 2020. Deep learning in business analytics and operations research: Models, applications and managerial implications. European Journal of Operational Research 281(3): 628–41. https://doi.org/10.1016/j.ejor.2019.09.018.

Mikalef, P., Krogstie, J., Pappas, I. O., and Pavlou, P. 2020. Exploring the relationship between big data analytics capability and competitive performance: The mediating roles of dynamic and operational capabilities. Information & Management 57(2): 103169. https://doi.org/10.1016/j.im.2019.05.004.

Park, A., Jabagi, N., and Kietzmann, J. 2021. The Truth about 5G: It's Not (Only) about Downloading Movies Faster! Business Horizons 64(1): 19–28. https://doi.org/10.1016/j.bushor.2020.09.

Singh, G., R. Aggarwal, S. Kumar, S. Nagpa, and S. A. Dhondiyal. 2024. Role of AI in enhancing health insurance penetration in rural India. Int. Conf. Comput. Intell. Comput. Appl. (ICCICA), Samalkha, India, pp. 198–202.

Zarifis, A., and Cheng, X. 2021. Evaluating the new AI and data driven insurance business models for incumbents and disruptors: Is there convergence? Business Information Systems, 199–208. https://doi.org/10.52825/bis.v1i.58.

Zarifis, A., Kawalek, P., and Azadegan, A. 2021. Evaluating If trust and personal information privacy concerns are barriers to using health insurance that explicitly utilizes AI. Journal of Internet Commerce, 20(1): 66–83. https://doi.org/10.1080/15332861.2020.1832817.

Chapter 2

The Dawn of AI in Insurance

A New Era Begins

Veerasankararao, R.[1] and *Shaiku Shahida Saheb*[2,*]

Introduction

Artificial Intelligence (AI) is a pioneering insurance and other sector business capable of duplicating human brain power and executing complex functions. AI is changing the insurance firm model with better efficiency, accuracy, and client engagement. AI applications have reshaped back-end activities like underwriting, danger estimation, burglary and cases settlement, which make it easier for insurers to deliver customized service at reduced business expense (Ikonomi et al., 2024).

The insurance industry handles enormous volumes of data, manual processes have been laborious and error-prone. AI avoids this by examining the data and automatically making decisions in real-time. Underwriting uses AI-based technologies to improve the evaluation of risk by taking into account enormous collections of data to provide competitive premiums and effective management of risk exposure (Eckert and Osterrieder, 2024). Artificial intelligence systems also continuously update risk profiles to act against changing risks.

Fraud detection, a source of concern to insurers in the past, has also been improved upon through AI. Machine learning computers that detect anomalies identify suspicious claims, and false alarms are minimized through learning from previous fraud patterns. Real-time verification in this way eradicates loss caused by fraud (Ikonomi et al., 2024). Customer

[1] Research Scholar, VIT School of Business, VIT-AP University, Amaravati, AP, India. Email: sankar.23phd7241@vitap.ac.in
[2] Associate Professor, VIT School of Business, VIT-AP University, Amaravati, AP, India.
* Corresponding author: shahid.sk@vitap.ac.in

DOI: 10.1201/9781003637301-2

experience is also improved by AI through 24/7 customer support chatbots, managing customers, and claim processing. Through repeated repetition of questions automatically, these virtual assistants achieve the maximum rate of response and allow the human representatives to address more complex issues (Cosma and Rimo, 2024).

But integration with AI comes with challenges such as data privacy, bias in algorithms, and regulatory compliance. Insurers would also need to reskill employees in such a way that they could be made to make better use of AI. The chapter also discusses the history of AI, primary technologies of insurance, challenges, and opportunities being offered by AI in making sustainable growth a success and improving customer experience.

Research Methodology

The research employs a qualitative, exploratory method in investigating the contribution of artificial intelligence in the insurance industry. The research relies on secondary data, including academic research, industry research, and case research, to determine the contribution made by AI in reshaping efficiency, risk management, and client satisfaction.

Data Gathering: Secondary data are collected from peer-reviewed articles, industry white papers, and expert reports (e.g., Ikonomi et al., 2024; Cosma and Rimo, 2024; Eckert and Osterrieder, 2024). The approach provides a general description of AI applications in insurance, ranging from underwriting to fraud detection, claims adjusting, to customer engagement.

Literature Review

The Roots of Artificial Intelligence and its Evolution

The term "artificial intelligence" (AI) was first applied by Dartmouth professor John McCarthy in 1955 as part of a grant to sponsor the Dartmouth Summer Research Project on Artificial Intelligence for 1956. This revolutionary conference was to train computers to perform tasks that would be termed intelligent if executed by humans (Ritchie, 2024). Though computers subsequently had modest processing capabilities and occupied entire floors in office buildings, this early work laid the foundation for AI research. Despite early hardware limitations, the concept of AI captivated scholars, writers, and computer scientists with visions of a future where machines could think like humans (Rose, 2020).

The enduring legacy of McCarthy's contribution is not his work per se but his choice of the terms "artificial intelligence." Those terms kindled several decades of innovative and creative activity in responsive computing. Russell and Norvig (2016) describe AI as the study of how to create machines that can perform things normally needing human intellect, such as perception, understanding language, making decisions, and translating.

AI's conceptual roots can be traced back to Alan Turing's famous "Turing Test" in 1950, which proposed an operational definition of intelligence based on a machine's ability to mimic human conversation. In 1952, Arthur Samuel created the first self-playing checkers program, demonstrating the possibility of machine learning. After his PhD at Dartmouth College, McCarthy organized the 1956 AI research workshop where he officially named the field "Artificial Intelligence" (Ritchie, 2024). This study was on the premise that learning and intelligence could be abstracted and replicated by machines.

McCarthy had developed LISP, the first AI-specific programming language, and a valuable resource in AI research, in 1958. Arthur Samuel first used the term "machine learning" in 1959, describing efforts to teach computers to learn to play games such as chess better (Ritchie, 2024). General Motors built "Unimate," the first industrial robot, which performed hazardous tasks on assembly lines in 1961. McCarthy kept working on AI technologies by establishing the Stanford Artificial Intelligence Lab (SAIL) in 1963, encouraging interdisciplinary AI research and innovation (Russell and Norvig, 2016).

Although AI was hampered by financial constraints in the 1970s, it went on to soar during the 1980s as it formed a new industry. AI has since accelerated at a lightning rate, evolving from a niche scholarly activity to a revolutionary technology revolutionizing industries across the world. AI in the modern era has capabilities that guarantee safety, efficiency, and intelligent decision-making, showcasing its enormous capacity to shape the future. This journey, from the early thought of AI to the present applications, demonstrates the capability of artificial intelligence to make life smarter, safer, and more efficient in numerous fields.

Understanding the Role of AI in Insurance

The insurance industry, with low customer involvement and long, complex processes (Sharma, 2019), is being transformed by digitalization and synergistic fusion of AI technologies. Artificial intelligence has revolutionized conventional insurance processes such as underwriting, risk evaluation, claims handling, and customer care to attain greater efficiency, decision-making, cost savings, and customer interaction (Rao and Tirumalaiah, 2024). By executive automation and application of big data, machine learning, predictive analytics, and IoT, insurers provide personalized products, prevent and detect fraud (McKinsey and Company, 2021), and drive regulatory compliance (Deloitte, 2022).

By virtual assistants and AI-based chatbots, human representatives are left to carry out challenging tasks only, driving service quality and overall productivity (Singh and Chivukula, 2020). In addition to this industry 4.0 technology advancements have also fueled subsequent growth in automation, reduction of errors, and globalization of economic activity, and AI has emerged as a vastly critical tool for insurers to achieve sustainable growth and competitiveness (Rai et al., 2021; PwC, 2021; EAIC, 2024).

Insights on AI Innovations Driving Value in Insurance

AI-Powered Automation: A Game Changer

Automation has transformed the insurance industry by improving insurance business processes from underwriting to customer services. AI and machine learning maximize operation effectiveness, decision-making, and accuracy of information. Big data enriches customers' data, while blockchain minimizes administrative costs and competitive pricing. AI-powered automation minimized processing time by a great margin and policy administration error to nearly zero, and RPA improves data accuracy by 95%. Blockchain will liberate $5 to $10 billion annually in insurers' costs by making them more efficient and reducing fraud. Some of the key benefits are improved efficiency, faster settlement of claims, reduced cost and error, and higher customer satisfaction (Pattnaik et al., 2024; Saeed and Arshed, 2022).

Risk Assessment and Underwriting

Risk assessment and underwriting become more precise by virtue of AI by analyzing high volumes of data as well as live data. Neural networks detect patterns and predict future claims from them, making possible customized premiums. Underwriting procedures have been changed before by conventional manual procedures aided by AI, thus removing human errors and allowing more accurate prices. Data mining is also a major function in risk assessment, with Learning Models heading to underwriting (Aswani et al., 2021). Big data improves pricing accuracy, reduces costs, and enables customer service.

Prevention of Fraud Detection

Insurance fraud presents enormous financial risk worth billions of dollars annually. AI and ML enable big data examination to detect fraud patterns and mark suspicious claims. Blockchain technology can enable traceability and decentralization, which can aid anti-fraud purposes. Cybercrime, the largest global business threat, is addressed through AI-based fraud detection. Insurers use advanced models like gradient boosting, Bayesian estimation, and hierarchical models to estimate losses and enhance fraud detection (Liu et al., 2019; Singh and Chivukula, 2020; Singh et al., 2024).

Computerized Claims Processing

It's through computerized claims processing by Artificial Intelligence powered with increased speed, efficiency, and accuracy. It reduces paper work to be performed under performing verification to the extent of time saving, reducing the scope for mistakes, and enhancing customer satisfaction. AI anticipates loss before its occurrence, makes timely payment, and reduces the quantum of claims since it employs NLP, ML, and IoT in order to accomplish that (Larson et al., 2022; Rao and Tirumalaiah, 2024).

Personalized Policy Recommendations

AI enables the insurer to communicate directly with customers, understand what they require, and develop personalized insurance products. Machine learning algorithms such as decision trees, ANNs and regression models forecast customer behavior accurately to retain customers and lifetime value (CLV). Cognitive systems use user behavior to suggest personalized policies, improving risk and customer interface levels (Ramnath et al., 2021; Kim and Park, 2019).

Enhanced Customer Experience

AI-driven chatbots and virtual assistants boost customer service through question answering, claims support, and 24/7 service. NLP enriches the interaction through response and correct understanding by chatbots. AI platforms boost customer experience through customer insights-based personalized products and strategies. Automated claim assessment maximizes efficiency, reduces errors, and creates a customer-focused experience (Komperla, 2022).

AI Application in the Insurance Sector

The companies target enhanced quality of services, enhanced customer penetration (women, low-income masses, and different clusters), and maximizing operations with the use of AI. Deployment of AI makes service less costly, boosts market share, and personalizes insurance coverage in relation to the customer's financial resources as well as lowering risks. Improved customer services ensure competition benefits insurers and insured alike (Table 1). Technological innovations such as AI reframe the

Table 1: Real-world Examples of AI Applications in the Insurance Industry.

Name of Company	Functional Area Applied	Tools/Technologies	Result Achieved
AXA-(France)	Underwriting	Predictive Modeling and Data Analytics	Improved efficiency and reduced errors
AXA-(Japan)	Prediction of Potential Loss	Google TensorFlow, ML and NLP	Accuracy Rate of 78%
Fukoku Life Insurance (Japan)	Claim Processing	IBM Watson	30% accuracy rate in payouts and Reduced claim Times
Transamerica (USA)	Customer Data Analysis	H2O.ai Machine Learning	Improved customer service and increased revenues
Lemonade (USA)	Underwriting Process	AI-powered chatbot 'Maya', and Jim	Enabled faster and more accurate underwriting
Root-Insurance (USA)	Personalized Auto Insurance Rates	AI-driven Algorithms	More accurate pricing and improved underwriting
Metro mile (USA)	Tailored Premium	"Pay-per-mile insurance," AI Technologies	Adjusting premiums accordingly
Allianz (Germany)	Cyber Security and Risk Management	AI-enabled cybersecurity tools and risk analytics	Strengthen data protection
Hippo Insurance (USA)	Tailored policies of homeowners	AI and Data Analytics	Customized coverage options and pricing
Haven Life (USA)	Life-insurance Underwriting	AI and Medical data analysis	Reduced approval time
Swiss Re (Switzerland)	Risk Assessment and Underwriting	IBM Watson Tool and ML	Adequate insurance premium
Progressive (USA)	Usage-based Insurance	AI, Telematics, and ML	Reduce claims
AIG (USA)	Underwriting, Customer experience	AI, ML and Big data	Streamline operations, increased profitability
Aviva (Canada)	Virtual Claim platform	AI, ML and Big data	Achieved 40% faster climes
Zurich Insurance (Switzerland)	Anomaly detection	AI-based anomaly detection and predictive modeling.	Reduced fraud-related losses and improved customer trust
Association of Serbian Insurers	Fraud Prevention	FROPS (Fraud Risk Operational Solution)	Calculates Risk of Fraud

Table 1 contd. ...

...Table 1 contd.

Name of Company	Functional Area Applied	Tools/Technologies	Result Achieved
LIC (India)	Electronic Policies	AI and Blockchain	42% Growth in the Premium Collection
ICICI Prudential Life Insurance (India)	Creation of Sales, Underwriting, and Claim Process and Data Process	My Coach -AI Platform, Bot Orchestration Layer Humanoid, Selfie Quote and, etc.	Policy Processes like pre-sales, customer service, claims, and marketing
SBI Life Insurance	Video-Based KYC	OCR, AI-enabled Facilities	Reduced Dependency on staff
HDFC Life Insurance (India)	Automate Processes, Customer support and service	Bots like SPOK, Etty, Zoey and Neo, 'Elsa', 'Ezra', etc. Machine Learning	Addressed 17 lakh Queries Achieved 25% more margin and prompt payments for claims
MAX Life Insurance (India)	Underwriting, Sales Team Support	Machine Learning NLP	Customer Segmentation and CRM
Kotak Life Insurance (India)	Customer Experience Distribution Ecosystem	Bots like KAYA	Served 53% more customers in a user-friendly way
ICICI Lombard (India)	AI for damage assessment	Computer vision and AI-powered algorithms	Speeding up the assessment process and improving accuracy

Source: (Sharma, 2019)

structure of the industry since studies bring into perspective tangible operating enhancements alongside prospects for increased future growth (Raikkonen et al., 2018).

Industry Challenges That AI Can Address

The adoption and implementation of Artificial Intelligence (AI) and Machine Learning (ML) in financial services like insurance, offers plentiful opportunities for enhancing competence, enhancing customer understanding levels, and driving technological innovation. However, it also permits a set of challenges that are necessarily addressed to yield the potential of these technologies. This set of challenges includes operational resilience, data quality and availability, Algorithmic Bias and Fairness, Data privacy, security, skill gap, and ethical considerations. The challenges

Table 2: AI Implementation Challenges and Solutions in Operational Contexts.

Challenge Type	Detailed Challenge	Solution
Operational Elasticity	1. Process automation 2. Predictive maintenance 3. Resource allocation, and 4. Security 5. Cutting time	1. AI-Driven Automation 2. Integration of AI, ML 3. Google Dataproc 4. Generative AI Approaches 5. Integration of DBT Tools
Implementing Challenges	1. Compatible with the inheritance system 2. Access and data quality 3. Impact on performance	1. Customized integrated solution 2. Gradual Modernization 3. Data purification and testing
Data Quality and Availability	1. Detecting data quality 2. Correcting data 3. Streamline Data	1. AI-technologies 2. Machine Learning 3. Predictive modeling 4. AI-driven data management solutions
Data Privacy and Security	1. The risk associated with data exposure 2. Model Flaws 3. Regulatory Challenges	1. Strong Data Governance 2. Repeated Security Audits 3. Acquiescent with data protection requirements
Algorithmic Bias and Fairness	1. Ensuring Fairness 2. Unfair Pricing 3. Sensitive Attributes like Race, Gender	Explainable AI (XAI) Models
Skill Gap	1. Expertise Requirements 2. Continuous learning needs	1. Inclusive training programs 2. Collaboration with institutions
Moral Aspects	1. Transparency and Bias in AI Judgments 2. Explainable	1. Follow ethical AI norms 2. Conduct Audits 3. Use of explainable AI approaches

Sources: (Akerkar, 2019); (Ramnath et al., 2021)

and corresponding solutions associated with AI integration across operational, data, ethical, and skill-based dimensions are summarized in Table 2.

Conclusion

By focusing on the latest AI-enabled technologies and utilizing advancements in innovation, the insurance business can address these challenges and harness the full potential of AI and ML to strengthen the industry, enhance operational efficiency, customer service, and satisfaction, and improve overall efficiency. However, these resolutions necessitate cautious accomplishment and continuous oversight to ensure they meet the multifaceted needs of the insurance industry globally.

Future Directions

The research points to areas where the limitations can emerge, including the available biases in research and the evolving nature of AI technologies. Future research can fill such lacunae by employing the synergy of primary data collection, e.g., in the form of interviews with practice experts, for testing and building upon the research.

Through it, the study attempts to deliver practical facts with respect to how business problems will be redefined by AI, enhance decision-making, and stimulate sustainable growth for the insurance sector.

References

Accenture. 2020. Why AI in Insurance Claims and Underwriting. https://www.accenture.com/in-en/insights/insurance/artificial-intelligence.

Aggour, K. S., P. P. Bonissone, W. E. Cheetham and Messmer, R. P. 2006. Automating the Underwriting of Insurance Applications. AI Magazine, 27(3): 36–50.

Akerkar, Rajendra. 2019. Artificial Intelligence for Business. Springer.

Alwyn, K. G., and R. J. Sera. 2007. Blockchain: A Road Ahead for India. College, 1.

Aswani, R., S. P. Ghrera, S. Chandra, and A. K. Kar. 2021. A Hybrid Evolutionary Approach for Identifying Spam Websites for Search Engine Marketing. Evolutionary Intelligence, 14(4): 1803–1815.

Butcher, Mike. 2014. Innovative Crowdsource Insurance Startup Friendsurance Raises New Cash.

Cao, S., H. Lyu, and X. Xu. 2020. Insurtech Development: Evidence from Chinese Media Reports. Technological Forecasting and Social Change, 161: 120277.

Cattaneo, M., R. S. Kenett, and E. Luciano. 2024. Adversarial AI in Insurance: An Overview. European Actuarial Journal, 14(1): 297–306.

Cortis, Dominic, Joseph Debattista, Jean-Paul Debono, and Mark Farrell. 2019. Insurtech. In Disrupting Finance: Fintech Strategy in the 21st Century, 71–84.

Cosma, S., and G. Rimo. 2024. Redefining Insurance through Technology: Achievements and Perspectives in Insurtech. Research in International Business and Finance, 102301.

Deloitte. 2022. India Inc. Weighs in on AI Investments: Deloitte Survey. https://www2.deloitte.com/in/en/pages/financial-services/articles/ai-regulatory-compliance-insurance.html.

Eckert, C., and K. Osterrieder. 2024. How Digitalization Affects Insurance Companies: Overview and Use Cases of Digital Technologies.

Egfjord, K. F. H., and K. J. Sund. 2020. Do you see what i see? How differing perceptions of the environment can hinder radical business model innovation. Technological Forecasting and Social Change, 150: 119787.

EY. 2020. Three Ways AI Will Transform the Insurance Industry. https://www.ey.com/en_in/insurance/revolutionizing-underwriting-with-ai.

Granados Franco, E. 2019. These Are the World's Top 10 Business Risks – By Region. World Economic Forum.

Gupta, R. 2020. Artificial Intelligence (AI) in Insurance: A Futuristic Approach. Shodh Drishti, 11(8): 6–10.

Gupta, S., W. Ghardallou, D. K. Pandey, and G. P. Sahu. 2022. Artificial intelligence adoption in the insurance industry: evidence using the technology–organization–environment framework. Research in International Business and Finance, 63: 101757.

Hassani, H., S. Unger, and C. Beneki. 2020. Big Data and Actuarial Science. Big Data and Cognitive Computing, 4: 1–29.

Ikonomi, A., B. Nast, L. Shi, L. Levrault, and T. M. Purcell. 2024. Artificial Intelligence in Insurance.

Imami, F. A. n.d. A Web-Based Interface for a Blockchain-Based Cyber Insurance Approach.

Jing, N., T. Jiang, J. Du et al. 2018. Personalized recommendation based on customer preference mining and sentiment assessment from a chinese E-commerce website. Electronic Commerce Research, 18: 159–179.

Kelley, C., and K. Wang. 2021. InsurTech: A Guide for the Actuarial Community.

Kim, I., and N. Park. 2019. Blockchain-Based Data-Preserving AI learning environment model for cyber security system. Journal of Korean Institute of Information Technology, 17(12): 125–134.

Komperla, R. C. A. 2022. AI Behind the Wheel: Innovations in Auto Insurance and Healthcare. International Neurourology Journal, 26 (4): 30–36.

KPMG. 2019. Artificial Intelligence in the Insurance Industry. https://home.kpmg/xx/en/home/insights/2019/03/india-ai-insurance.html.

Kumar, N., J. D. Srivastava, and H. Bisht. 2019. Artificial intelligence in insurance sector. Journal of the Gujarat Research Society, 21(7): 79–91.

Kumar, N., J. D. Srivastava, G. G. Singh, and H. Bisht. n.d. Artificial Intelligence in Insurance Sector. https://www.researchgate.net/publication/337305024.

Lamberton, C., D. Brigo, and D. Hoy. 2017. Impact of Robotics, RPA and AI on the insurance industry: challenges and opportunities. Journal of Financial Perspectives, 4(1).

Lasi, Heiner, Peter Fettke, Hans Kemper et al. 2014. Industry 4.0. Business and Information Systems Engineering, 6(4): 239–242. https://doi.org/10.1007/s12599-014-0334-4.

Liu, W., Q. Yu, Z. Li, Z. Li, Y. Su, and J. Zhou. 2019. A blockchain-based system for anti-fraud of healthcare insurance. 2019 IEEE 5th International Conference on Computer and Communications (ICCC), 1264–1268.

McKinsey and Company. 2021. Using Advanced Analytics for Fraud Management. https://www.mckinsey.com/business-functions/risk-and-resilience/our-insights/ai-in-fraud-detection-protecting-insurers.

Meindl, B., N. F. Ayala, J. Mendonça, and A. G. Frank. 2021. The Four Smarts of Industry 4.0: Evolution of Ten Years of Research and Future Perspectives. Technological Forecasting and Social Change, 168: 120784. https://doi.org/10.1016/j.techfore.2021.120784.

Mitchell, T. M. 1997. Machine Learning. New York: McGraw-Hill.

Mulgan, T. 2016. Superintelligence: Paths, Dangers, Strategies.

Patel, R., M. Migliavacca, and M. E. Oriani. 2022. Blockchain in banking and finance: a bibliometric review. Research in International Business and Finance, 62: 101718.

Pattnaik, D., S. Ray, and R. Raman. 2024. Applications of Artificial Intelligence and Machine Learning in the Financial Services Industry: A Bibliometric Review. Heliyon.

Pilote, M., and M. Fillion. 1991. Automated Underwriting at Continental Canada: Results and Major Obstacles. Artificial Intelligence Applications on Wall Street, 1991. Proceedings. First International Conference, IEEE.

PwC. 2021. AI in Customer Service: A Game Changer for Indian Insurers. https://www.pwc.in/industries/financial-services/insurance.html.

Rai, R., M. K. Tiwari, D. Ivanov, and A. Dolgui. 2021. Machine learning in manufacturing and Industry 4.0 applications. International Journal of Production Research, 59(16): 4773–4778. https://doi.org/10.1080/00207543.2021.1956675.

Ramnath, B., L. Ari, and M. Doug. 2021. Insurance 2030 – The Impact of AI on the Future of Insurance.

Rao, K. M., and G. Tirumalaiah. 2024. Future Insurance Implications of Artificial Intelligence: A Meta-Analysis. Business, Commerce and Management, 27.

Rathi, T., and V. Ravi. 2017. Customer lifetime value measurement using machine learning techniques. In Artificial Intelligence: Concepts, Methodologies, Tools, and Applications, 3013–3022. IGI Global.

Rawat, S., A. Rawat, D. Kumar, and A. S. Sabitha. 2021. Application of machine learning and data visualization techniques for decision support in the insurance sector. International Journal of Information Management Data Insights, 1(2): 100012.
Report, A. 2019. Delivering Value Sustainably: Fulfilling Commitments.
Revathi, P. 2020. Technology and Innovation in Insurance – Present and Future Technology in Indian Insurance Industry. International Journal of Engineering and Management Research, 10.
Riikkinen, M., H. Saarijärvi, P. Sarlin et al. 2018. Using Artificial intelligence to create value in insurance. International Journal of Bank Marketing, 36: 1145–1168.
Ritchie, Ian. 2024. AI History.
Rose, D. 2020. Artificial intelligence for business. FT Press.
Russell, S. J., and P. Norvig. 2016. Artificial Intelligence: A Modern Approach. 3rd ed. Pearson.
Russell, S., and P. Norvig. 2020. Artificial Intelligence: A Modern Approach. 4th ed. Pearson.
Saeed, M., and N. Arshed. 2022. Revolutionizing insurance sector in india: a case of blockchain adoption challenges. International Journal of Contemporary Economics and Administrative Sciences, 12(1): 300–324.
Seekings, C. 2017. Amazon Set to Shake-Up UK Insurance. The Actuary.
Shamsuddin, J. N., C. Gan, and D. L. T. Anh. 2023. Bibliometric analysis of InsurTech. Journal of Advanced Research in Applied Sciences and Engineering Technology, 30(2): 103–132.
Sharma, S. 2019. Artificial Intelligence in the Insurance Sector. The Journal of Insurance Institute India, 59–61.
Simester, D., A. Timoshenko, and S. I. Zoumpoulis. 2019. Targeting prospective customers: robustness of machine learning methods to typical data challenges. Management Science.
Singh, G., R. Aggarwal, S. Kumar, S. Nagpa and S. A. Dhondiyal. 2024. Role of AI in enhancing health insurance penetration in rural India. Int. Conf. Comput. Intell. Comput. Appl. (ICCICA), Samalkha, India, pp. 198–202.
Singh, S. K., and M. Chivukula. 2020. A Commentary on the application of artificial intelligence in the insurance industry. Trends in Artificial Intelligence, 4(1): 75–79.
Thomas, R. W., D. H. Friend, L. A. Dasilva, A. B. Mackenzie, and V. Tech. 2006. Cognitive Networks: Adaptation and learning to achieve end-to-end performance objectives. 51–57.
Vafeiadis, T., K. I. Diamantaras, G. Sarigiannidis et al. 2015. A comparison of machine learning techniques for customer churn prediction. Simulation Modelling Practice and Theory, 55.
Vahdati, M., K. G. HamlAbadi, A. M. Saghiri, and H. Rashidi. 2018. A self-organized framework for insurance based on internet of things and blockchain. 2018 IEEE 6th International Conference on Future Internet of Things and Cloud (FiCloud), 169–175.
Verhoef, P. C., and B. Donkers. 2001. Predicting customer potential value: an application in the insurance industry. Decision Support Systems, 32: 189–199.
Zhang, Y., and V. Dukic. 2013. Predicting multivariate insurance loss payments under the bayesian copula framework. Journal of Risk and Insurance, 80(4): 891–919.

Chapter 3

Visualizing the Global Research Trends of Artificial Intelligence in Insurance

A Bibliometric Review

Anil Kumar,[1,*] *Vineet Pathak*,[1] *Shikha Tiwari*[1] and *Bhuwan Melkani*[2]

Introduction

One definition of artificial intelligence (AI) is that it is a simulation of human brains that is implemented in machines that have been built to behave and think in the same way that people do. Artificial intelligence has been gaining popularity since 2015, with various tools such as robots, chatbots, and others. AI helps to improve governance by facilitating improved decision-making, which in turn helps to improve efficiency and reduce time. The purpose of artificial intelligence is to simulate the functioning of the human brain and to arrive at conclusions that are comparable to those reached by humans in a range of contexts. The use of artificial

[1] Assistant Professor, School of Management Graphic Era Hill University, Haldwani Campus, Uttarakhand, India. Emails: vntpathak@gmail.com; shikha.tewari1357@gmail.com
[2] Assistant Professor, Department of Commerce, MBGPG College Haldwani, Uttarakhand, India. Email: bhuwanmelkani1980@gmail.com
* Corresponding author: anilbahuguna123@gmail.com

DOI: 10.1201/9781003637301-3

intelligence is a method that provides companies with the opportunity to gain a competitive advantage by employing enormous amounts of data to directly address the requirements of their customers through the provision of tailored services. It is a gadget that behaves, thinks, and learns exactly like a human. The world became a web of interconnected networks as technology advanced. The field of artificial intelligence offers a wide range of applications that can be utilized in a variety of different industries, including investment opportunities. There is a dynamic expansion taking place in the worldwide insurance sector. According to Businesswire (2020b), the total amount of premiums paid for insurance throughout the world in 2017 topped 4.9 trillion USD. Additionally, in 2018, they surpassed the threshold of USD 5 trillion for the very first time. Similar to more than six percent of the total gross domestic product of the whole world, this statistic is equivalent to that amount (Forinsurer, 2019). The continued increase in the non-life insurance market was the primary factor that contributed to the total business expansion. At this very moment, the insurance business is at a crucial crossroads of transformation, although it is inherently conservative. InsurTech is considered a significant opportunity for innovative growth by several industry professionals. The COVID-19 epidemic has substantially accelerated the development of new technologies in the insurance business, and it is now justifiable to assert that it will be a major element driving this expansion.

Literature Review

The shift that has taken place from traditional efficiency evaluations to more holistic models that incorporate advanced methodologies, including Artificial Intelligence (AI), represents a significant development. The global adoption of AI has accelerated in the wake of the pandemic. The public's awareness of cyber hazards is inextricably linked to scientific advancements in the insurance sector that pertains to cyber insurance. In their article "Cyber Risk and Insurance Coverage: An Actuarial Multistate Approach", In their opinion they suggest a manner to cover cyber risk: "Three levels of damage will be identified regarding the functionality of the terminal, analogous to the coverage regarding health insurance" (Barracchini and Addessi, 2014). A supportive statement came as "AI has the potential to significantly impact this sector, from predicting risk more accurately than actuaries to comprehending the new vulnerabilities in the system infrastructure and processes". Several studies which focus on the link between cyber risk and cyber insurance now see it differently because of AI. "The great difficulties to insure cyber risk, especially due of a lack of data and modeling approaches, the risk of change, and incalculable accumulation risks". A special issue that was published in the Geneva Papers in 2020 also raised concerns about cyber hazards and cyber insurance. Amanda Hoxell's paper "Observable Cyber Risk and Market Concentration" also shows a link between cyber hazards in the market. In the framework of cyber insurance, she explains the basic price ideas that apply to every valuation. Data integrity and availability define the main obstacles in the cyber insurance business, according to Hoxell (Hoxell, 2020). "Using artificial intelligence not only creates fresh revenue sources for insurance firms but also increases their cost-effective performance". By use of artificial intelligence, computer systems may detect trends in insured data, therefore enabling them to engage in a more accurate computation of the likelihood of a loss. Through this, the insurance firm easily automates the underwriting work process and raises the effectiveness with which they manage claim settlements. Moreover, the special knowledge acquired by artificial intelligence helps insurance plans to be customized to every customer.

An artificial intelligence system has been developed by Lapetus Solutions, an InsurTech start-up based in the United States. This system is comprised of sensory analytics and dynamic inquiry. To obtain a quote, the consumer is required to submit a self-portrait photograph (a "selfie"). This method will use an image and will analyze it to determine the health condition, ailment susceptibility, and expectancy of the individual (Lapetus Solutions, 2017). Assert that AI enhances cost efficiency and creates new insurance money. AI-powered computers may spot insured data patterns and evaluate loss risk more accurately. This helps insurers manage claim settlements and automate underwriting. Using personal data from artificial intelligence, insurance plans are customized as per individual customer requirement and their current state.

Research Objectives

1. Examining publication trend of AI and Insurance.
2. To examine performance of sources, authors, countries.
3. To discover underlying themes.

Methodology

Present work incorporated bibliometric analysis to illustrate worldwide research dimensions and prospective research trajectories in AI and Insurance. "Bibliometric analysis is a quantitative approach for examining scientific literature to discern patterns, trends, and structures within a designated research domain." We utilized Scopus to get the data because it is the most complete and commonly used bibliometric database (Table 1).

Data Collection

Table 1: Criteria of article selection.

Criteria of Selecting Articles	Exclude	Include
Database- Scopus		
Search Date- 14-10-2024		
Search Strings- (TITLE-ABS-KEY ("Artificial Intelligence") AND TITLE-ABS-KEY ("Insurance"))		1967
Publication Period: 2000–2024	53	1914
Language: English	61	1853
Subject area "Business, management and accounting, Economics, Econometrics and Finance"	1611	242
Document type: "Articles", " Book Chapter ", and "Reviews"	73	169

Source: Author Compilation

Data Analysis Tool

R Bibliometrix via Biblioshiny was used for analyzing the data for the analysis part.

Data Analysis and Interpretation

Descriptive Statistics

Table 2 is a summary table showing that 116 sources and 169 articles were analyzed which were having annual growth rate below twenty percent average citation per document found to be 10.63 with total references 77882 with plus keyword count of 374 and author keyword as 472.

Annual Scientific Production (Fig. 1) demonstrates the productivity or scientific publications from 2005 to around 2024. The graph represents an upward trend suggesting an immense scope in the field of artificial intelligence in the insurance sector.

Table 2: Summary of Dataset.

Information Summary	
Time Space	2005:2024
Sources	118
Documents (Articles, Books and Reviews)	169
Annual Growth Rate Percentage	16.76
Average age per document	2.93
Citation average per document	10.63
References	7882
CONTENT OF DOCUMENTS	
Keywords Plus	374
Author Keyword	482
Authors	460
Authors of single-authored document	39
Collaboration	
Single-authored documents	42
Co-Authors per Doc	2.85
International co-authorships %	26.04
Documents	
article	85
book chapter	69
review	15

Source: Author's Creation

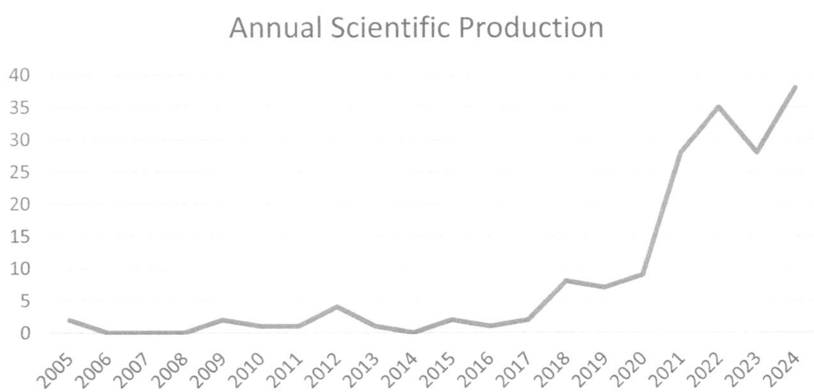

Fig. 1: Scientific Production.

The ups and down of citations (Fig. 2) shows average citation and it can be concluded that somehow the productivity is there but the usage of these articles is still underutilized.

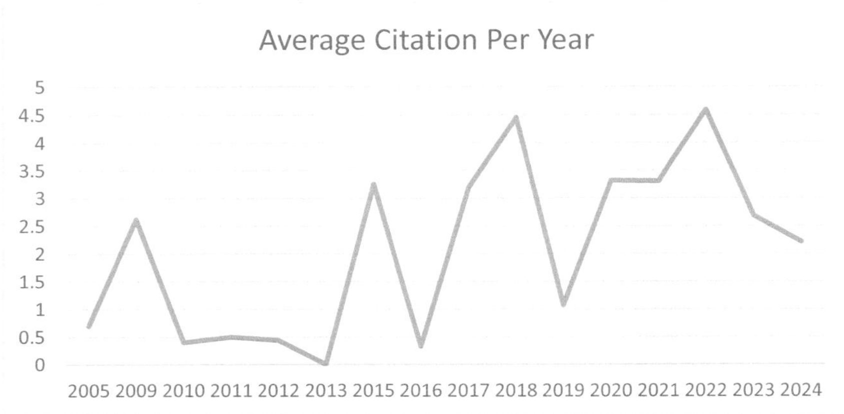

Fig. 2: Average Citations per Year.

Source of Impact

The impact of Sources (Table 3) as measured by the h-index. Higher h-index values suggest influence and impact of sources. "Risk", and "Big data: a game changer for insurance industry", are impactful sources.

Table 3: Impactful Sources.

S. NO	Element	h_index	g_ index	m_ index	TC	TP	PY_start
1	Risks	5	6	1	85	6	2020
2	Big data: a game changer for the insurance industry	4	5	1.33	32	7	2022
3	Annals of Actuarial Science	3	3	0.23	48	3	2012
4	Computer law and security review	3	4	0.75	35	4	2021
5	International journal of bank marketing	3	4	0.42	241	4	2018
6	Big data analytics in the insurance market	2	2	0.66	12	2	2022
7	Big data and cognitive computing	2	2	0.4	19	2	2020
8	Decision support systems	2	2	0.2	41	2	2015
9	Geneva papers on risk and insurance: issues and practice	2	2	0.66	68	2	2022
10	Insurance markets and companies	2	3	0.4	52	3	2020

Source: Author Cimpilation

Most Relevant authors

The top ten cited and productive authors (Table 4) of AI and insurance. Riikkinen m is the top cited author with 146 citations, Rajaobelina l with 99 citations, Hentzen j.k with 78 citations, Ince h with 72 citations, Taymouri f with 63 citations, Agarwal p with 51 citations, Aslam f with 50 citations and remaining with 45, 44 and 44 citations.

Table 4: Top Authors.

Author	Citations	Authors	Articles	Articles fractionalized
Riikkinen m	146	Kumar B	2	2
Rajaobelina l	99	Nwogugu M	2	2
Hentzen j.k	78	Richman R	2	2
Ince h	72	Chen K	2	1.5
Taymouri f	63	Grassi L	2	1.5
Agarwal p	51	Kukreja G	2	1.33
Aslam f	50	Li S	2	1
Volosovych s	45	Eckert C	2	0.83
Eling m	44	Osterrieder K	2	0.83
Menon v.g	44	Zarifis A	2	0.83

Source: Author Creation

Assessing the top productive nation we found India is at the top with 97 articles, Italy with 45 articles (Table 5). The United States is the top-cited country with 270 citations.

Table 5: Top Countries.

Top 10 Cited Countries		Top 10 Productive Countries	
Country	**Citations**	**Country**	**Articles**
United States	270	India	97
Italy	259	Italy	45
India	230	USA	40
Australia	179	Germany	35
Canada	163	Uk	23
Finland	159	Australia	18
Turkey	145	Ukraine	16
Germany	128	China	14
United Kingdom	99	Canada	13
France	79	Turkey	11

Source: Author Creation

Co-occurrence network (Fig. 3) is an analysis method to assess clusters. The Red cluster identify theme 'Artificial Intelligence', the blue cluster identify theme 'Insurance', the Green cluster identify theme 'Machine Learning', Orange Color identify theme 'Risk Management', and the Violet cluster identify theme 'Chatbot'.

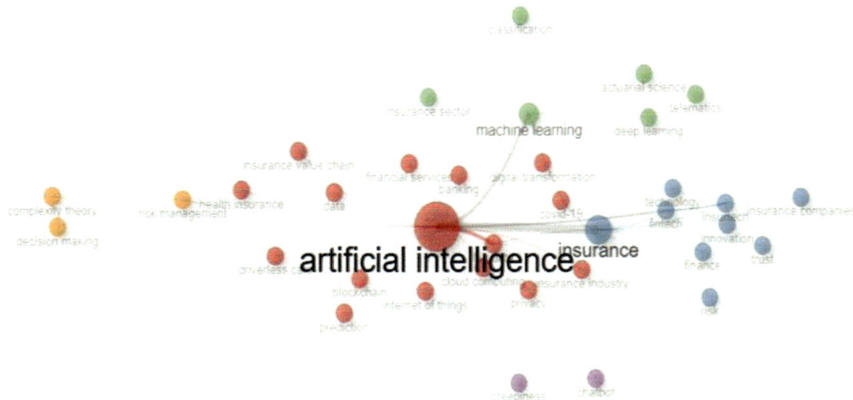

Fig. 3: Co-occurrence Network.

Thematic Map: "A Thematic map is a two-dimensional plot which plots the typological themes based on centrality and density" (Cobo et al., 2011).

"The Top right quadrant in Fig. 4 showcases the Motor themes that are highly discussed and are highly developed in the research domain due to which they are the core themes, The top left quadrant showcases Niche themes that are well developed internally but have a wide scope of discussion in the research domain, The quadrant at the lower

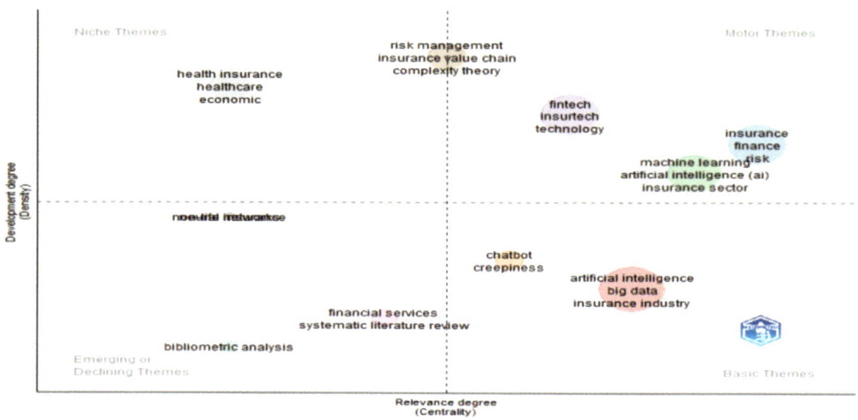

Fig. 4: Thematic Map.

right demonstrates basic themes that are of utmost importance for the development of the research field but are less developed internally, The last quadrant at lower left consists of themes that are either emerging or may disappear with time". The themes of risk Management, 'Insurance Value Chain', and 'Complexity Theory lie between niche and Motor themes.

Discussion and Future Research Directions

Results of the study demonstrates ups and downs in publication till 2018 and from there onward there was a steady increase in it. "Risks", and "Big Data: A Game Changer for Insurance Industry" were impactful sources. Riikkinen M., and Rajaobelina L., were top cited authors in the domain. In terms of productivity among nations India is at top. The United States is the top-cited country. Five clusters 'Artificial Intelligence, Insurance, Machine Learning, Chatbot, and Risk Management'. The thematic map which was used to analyze emerging and trending themes explains that 'Fintech', 'Insuretech', 'Insurance', 'Risk', 'Machine Learning', 'Artificial Intelligence', and 'Insurance Sector' are the motor themes. Niche themes consist of keywords such as 'Health Insurance', 'Healthcare', and 'Economic'. Basic themes include keywords such as 'Chatbot', 'Artificial Intelligence', 'Big Data', 'Insurance Industry', and 'Creepiness'. Themes that are either emerging or which may disappear with time include keywords such as 'Financial Services', 'Systematic Literature Review', and 'Bibliometric Analysis'. 'Risk Management, 'Insurance Value Chain', and 'Complexity Theory' lie between niche and Motor themes. Future studies could incorporate inclusion of further databases and a mixed methodology to analyze the AI and Insurance relation.

Conclusion

From 2000 to 2024, this bibliometric study elucidates the research patterns, key Figs., and new subjects in the domains of AI and insurance. The results show that over the past 20 years, publications on AI in insurance have steadily increased, reflecting both growing scholarly interest and technical developments in the field. There is a concentration of research coming from economically advanced places, particularly in the domains of business, management, and finance. Several influential countries, journals, and writers have shaped the discourse. New areas, like AI-powered risk assessment, fraud detection, and consumer experience enhancement, are starting to make waves, according to an examination of recurring themes and phrases. In the future, these themes suggest that AI will revolutionize many insurance operations by making them more efficient, accurate, and personalized. The findings also point to knowledge gaps in the field, which calls for more investigation into the insurance industry's long-term effects of AI as well as its ethical and regulatory ramifications.

In conclusion, the use of AI in insurance is a developing area that has important theoretical and practical consequences. Both the present and future of the field are laid out in this paper, which serves as a roadmap for researchers.

References

Acosta-Prado, J. C., C. G. Hernández-Cenzano, C. D. Villalta-Herrera, and E. W. Barahona-Silva. 2024. Three horizons of technical skills in artificial intelligence for the sustainability of insurance companies. Administrative Sciences, 14: 190. https://doi.org/10.3390/admsci14090190

Aleksandrova, A., V. Ninova, and Z. Zhelev. 2023. A survey on AI implementation in finance, (cyber) insurance and financial controlling. Risks, 11: 91. https://doi.org/10.3390/risks11050091

Alhitmi, H. K., A. Mardiah, K. I. Al-Sulaiti, and J. Abbas. 2024. Data security and privacy concerns of AI-driven marketing in the context of economics and business field: an exploration into possible solutions. SSRN. https://doi.org/10.2139/ssrn.4737943

Amerirad, B., M. Cattaneo, R. S. Kenett, and E. Luciano. 2023. Adversarial artificial intelligence in insurance: from an example to some potential remedies. Risks, 11: 20. https://doi.org/10.3390/risks11010020

Cobo, M. J., A. G. Lopez-Herrera, E. Herrera-Viedma, and F. Herrera. 2011. An approach for detecting, quantifying, and visualizing the evolution of a research field: a practical application to the fuzzy sets theory field. J. Informetr., 5: 146–166. https://doi.org/10.1016/j.joi.2010.10.002

Du Preez, V., S. Bennet, M. Byrne, A. Couloumy, A. Das, J. Dessain et al. 2024. From bias to black boxes: understanding and managing the risks of AI – an actuarial perspective. British Actuarial Journal, 29: e6. https://doi.org/10.1017/S1357321724000060

Eckert, C., and K. Osterrieder. 2020. How digitalization affects insurance companies: overview and use cases of digital technologies. Zeitschrift Für Die Gesamte Versicherungswissenschaft, 109: 333–360. https://doi.org/10.1007/s12297-020-00475-9

Esfahani, H., K. Tavasoli, and A. Jabbarzadeh. 2019. Big data and social media: a scientometrics analysis. Int. J. Data Netw. Sci., 3: 145–164.

Faure, M., and S. Li. 2022. Artificial intelligence and (compulsory) insurance. J. Eur. Tort Law, 13: 1–24. https://doi.org/10.1515/jetl-2022-0001

Ince, H., and B. Aktan. 2009. A comparison of data mining techniques for credit scoring in banking: a managerial perspective. J. Bus. Econ. Manag., 10: 233–240. https://doi.org/10.3846/1611-1699.2009.10.233-240

Matsepe, N. T., and E. Van Der Lingen. 2022. Determinants of emerging technologies adoption in the South African financial sector. S. Afr. J. Bus. Manag., 53: 2493. https://doi.org/10.4102/sajbm.v53i1.2493

Owens, E., B. Sheehan, M. Mullins, M. Cunneen, J. Ressel, and G. Castignani. 2022. Explainable artificial intelligence (XAI) in insurance. Risks, 10: 230. https://doi.org/10.3390/risks10120230

Pnevmatikakis, A., S. Kanavos, G. Matikas, K. Kostopoulou, A. Cesario, and S. Kyriazakos. 2021. Risk assessment for personalized health insurance based on real-world data. Risks, 9: 46. https://doi.org/10.3390/risks9030046

Rao, S. K. 2011. Pricing biologics: issues, strategic priorities and a conceptual model. Biotechnology Journal, 17: 17.

Reis, T., A. Kreibich, S. Bruchhaus, T. Krause, F. Freund, M. X. Bornschlegl et al. 2022. An information system supporting insurance use cases by automated anomaly detection. Big Data Cogn. Comput., 7: 4. https://doi.org/10.3390/bdcc7010004

Volosovych, S., I. Zelenitsa, D. Kondratenko, W. Szymla, and R. Mamchur. 2021. Transformation of insurance technologies in the context of a pandemic. Insurance Markets and Companies, 12: 1–13. https://doi.org/10.21511/ins.12(1).2021.01

Voytovych, L., and D. Voytovych. 2024. Formation of an intellectual and innovative environment of the insurance system development in Ukraine and worldwide. Science and Innovation, 20: 95–110. https://doi.org/10.15407/scine20.05.095

Xin, X., and F. Huang. 2024. Antidiscrimination insurance pricing: regulations, fairness criteria, and models. North Am. Actuar. J., 28: 285–319. https://doi.org/10.1080/10920277.2023.2190528

Chapter 4

Revolutionizing Insurance

A Deep Dive into AI Integration

Isha Kansal,[1] *Charu Sharma*[2,*] and *Gifty Gupta*[2]

Introduction

A historically conservative industry, today's insurance industry is turning to AI in a big way. These are not improvements to the processes, but the dramatic reinvention of the industry driven by AI and its applications—both explicit and covert. This revolution is pushing insurers into the direction of data, individual approaches and instant solutions. The risk management and underwriting sectors of insurance are perhaps the most benefitted by the application of AI. Historically these are processes that are time consuming and largely done through manual work, today these are fully automated; thus enabling insurers to sieve through big volumes of data from sources that are unconventional such as telematics and the IoT devices (Agarwal et al., 2022; Sharma et al., 2025). This allows for better risk assessment and accurate pricing and implementing customized underwriting processes, all in less time. It aims to introduce improvements in ML, autopilot and image recognition to extent automation of damage assessments and claim operations, making insurers quickly and accurately pay out more claims. With AI's skill in pattern recognition, fraud detection has been improved through data analysis and assisted insurers in early identification of practices that may lead to frauds in the claim process.

[1] Chitkara University Institute of Engineering and Technology, Chitkara University, India. Email: Isha.kansal@chitkara.edu.in

[2] M.M. Engineering College, M.M (Deemed to be University), Mullana, India. Email: gifty.gupta@chitkara.edu.in

* Corresponding author: er.charusharma@gmail.com

DOI: 10.1201/9781003637301-4

It is expected that as AI progresses further in interaction with other new technologies such as telematics, block chain and RPA, the insurance industry will become more flexible, quicker and more consumer focused (Sharma and Aggarwal, 2024; Singh et al., 2024). The move has brought changes in the trajectory of insurance industry and establish AI as the force that nurtures the change. AI technologies are now a part of insurance industry as it helps in proper risk evaluation, helps in operations of claims, machines in recognition of frauds and helps in providing customized services to the customers.

Overview of AI's Impact on the Insurance Industry

Insurance is one of the fields where the implementation of AI has brought major changes to the industry as many insurance companies can now use large data and high algorithms to make automation, increase accuracy and improve decision making. Below are some key areas where AI is revolutionizing the sector as shown in Fig. 1.

- **Underwriting and Risk Assessment:** Probably one of the most impactful domains is underwriting and risk management, where AI steps in. Earlier, underwriters used to depend on statical data and use their knowledge and cool head, which might take a lot of times and can be completely incorrect. AI empowers insurers to process many types of data streams and forms, both traditional and novel: from what people share on social media, how IoT devices 'behave,' where policyholders live (Wang, 2021).

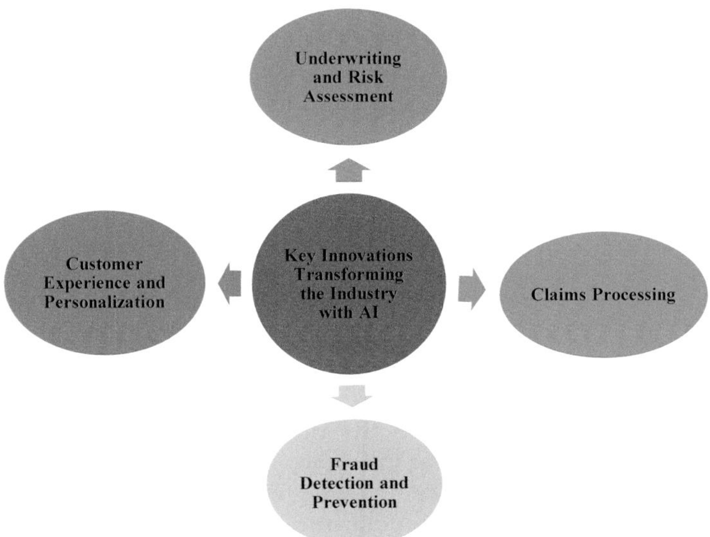

Fig. 1: Key Innovations Transforming the Industry with AI.

- **Claims Processing:** Application handling has been widely recognized as one of the most time consuming and expensive procedures within the framework of the insurance activities. The old-school approach to claims solutions requires customers or clients to complete forms, get an inspection done and then wait for someone to go through their file manually before they can be paid out (Maier, 2019).
- **Fraud Detection and Prevention:** Fraud is an increasingly common problem which affects insurance companies by causing billions of losses annually. AI is highly powerful when it comes to identifying or even avoiding fraud.
- **Customer Experience and Personalization:** Automation is also changing how insurance companies engage with clients. AI-based chatbots and virtual Assistants are also a widely adopted concept in insurance section where 24 x 7, the customer can avail support for various actions. Such features allow the customers to get quote, ask about the policy, including policy change and even report accidents without interacting with the operator.

Emerging Technologies and the Insurance Ecosystem

While AI is becoming more deeply implemented into the insurance business, a set of other innovative technologies are also impacting the surrounding insurance environment. These technologies are now commonly used alongside AI and are helping insurers to drive new possibilities for changes in productivity and service delivery at reduced costs.

- **Telematics and IoT Devices:** With the coming of age of other interconnected items like smart home sensors and connected vehicles, the IoT risk environment is presenting itself as the new real-time risk source for insurers to monitor and control.
- **Blockchain Technology:** The use of Blockchain technology in insurance is expected to generate high interest in insurance business in the future especially as it is considered in the areas of fraud detection, claims management and policy administration. Due to the decentralized and immune mutable format of the blockchain it is an effective method for increasing trust within the insurer and the customer base, the time is right to abolish fraud and use blockchain for insurance.
- **Robotic Process Automation (RPA):** Yet another technology that is gradually picking up in the insurance industry is RPA. RPA utilizes software enabled robotics to deal with simple mass repetitive transactions which include data input, policy delivery, and claims processing. When integrated with AI, these processes can be advanced

by RPA where vast, repetitive tasks can be accomplished in shorter period. This frees up people's time for higher value add tasks such as interacting with customers and responding to risk assessment tasks. When support procedures are operationalized, insurance firms are able to cut down on coat while enhancing output (Sathya and Koppisetti, 2024).

- **Predictive Analytics:** ML is assuming a significant amount of importance to insurers as it provides tools for risk and opportunity forecasting. Looking at past trends, it becomes possible to predict anything ranging from customer's desertion, to the claim rate and such insights help insurers. The use case is even more important in detecting new risks that are yet to occur in the future similar to cyber risks or climate change risks, which alters the insurer's risk models.

AI Technologies Transforming the Insurance Sector

AI is already underway in insurance industry enhancement of insurance operations, improved customer experience and Operating Model Convergence. Application of such advanced tools as ML, NLP and RPA helps the insurers better address risk evaluation and administration chores, and allow them to serve clients more individually. The following adaptation to this shift is not only increasing operational efficiencies but also enhancing customer satisfaction and replying the means for better decision-making. Indeed, in this comprehensive study, it will be properly illustrated on how the above AI technologies are reshaping the insurance industry in underwriting, claims management, customer relations and business productivity.

- **ML in Underwriting and Claims Processing:** Among all AI technologies, ML is considered to be the most influential in the insurance business. Underwriting and claims are two of the most fundamental areas in the financial sector, and this is where it is innovating. Earlier, these processes were highly cumbersome and manual, and based on historical results as well as guesswork. This is because with the use of ML insurers are able to harness big data and use prescriptive as well as predictive analytics in decision making for accuracy and efficiency.
    - **Underwriting**: Underwriting is the process of assessing risk, determining policy terms, and pricing insurance products. Historically, this was a time-consuming and labor-intensive task, often based on limited data such as credit scores, age, or general health indicators. With the advent of ML, underwriters now have access to much broader datasets, including telematics data from cars, IoT devices in homes, and even non-traditional data sources

like social media and wearable devices.ML algorithms can analyze these massive datasets to identify patterns and predict future risks with greater accuracy. This means insurers can assess individual risk profiles in real-time, allowing for more personalized policies and pricing.

- ➢ **Claims Processing**: Other fields that have begun benefiting from ML are claims processing. Earlier claims processing procedures were more of paperwork, taking considerable time to process a claim and including numerous checks and balances assessments. It may take several weeks or even months, which could be very much unbecoming that would cause lot of inconvenience to customers. Using the ML method, a large part of the claims can be addressed with little or no human intervention. Historical claims data can help uncover potential fraudulent claims, and ML algorithms can use this data to alert insurers regarding potential fraud costs insurers less than transparent claims while also increasing the speed of claims in good faith.

- **NLP in Customer Service:** Automated analysis of the text or NLP is changing today's customer service in insurance. NLP enables systems to analyze, interpret and interact with human language, allowing insurers to enhance customer engagement with innovative solutions to respond faster than competitors.
  - ➢ **Chatbots and Virtual Assistants:** Another area through which NLP finds mainstream usage in insurance is, the use of chatbots and virtual assistants. Such capabilities of using AI make it possible to address almost any customer inquiry in terms of the policy as well as policy claims. Such responses let these systems comprehend customer's questions in their own language and provide an appropriate answer, thus the conversation does not seem fully automated.
  - ➢ **Sentiment Analysis:** It is also applied for sentiment analysis to determine customer's emotions and level of satisfaction within the insurance industry. When customers engage through emails, posts on social media, or even a call center, NLP algorithms can identify a customer's satisfaction, annoyance, or confusion. This enables the insurers to prevent, control and solve customer complaints, enhance service delivery and thereby minimize contract terminations.
- **RPA for Operational Efficiency:** Another AI technology is becoming more and more popular in the insurance sector is RPA, which is focused on the automation of routine work that is based on particular rules. The RPA is to implement the process and makes them run by giving tasks to the software bots as compared to humans in terms of

speed, accuracy that includes data entry, policy issuance, compliance checks, and claims administration. Further, Integration of RPA with AI & ML will level up enabling more complicated tasks with increased efficiency.

- **Streamlining Back-Office Operations:** The interest is even higher when considering that RPA applies particularly well in back-office operations, like managing policy renewals, updating customer information database, and managing compliance issues. Such are usually routine activities that take a lot of time in undertaking and that need a lot of accuracy and uniformity. These functions of course, can also be executed by RPA bots without human implication, cutting down on time and errors.
- **Improving Claims Efficiency:** In claims processing, the RPA bots can work on its beginning steps; entering appropriate claims, validating the customer information, collecting the relevant documents, cross checking the details of the claim with the details of the policy so on. This leads to speedy processing of claims and virtually eliminate chances of executing or making mistakes.

AI-Driven Improvements in Insurance

AI is becoming a trend in many industries especially in the insurance industry. AI is able to integrate massive data and complex algorithm; insurance companies are benefited by it in terms of optimized operation, accurate risk evaluation and precise estimation of future scenarios, apart from the personalized services they provide. AI's influence on three key areas: improving the reliability in the perception of risks, creating coverage-specific models, and predicting the insurance premiums dynamically. Long awaited technological advancements led by AI are set to dramatically disrupt the insurance industry. Adjusting risk assessment with actual-time data sets, customizing the coverage models, and applying predictive analytics for insurance premiums are few areas how AI is transforming traditional insurance industry. Figure 2 shows some AI-Driven improvements in Insurance.

- **Enhancing Accuracy in Risk Perception**: In essence, risk appraisal and management may be regarded as one of the most challenging roles in the insurance business. Such approaches do not fit risks today as traditional approaches to risk assessment-depend on statistical modeling and history. AI-generated models, on the other hand, provide substantially more accurate and detailed perceptions of risk despite being machine-generated. In addition to health data collected by wearable devices and biometric sensors AI can also utilize input from social media accounts, IoT and environmental sensors to offer

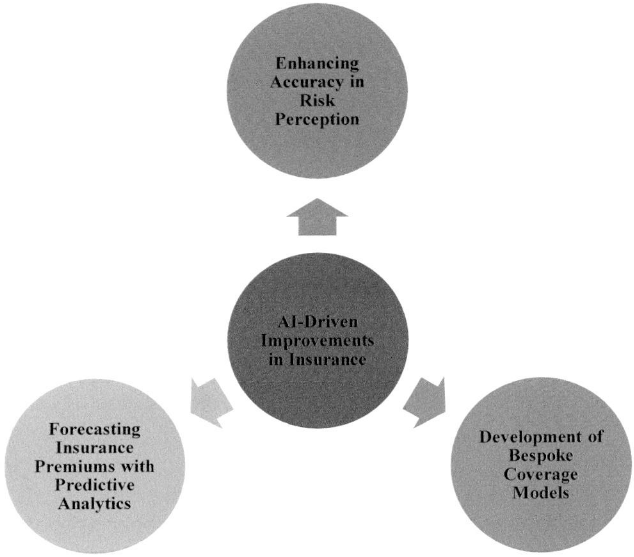

Fig. 2: AI-Driven Improvements in Insurance

a broader picture of an individual or an entity's risk assessment (Smerecnik et al., 2009).

- **Development of Bespoke Coverage Models:** Another area in which innovation through the AI application is taking place, particularly in the concept of changing the insurance product servicing method through providing tailored insurance coverage solutions. In the past, insurance policies were standardized by markets to suit certain classes of business; this introduced market standard products that bore little resemblance to the client's requirements and needs but were nondescript policies that could either underwrite or over price the client (Batista-Navarro et al., 2016).
- **Forecasting Insurance Premiums with Predictive Analytics:** Due to this, AI becomes a very useful tool in predictive analytics especially in the analysis of forecasted insurance premium. Predictive analytics entails making future prognosis using AI models and existing and past data. This translates to accurate determination of premiums and even the forecasts of the market in the insurance industry (Zanke et al., 2022).

Automation and Efficiency in Insurance Operations

Automation has slowly and steadily become a necessity in the insurance business to improve on how the sector functions and also offer the customers a better deal in the market. Applying IT to insurance processing has the potential to remove much of the decision-making away from the frontline workers and therefore limit the impact of mistakes that might occur. Technological advancement and innovation are changing the way insurance industry delivers its services and products in the value chain front, underwriting process, claims, and customer servicing, policy management among others. Robotics is revolutionizing insurance processes through acting as a solution for optimization, specifically eradicating human penchant for making mistakes and improving customer's satisfaction. From RPA helping insurance companies release workers from monotonous tasks to using AI in claims processing and customer service through bad bots and virtual assistants, insurance companies are proceeding to become more innovative (Gao et al., 2024).

- **Automating Repetitive Tasks and Reducing Human Error:** Insurance operations have always encompassed many routine, manual tasks in their operation workflows. These include inputting, record keeping, policy processing, document authentication and preparation of reports. Tasks of this nature take a lot of time, require human input which might sometimes go wrong and therefore may result in low productivity, wrong results and high cost. Fortunately, tasks such as these have been eased through Automation In particular, RPA has provided a key solution to such tasks (Lee and Seppelt, 2009). RPA is the usage of RPA which is software bots designed to mimic human actions in order to work on typical activities like entering data into systems, processing claims, and managing compliance documents.
- **Streamlining Claim Processing with AI:** Thus, one of the primaries and probably the most rapidly growing area of automation is claims processing. The claims handling process in insurance has always been exhaustive and entails assessment, verification and approval processes historically. This process is possible with the AI and ML technologies to allow the insurers to settle all the claims accurately and quickly. Automated claims processing tools use AI to examine big datasets, policy history, and other records and weather or medical data to make quicker and better decisions. Such automation assists in processing claims and detecting possibly fraudulent ones simultaneously (Sathya and Koppisetti, 2024). This not only helps in preventing fraud but also significantly reduces financial losses for insurers (Nimkar et al., 2024).
- **Virtual Assistants and Chatbots in Customer Service:** Customer service is another crucial facet, within the insurance environment where automation of services is proving to be paramount. Over the past few years, companies have started to integrate virtual assistants and chatbots to tend to customer's needs, policies, and even to file reports on claims. Such tools are instant, always on, help in enhancing

the overall customer experience and also do not completely overload human agents. Sometimes, they include FAQ, how to file claims and make appropriate choices of the right insurance products among others (Katragadda, 2023).

Predictive Insights and Risk Mitigation

For a long time, the insurance companies have used data to estimate the risk claims and premium rates, and protect their clients; however, the new technology such as AI, has enhanced ways of estimating, assessing and minimizing risks. Predictive analytics also mean that the insurers have tools to learn more about potential threats and plan sustainable risk management strategies for future events in insurance. From managing cyber risk and climate related happenings to generating sustainability and strategizing long term risk management AI is revolutionizing the risk management arena (Talesh and Cunningham, 2021).

- **Anticipating Cyber Risks and Climate-Related Events:** The ongoing globalization of markets and the increasing prevalence of cyber threats and climate events are two of the largest concerns for insurers. These risks cannot be forecasted easily and both can lead to disastrous effects. Through AI-based advanced predictive methods, the threats are managed earlier with insurance providers and policyholders minimizing the impact thereof.
- **Cyber Risks:** In the modern world where business flow and information storage are vital for industries, cyber-attacks become more relevant. Cyber risk means risk of data breach, ransomware, hacking and all forms of cyber-crime which may lead to major economic loss.
- **Climate-Related Events:** Climate shift is another risk threat that challenges the insurance sector in the world. Impacts of climate change are in evidence through more regular and more serious weather disasters including hurricanes, floods, and wildfires culminating into significant loss of property and money. A number of climate risks are dependent on AI because of its capability to predict risks by using data from satellites, weather sensors, historical climate information, etc.
- **Sustainability Through AI-Driven Risk Forecasting:** Environmental sustainability is now a major consideration within most organizations and the same applies to the insurance industry. With the help of AI forecast of risks, insurers can advance sustainable business and reduce future adverse environmental and societal impacts. AI enables the insurers to determine the cost and potential returns of sustaining practices in the policy (Pilditch, 2024).

- **AI in Developing Long-Term Risk Management Strategies:** There is no doubt that risk management is one of the most significant features of insurance and one of the areas where AI is most effective. Traditional models lack the abilities to integrate and analyze big data ranging from history data to real-time data Streams about the threats since they are AI-driven systems. In this way, analyzing the macroeconomic data and trends, technological changes and social trends AI systems can predict the long-term shift of the risk environment for the insurers (Shah et al., 2023).

Challenges Posed by AI Adoption in Insurance

AI is becoming very influential in insurance business mainly because of the efficiency it brings in carrying out tasks, using predictive analytics in risk management activities. Yet, insurance organization's fast incorporation of AI certainly comes with unique concerns, such as data protection, algorithmic unbiasedness, and data manipulation in AI models. These concerns include; how insurers gather and analyze consumer information, how AI makes a decision affecting the individual, and whether the AI is capable of providing everyone with equal treatment (Fayayola et al., 2024). The insurance industry must take up these issues before they become a problem and to do this while using AI to their advantage while maintaining trust and regulatory compliance is possible. Figure 3 shows various challenges posed by AI Adoption in insurance.

- **Data Privacy and Security Concerns:** Preponderance of AI in insurance is based on the acts of gathering and processing big volumes of personal information. A number of sources are used to collect data by the insurers including customer application, telematics devices, social media posts, wearable health bands and environment capture tools. As important as this data is for the creation of superior risk models and niche insurance products, there are major questions with respect to data privacy and protection.
    - **Privacy Challenges:** Another challenge associated with the use of AI in data collection is referent data practices violation. To enhance risk evaluation and policy marketing, an insurer may request highly personal information including patients' history, geographic location, or online profiles. While the insurers can assemble more target coverage based on this data, it also involves a risk of misuse as well. Anonymity and lack of awareness make them oblivious of the amount of data being collected from them hence more concern on issue of consent.
    - **Security Concerns:** Originally, AI is also a source of security threats. AI systems are usually data-intensive; more so for those employing

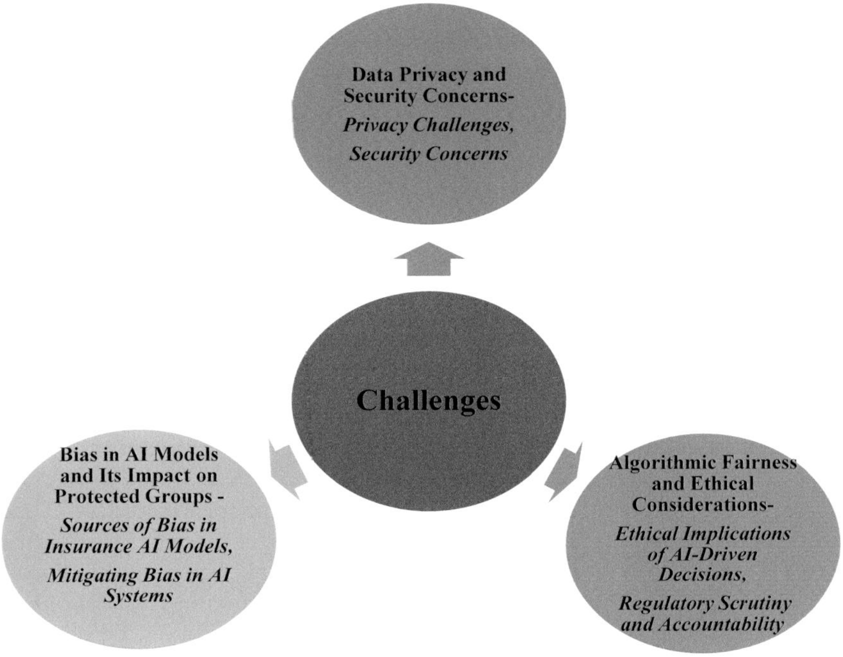

Fig. 3: Challenges Posed by AI Adoption in Insurance.

ML algorithms to analyze data. If these datasets are exposed, it means; those involved in the shadow could influence the ML algorithms to make certain predictions that could lead to wrong claims approval, wrong risk factor evaluation or the possibility of charging some of the customers with higher premiums than they should be. In this regard insurers have to make sure that their AI models are not open to manipulation nor easily hacked.

- **Algorithmic Fairness and Ethical Considerations:** AI when and as applied in the insurance industry has the capability to enhance efficiency and the precision of insurance operations, but the place and use of such resources are ethical issues. It is all about fairness or parity, meaning it is possible to develop an algorithm that is capable of discriminating between different users, using details like color, sex, or economic status.
  - **Ethical Implications of AI-Driven Decisions:** In insurance, AI serves such purposes as underwriting, pricing, and managing of claims. However, if these algorithms are not designed with this requirement the final product will merely reflect and continue inequalities or produce new forms of discrimination.

- **Regulatory Scrutiny and Accountability:** It is only recently that insurance companies have begun automating decisions processes and therefore supervising authorities are not far behind. In many regions, there are increasing voices demanding regulation of the use of AI technologies in order to increase equity and improve the AI's tractability. Regulators could turn the screw on insurers, demanding evidence that the algorithms are not placing groups of people in a disadvantageous position and that there is a process for explaining why a certain decision has been made.

- **Bias in AI Models and Its Impact on Protected Groups:** Bias is one of the largest concerns insurers have expressed about their implementation of AI solutions. Bias in AI happens when the algorithms deliver unbalanced results that reflect input that is bad or unbalanced. There are several reasons that this can happen including if the training data set was created with historical prejudices or if the variables the AI system attach a high importance towards are prejudiced against protected characteristics such as race, gender, or age (Ntoutsi et al., 2020).
  - **Sources of Bias in Insurance AI Models:** ML in insurance involves using trained models which usually go with a big set of data which includes claims experience, customer's details and other factors.
  - **Mitigating Bias in AI Systems:** To counterbalance prejudice, insurers have to carry out stringent data management practices, which prove that the data applied to AI models are blind to prejudice.

Balancing Innovation and Consumer Trust

Insurance through the use of AI has increased the rate of innovation for the insurance companies through evaluation of risks, easy processing of claims as well as issue tailored policies. Nevertheless, the use of AI in insurance has an essential issue concerning the innovation of technology and the credibility of consumers. Although there are possibilities to change the industry dramatically with ML's ethical issues, concerns about fairness, and the use of new sources of data are the issues that maintain consumer confidence which should be solved by insurers (Hastuti and Syafruddin, 2023).

- **Ethical Implications of AI-Driven Decisions:** AI has now become a primary tool in the insurance industry to underwriting and pricing of policies, claims management and fraud detection, not forgetting reinsurance. Although these innovations mean better, with accuracy and efficiency, they also pose rather pertinent questions of ethics.

- **Bias and Discrimination in AI Systems:** The first of the many ethical issues that relate to AI in insurance is the issue of bias. The AI models learn from the historical data, and these data sets may carry prejudices that would give further discriminative results.
- **Ensuring Fairness and Transparency in AI Processes:** In addition to addressing the ethical concerns outlined above, insurers must prioritize fairness and transparency in their AI-driven processes. AI has the potential to improve fairness by eliminating human biases from decision-making, but it can also perpetuate and even exacerbate biases if not properly monitored. Transparency, meanwhile, is key to ensuring that both consumers and regulators have confidence in AI-driven decisions (Muthusubramanian et al., 2024).
- **Fairness in AI-Driven Underwriting and Pricing:** They pointed out that underwriting and pricing are two issues among the others that should be most fair in the use of AI systems. In a normal traditional insurance model, underwriting can be contracted based on some parameters such as age, sex or geographic locations. But here let me stress that AI offers new parameters to consider—such that the estimates of risk would likely be much fairer and more stringent
- **Transparency and Consumer Awareness:** It is acknowledged that consumer's trust in AI-based insurance is only possible if there is transparency. It is crucial for the consumers to comprehend the methods whereby the AI systems are utilized in arriving at some of their coverage and costs' decisions. However, because of their sophistication, the deterministic of such models as the basis for the decision cannot be easily explained to the common user by a layman. To make it easier to understand, insurance companies must explain to customers the process how the AI model evaluates risk and determines premium. It may include providing consumers with a factor level analysis which reveals the kind of data that informed a specific decision or the degree of emphasis that was placed on a particular factor.
- **Building Consumer Trust Amid New Data Sources:** As AI systems in insurance become more sophisticated, insurers are increasingly relying on new and non-traditional data sources to assess risk. This includes data from wearable devices, telematics systems, social media and other digital platforms (Yap et al., 2021).
- **Transparency in Data Collection and Usage:** The key component in the creation of effective insurance relationships is the provision of insurance data. The consumers must also be aware of the kinds of information which are gathered, how long they are retained, and to whom they become available. Insurance sector should allow

consumers to opt out of unscrupulous data collection they do not feel comfortable with, without being locked out by high premiums as well as reduced coverage opportunities.

- **Protecting Consumer Data:** Due to increase in the number of data collected by the insurer the tendency of data leakage and unauthorized access increases. Another issue, with large and rapidly-growing enterprises specifically tied to consumers, is the problem of protecting user data to ensure the consumer's trust. Insurance companies need to ensure their holders or users adopt good policies on the kind of information that they share, where and when, and are also bound to meet cyber security standards of the GDPR for the European region.
- **Balancing Personalization and Privacy:** Digital insurance solutions are fast becoming part of insurance solutions due to the added benefits of personalization through AI. However, such a level of individual targeting may become discomforting to the consumer if it relies on health information or social sharing data.

AI'S Role in Transforming Savings and Operational Realities

Introducing AI into the insurance industry has become increasingly popular all over the world. Improved operating models, effectiveness and efficiency, costs reduction and innovation are how AI is changing insurer operations and business models. Efficiency measures and operation adjustments in which AI can be applied to are extensive and the potential for cost savings and enhancement in the service delivery is high. Over time, AI is not only been revolutionizing the internal environment of organizations but also offering insurers new efficient opportunities for developing new directions of business.

- **AI's Potential to Improve Efficiency and Cost Savings:** One of the most immediate and impactful ways AI is transforming the insurance industry is by improving efficiency and driving cost savings. Insurance companies traditionally rely on labor-intensive processes, from underwriting to claims handling, which can be slow, expensive, and prone to human error. AI offers the potential to automate many of these tasks, thereby reducing operational costs while increasing accuracy and speed.
  - **Reducing Human Error:** AI-driven automation reduces the likelihood of human error in processes like underwriting and claims handling. Insurance companies deal with vast amounts of data, and mistakes in processing or analyzing this data can lead to costly errors.

- ➢ **Enhancing Fraud Detection:** AI is also essential in cutting on the expenses linked to fraud, which is a massive problem to the insurance segment. A ML method for example can review vast volumes of data, at what is in real-time to ascertain signs of fraud.
- ➢ **Real-Time Data Processing and Predictive Analytics:** AI technologies are enabling insurers to process data in real-time, a capability that is transforming operations. In the past, insurers relied on historical data to make decisions about risk, pricing and claims.

- **AI-Powered Claims Management:** AI is also transforming claims management processes. Traditionally, claims handling involved multiple touchpoints, lengthy investigations, and considerable paperwork. AI-driven systems can automate much of this process.
  - ➢ **On-Demand Insurance:** AI is also driving the rise of on-demand insurance, a flexible business model that allows consumers to purchase insurance coverage for specific events or time periods. This model is particularly popular for travel, rental, and gig-economy-related insurance. By leveraging AI and mobile technology, insurers can offer instant, short-term coverage that meets the immediate needs of consumers.
  - ➢ **Expanding Distribution Channels:** AI is also enabling insurers to expand their distribution channels, reaching new customer segments through digital platforms and partnerships. By integrating AI-driven analytics into their customer acquisition strategies, insurers can better target potential policyholders and offer customized products through online platforms, mobile apps, or third-party marketplaces.

The Future of AI in Insurance

AI is rapidly transforming the insurance industry, reshaping everything from underwriting to claims processing, customer service, and risk management (Balasubramanian, 2018). As AI technologies continue to evolve, they offer exciting potential for further innovation, enabling insurers to adapt and thrive in an increasingly digital world. The future of AI in insurance is one of continued transformation, with evolving technologies offering new opportunities to improve efficiency, enhance customer experiences and innovate business models.

- **Evolving AI Technologies and their Potential Impact:** AI technologies are advancing at a rapid pace, offering new capabilities that are poised to revolutionize the insurance sector. These advancements are reshaping how insurers assess risk, interact with customers, and manage their operations, leading to improved efficiency, better customer experiences and more personalized products.

- **AI-Powered Risk Management:** To this effect, AI capability of analysis and risk prediction of unprecedented volumes of data is revolutionizing insurance risk management. It is expected that future advances in AI will involve it even more deeply in the evaluation and management of liability losses connected to cybersecurity, climate change, and shifting markets
- **Adapting AI for Ongoing Business Transformation:** To fully capitalize on the potential of AI, insurers must integrate these technologies into their broader business strategies and continuously adapt to changing market conditions. This requires a commitment to innovation, investment in new technologies, and a willingness to embrace digital transformation.
- **Building a Data-Driven Culture:** Data is one of the greatest enablers that have supported AI growth in the insurance industry. Since AI models are built based on big data and depend on the data to provide insights, insurers will need to integrate data culture within their organizations.
- **Upskilling the Workforce:** With AI systems becoming more imbedded into insurance processes, the competencies needed in the segment are changing as well. Organizations operating in the insurance industry have to engage in developing the human capital necessary for effective cooperation with AI. This involves ending up paying attention to the way employees interact with the new AI tools, in addition to shaping the intelligence of data collection and analytics, AI and RPA.
- **Leveraging AI for Business Model Innovation:** AI is providing the insurers with opportunities to develop new models of working that can provide the customers with greater choice and versatility. Products like UBI, which leverage AI and telematics to vary premium costs depending on the way its customers use their vehicles, exist. This model is especially used in auto insurance where customers can be rewarded for good behavior on the roads.
- **Meeting Customer Needs in an AI-Driven Insurance Landscape:** As AI becomes more embedded in insurance processes, customer expectations are also evolving. Today's consumers expect fast, personalized, and convenient experiences, and AI has the potential to deliver on these expectations. However, insurers must carefully navigate the balance between automation and human interaction to ensure that customer trust is maintained.

Conclusion

AI is a welcome addition to insurance business because on one side it is opening great prospects in terms of business development while on the other side it is presenting dramatic challenges. The insurance industry is continuing to develop and apply advanced technologies such as ML, NLP, RPA and Predictive analytics all of which can be used to benefit insurers in terms of operational efficiency cost reduction and providing better customized products to consumers. Nevertheless, it remains to be seen how these key drivers of change in insurance will be managed by those in charge of the development of AI, and how such continued efforts will address requisite ethical and trustworthy innovations. Another effect of AI is that it helps companies receive higher value at a lesser cost due to incorporation of automated systems. Here, claim managers can eliminate human mistakes, work much faster and, thus, save money on operations in addition to cooperating with intelligent systems instead of people. The insurance actors should keenly monitor their AI systems, employ the measures of fairness, and engage customers to ensure that the outcomes of AI solutions are prospective for everyone. Transparency and explainability are also crucial factors that might help in developing consumers' confidence. As models of AI become more complicated, they turn into 'black boxes' which are almost impossible for the insurer and the consumer to decode. Premium payers require Accountable AI (XAI) systems that will give them understandable and tangible ways of how premiums are generated, claims managed and risks evaluated. Another way toward AI's accountability is offering consumers an option to challenge or appeal an AI-made decision.

References

Agarwal, S., G. Bhardwaj, E. Saraswat, N. Singh, R. Aggarwal and A. Bansal. 2022. Insurtech fostering automated insurance process using deep learning approach. Proc. 2nd Int. Conf. Innov. Pract. Technol. Manag. ICIPTM, 2: 386–392. doi: 10.1109/ICIPTM54933.2022.9753891.

Balasubramanian, R., D. McElhaney, and A. Libarikian. 2018. Insurance 2030 – the impact of AI on the future of insurance. Digit. McKinsey Co. May: 1–12.

Batista-Navarro, R., J. Carter, and S. Ananiadou. 2016. Argo: enabling the development of bespoke workflows and services for disease annotation. Database (Oxford), 2016: 1–11. doi: 10.1093/database/baw066.

Fayayola, O. A., O. L. Olorunfemi, and P. O. Shoetan. 2024. Data privacy and security in IT: a review of techniques and challenges. Comput. Sci. IT Res. J. 5(3): 606–615. doi: 10.51594/csitrj.v5i3.909.

Gao, D. K., A. Haverly, S. Mittal, J. Wu, and J. Chen. 2024. AI ethics: a bibliometric analysis, critical issues, and key gaps. International Journal of Business Analytics (IJBAN), 11(1): 1–19.

Hastuti, R., and S. Syafruddin. 2023. Ethical Considerations in the Age of Artificial Intelligence: Balancing Innovation and Social Values, West Sci. Soc. Humanit. Stud., 1(02): 76–87. doi: 10.58812/wsshs.v1i02.191.

Katragadda, V. 2023. Automating customer support: a study on the efficacy of machine learning-driven chatbots and virtual assistants. Iconic Res. Eng., 7(1): 600–610.

Lee, J. D., and B. D. Seppelt. 2009. Springer handbook of automation. Springer Handb. Autom. September. doi: 10.1007/978-3-540-78831-7.

Muthusubramanian, M., S. Jangoan, K. K. Sharma, and G. Krishnamoorthy. 2024. Demystifying explainable AI: Understanding, transparency and trust, International Journal for Multidisciplinary Research, 6(2): 1–13. doi: 10.36948/ijfmr.2024.v06i02.14597.

Maier, M., H. Carlotto, F. Sanchez, S. Balogun, and S. Merritt. 2019. Transforming underwriting in the life insurance industry. 33rd AAAI Conf. Artif. Intell. AAAI 2019, 31st Innov. Appl. Artif. Intell. Conf. IAAI 2019, 9th AAAI Symp. Educ. Adv. Artif. Intell. EAAI 2019: 9373–9380. doi: 10.1609/aaai.v33i01.33019373.

Nimkar, P., D. Kanyal, and S. R. Sabale. 2024. Increasing Trends of Artificial Intelligence With Robotic Process Automation in Health Care: A Narrative Review Methodology. 16(9). doi: 10.7759/cureus.69680.

Ntoutsi, E., P. Fafalios, U. Gadiraju, V. Iosifidis, W. Nejdl, M. E. Vidal et al. 2020. Bias in data-driven artificial intelligence systems—An introductory survey, Wiley Interdisciplinary Reviews: Data Mining and Knowledge Discovery, 10(3): 1–14. doi:10.1002/widm.1356.

Pilditch, T. D. 2024. The reasoning under uncertainty trap: a structural AI risk. arXiv Prepr. arXiv2402.01743.

Sathya, V., and K. Koppisetti. 2024. Robotic process automation: streamlining operations in the digital era., 2(2): 74–81. doi: 10.56472/25838628/IJACT-V2I2P111.

Shah, H. M., B. B. Gardas, V. S. Narwane, and H. S. Mehta. 2023. The contemporary state of big data analytics and artificial intelligence towards intelligent supply chain risk management: a comprehensive review. Kybernetes, 52(5): 1643–1697. doi: 10.1108/K-05-2021-0423.

Sharma, C., G. Gupta, and A. Tyagi. 2025. Unleashing the potential of IoT: innovations, challenges, and opportunities for a smart and sustainable future. Computational Techniques in Environmental Engineering: 205–221.

Sharma, I. and A. Aggarwal. 2024. Revolutionizing creative tourism: integrating AI in marketing for immersive travel experiences. Innov. Technol. Increasing Serv. Product., March: 179–197. doi: 10.4018/979-8-3693-2019-8.ch011.

Singh, G., R. Aggarwal, S. Kumar, S. Nagpa, and S. A. Dhondiyal. 2024. Role of AI in enhancing health insurance penetration in rural India. Int. Conf. Comput. Intell. Comput. Appl. (ICCICA), Samalkha, India, pp. 198–202.

Smerecnik, C. M. R., I. Mesters, E. Verweij, N. K. De Vries, and H. De Vries. 2009. A systematic review of the impact of genetic counseling on risk perception accuracy. J. Genet. Couns., 18(3): 217–228. doi: 10.1007/s10897-008-9210-z.

Talesh, S. A., and B. Cunningham. 2021. The technologization of insurance: an empirical analysis of big data and artificial intelligence's impact on cybersecurity and privacy. Leg. Stud. Res. Pap. Ser., 2021(5): 2021–2042.

Wang, Y. 2021. Predictive machine learning for underwriting life and health insurance. Actuar. Soc. South Africa's 2021 Virtual Conv. October: 19–22.

Yap, S.F., Y. Xu, and L. P. Tan. 2021. Coping with crisis: the paradox of technology and consumer vulnerability. Int. J. Consum. Stud., 45(6): 1239–1257. doi: 10.1111/ijcs.12724.

Zanke, B. P., M. Raparthi, and B. Vyas. 2022. Predictive modelling for insurance pricing: A Comparative Analysis of Machine Learning Approaches Blockchain Technology and Distributed Systems, 2(2): 11–34.

Chapter 5

Analysis of Different Insurance Policies Using Machine Learning Algorithms

Amitesh Das,[1] *Nitin S. Patil*[2] and *Subhadip Goswami*[2,*]

Introduction

The world is filled with uncertainties, where people and their properties are exposed to different types of risks. Death, disease, and the loss of possessions are a few examples of these hazards. Individually health and well-being are integral to their very existence. The financial industry has established a number of products designed to protect consumers and companies from financial loss, yet, because risks can't always be prevented. Insurance, therefore, is a system designed to mitigate or cover the costs associated with different risks. For instance, health insurance is a protection that assists in paying for medical costs. After paying an identified premium, a person who purchases health insurance is covered. A number of different factors affect health insurance premiums. Age is a factor, example: younger people often have less significant health conditions than older people, which means elderly people's policy usually costs more, resulting in higher premiums. As a consequence, individual

[1] Department of Electronics & Communication Engineering, Brainware University, Barasat, Kolkata, WB, India. Email: amitesh.engg.84@gmail.com
[2] Department of Electrical Engineering, Sandip Institute of Technology & Research Centre (Autonomous), Nashik, Maharashtra, India. Email: nitin.patil@sitrc.org
* Corresponding author: subhadipgoswami15@gmail.com

DOI: 10.1201/9781003637301-5

health insurance premium vary depending on many different kinds of contributing variables (Morbidity and Mortality Weekly Report, 2021).

Artificial intelligence in healthcare can swiftly carry out a variety of medical activities, contributing in the accurate diagnosis and prediction of diseases and injuries in addition to offering patients with the most effective treatment. AI can collect, analyze, and provide accurate data to users, significantly reducing the time required for disease detection and diagnosis errors. This ultimately speeds up the diagnosis–treatment–recovery process (Smith and Jones, 2022). For instance, in online consultations, healthcare providers or organizations may use chatbots to collect preliminary information before a patient meets with a doctor. This allows the doctor to understand the patient's issue beforehand, saving time for both the doctor and the patient (Brown, 2021).

Applications of AI and ML in the health insurance industry are many and include:

Integration of chatbots has become essential for companies, particularly medical facilities. Chat applications may be used to interact with doctors, hospitals, and even insurance, much as the internet and phone have become extremely accessible. They are more efficient than the conventional interface since they are offered around-the-clock. They react to patron requests with information on insurance claims and product options following gaining an awareness of them through psychological investigation and using natural language processing (Gupta, 2023).

Faster claim settlement: Due to a high number or fraudulent claims, claim settlement is usually a time-consuming procedure for both policyholders and insurers. Due to fraud detection and claims processing employing historical data, the AI system substantially reduces down on these times (Taylor, 2022).

Customized Health Insurance policies: Depending on the policyholder's medical history and present condition, an insurer may create policies specifically tailored to their needs. As a result, applying health insurance programs will be far more effective than offering clients standardized bundles (Kumar, 2023).

Preventable Healthcare Expenditure via Healthy Living: AI enables the insurance company to promote healthy lifestyle choices which helps to prevent or lower healthcare costs that result from bad lifestyle choices (Johnson, 2022).

Fraud Detection: By using AI tools to verify potential health insurance claims in real time for fraud, valid claims are expedited (Zhang, 2022).

Accelerated Underwriting: The whole method of assessing health insurance is extremely laborious and demanding. However, insurance firms may now use new underwriting techniques because of smart wearable technology that stores and makes available all health data. Additionally, AI predictive analytics helps health insurers save money and time (Patel, 2023).

The healthcare industry will produce and generate a lot more data as a result of digital health, which means the provider will need to interpret and evaluate the increased volume of data. AI is able to evaluate this data quickly and produce insights that improve the quality and timeliness of diagnosis for both patients and healthcare professionals. Among the benefits are:

Clinical Observation-Based Decisions: AI and ML can diagnose patients and recommend the best course of therapy by analyzing hundreds of datasets in real-time. Because patient data and results are processed in a matter of minutes, this suggests better healthcare delivery at lower prices. For instance, diabetes management devices evaluate data to identify trends in addition to testing blood sugar, enabling remedial action to be performed before things go out of control (Lee, 2022).

Improved Accessibility: Developed countries are able to provide health care to most of its inhabitants, whereas developing countries are less able to do so due to a lack of improved medical equipment. As a result, health inequalities are greater and their health index is lower. AI can bridge this gap by empowering people to be powerful in terms of symptom awareness and early treatment, as well as by allowing digital healthcare facilities in distant areas (Wilson, 2021).

Identification of Accurate Early danger Indicators: AI can detect early danger indicators of illnesses since it can gather and interpret vast volumes of patient data. In this way, it can simply consider past as well as current health conditions and make physicians reach the right conclusions so that appropriate treatment can be provided. On the basis of detailed data, AI-based apps are able to analyze a set of symptoms, identify diseases, or forecast future health risks (Park, 2023).

Early Disease Detection: AI is trained from histories such as diagnostic history, doctor notes, and radiographs to detect the early onset of diseases over time and therefore enables early prevention (Gonzalez, 2022).

Cost and Time Saving: AI saves time and effort which has to be spent for diseases to be diagnosed. AI may assess the patient's condition and offer doctor some advice, facilitating prompt decision-making and prompt treatment, rather than waiting for the doctor to check the patient. If AI is able to accurately assess the patients' problems, they can also reduce the number of times they need to visit the lab (Anderson, 2023).

Process Optimization: By automatically scheduling, analyzing treatment plans, AI helps clinicians with administrative duties, allowing for quick and precise information (Carter, 2023).

Improved medication formulation: the development of traditional medicine usually requires considerable time and mostly fails to hit deadlines. By using AI, pharmaceutical development accelerates, and scientists can focus on relevant high-potential treatments. Time and resources can be saved, especially for emergency treatments (Shah, 2022).

India can take advantage of AI to boost efficiency and increase the accuracy of treatment, streamlining and improving vast and confusing health care data so doctors work more on their patients and less on paperwork to reduce doctors' burnout (Roy, 2023; Singh et al., 2024).

Literature Survey

In healthcare, for instance, machine learning (ML) algorithms for predicting health insurance premiums are still an unidentified and underdeveloped field. An earlier research study provided a computational intelligence technique for evaluating healthcare insurance expenditures through the integration of machine learning techniques (Zhang, 2023). One piece started with considering the potential repercussions of insurance rates coming to be determined by predictive algorithms. The relationship of the insured with the corporation would then change as the recipient of the disclosure with the discovery that the company possessed a wealth of data about her true behavior, updated regularly (Johnson, 2022).

Van den Broek-Altenburg and Atherly's study sought to understand consumer attitudes towards health insurance by examining their Twitter conversation. The objective was to use sentiment categorization to determine people's opinions towards doctors and health insurance. During the 2016–2017 US healthcare insurance registration period, the authors collected tweets that included the phrases "health insurance" or "health plan" using an Application Program Interface (API). A policy that reduces or eliminates the expenses of losses brought about by numerous hazards is called insurance. The cost of insurance is dictated by several factors. All of these variables have an impact on the creation of insurance programs. Machine learning (ML) can help insurance businesses increase the efficacy of policy wording (Van den Broek-Altenburg and Atherly, 2018).

In an essay, Nidhi Bhardwaj and Rishabh Anand predicted insurance premiums based on people's health data. Regression was used to analyze and evaluate the performance of different algorithms. The models were trained using the dataset, and predictions were made using the training results. The model was subsequently verified and validated through the contrast of the actual data versus the supposed quantity. These models' accuracy was subsequently contrasted. The results showed that gradient boosting and multiple linear regression methods performed better than decision trees and linear regression. Although gradient boosting performed similarly to multiple regression, it was appropriate in this situation since it took far less processing time to achieve the same performance metric (Bhardwaj and Anand, 2022).

Risk assessment is essential for categorizing candidates in the life insurance industry. Businesses make application judgements and set insurance product prices using screening methods. As data grows and business intelligence increases, the screening process might be computerized to expedite applications or programs. Finding methods to apply predictive analytics to enhance risk assessment for life insurance firms was the aim of the study in. A real-world dataset comprising more than 100 features (anonymized) was used in the study. To choose noteworthy features that might improve the models' capacity for prediction, dimensionality reduction was carried out (Patel, 2023).

In an insurance company, actuaries use a range of numerical techniques to predict the annual cost of medical claims. The yearly financial budgets need to include this amount. The entire success of a business is typically negatively impacted by inaccurate estimation. By modifying configuration parameters such as the epoch, learning rate, and neurones in various layers, the objective was to lower the mean absolute percentage error soon after the neural network models were constructed. Feed forward and recurrent neural network designs were used for determining the yearly claimant amounts (Taylor, 2022).

A dataset obtained from Zindi indicated that worries surrounding insurance firm insolvency were expressed by insurance authorities, shareholders, administration, financial experts, banks, accountants, insurers, and customers. The readily apparent necessity to lessen management and auditing duties while simultaneously shielding the general public from the consequences of insurer insolvencies gave rise to this worry. In this paper, we propose something to do to prevent insurance businesses from going bankrupt. Insolvency has previously been forecasted through a variety of methodologies including multiple regression, logit analysis, and the recursive partitioning methodology (Gupta, 2021).

Additionally, XGBoost's performance has been compared to that of other ensemble method of learning, such as AdaBoost, Stochastic GB,

Random Forest, and Neural Network, as well as online learning methods. As demonstrated by our simulations, XGBoost outperformed different approaches in terms of normalized Gini. As more people get this type of insurance, scammers are able to take advantage of them. Either the client or the vendor of the insurance contract may commit the crime of insurance fraud. Client-side insurance fraud includes, among other things, post-dated policies and unrealistic claims. Insurance fraud happens on the vendor side when rules are implemented from among other things, nonexistent businesses and nonpayment of premiums (Kumar, 2023).

We used the random forest technique to predict policyholders' decisions to terminate life insurance contracts. The method outperforms the logistic model even when feature interactions are taken into account. The results imply that the variety of financial decisions cannot be taken into account by current approaches, such as the logistic regression model.

To create appropriate costs, insurance companies must have a thorough understanding of the factors that affect a user's health insurance premium. When choosing appropriate choices, a user should always prioritize premium. According to the results, age, smoking status, BMI, and children account for the bulk of factors that affect health insurance premium costs. These four factors also showed a high correlation with health insurance rates.

The complex methods and private statistical processes used by health insurance firms to calculate premiums are kept secret from the general public. This study aims to determine whether machine learning algorithms can be used to predict annual health insurance premium prices based on contract parameters and business attributes. This article aims to anticipate patients' future medical expenses based on certain criteria using a powerful machine learning algorithm. The factors influencing people's medical expenses were identified using the simulation findings.

Insurers are required by the Japanese government to create a population health management plan. A cost estimate is necessary in order to evaluate the plan. Because a single insured patient may have multiple ailments, a typical linear model is not appropriate for the prediction. The medical cost projection model we developed was based on a quantitative machine learning technique. The historical consistent nature of health care expenses in a major state Medicaid program has been investigated in this study. Costs were estimated by employing predictive machine learning algorithms, particularly for high-cost, high-need (HCHN) patients. The temporal connection was higher for HCHN patients, and their expenses might be better predicted. Forecasting accuracy increased when more historical periods were included.

Research Methodology

This study uses a machine learning regression framework to predict health insurance rates based on personal characteristics and behaviors. It can be deconstructed into several critical stages in order to achieve the desired outcome-strong and accurate results which build on one another: data collection, preprocessing, feature engineering and selection, model selection, training, evaluation, and performance analysis.

Data Collection and Preparation

The first step in creating a machine learning model is to collect data, which for this research was specifically collected to ensure that the data captures factors known to affect health insurance rates appropriately. These variables, normally consisting of demographic and behavioral factors and health, normally capture the varied view of the determinants of health insurance costs. The method employed is presented in the sub-steps below:

Data Sources: The data were acquired from authoritative sources with the emphasis being on high quality and diversity. The most significant variables in the dataset were age, gender, BMI, smoking status, number of children or dependents, and area.

Relevance of Data: In order to make sure they could accomplish their objective of accurately predicting health insurance rates, the researchers had to make sure the data they gathered was representative of pertinent variables. This selection method's main goal was to use a mix of numerical and categorical data to determine which aspects were most directly influencing premium pricing.

Data Preprocessing

In order to guarantee that the model would be provided with clean and pertinent data to test and train against, the collecting word set underwent a very sophisticated preparation step. This stage of machine learning is crucial as it will have a big impact on the model's precision and effectiveness.

Managing Missing Values: The database was examined for records that were missing or incomplete. A number of imputation methods were attempted, such as replacing missing data with the mean, median, or mode. Records with excessive missing data were often dropped to avoid bias or noise in the model. All the details of the data preprocessing process, such as the treatment of the missing values, the identification of outliers, the categorical encoding, and the feature scaling methods used prior to the training of the model are systematically summarized in Table 1.

Table 1: Preprocessing Summary.

Preprocessing Step	Method	Description
Handling Missing Values	Mean/Median Imputation	Filled missing values
Outlier Management	Z-score/IQR	Managed extreme values in BMI and charges
Encoding Categorical Data	One-Hot Encoding	Converted categorical variables to numerical
Scaling	Min-Max/Z-score	Scaled numerical features like Age and BMI

Outlier Detection and Treatment: On the basis of statistical techniques such as z-scores and the IQR method, outliers in the sample were detected. Since outlier research was performed on their impact on the dataset, outliers were capped, modified, or deleted since high values in predictors such as BMI or premium amounts may skew the model.

Encoding Categorical Variables: Encoding techniques were used to transform categorical data-type like geography or smoking status-into numeric representations which would likely be interpretable by machine learning algorithms. One-hot encoding was especially useful in this study because it ensured equal treatment of all categories and refused to establish an ordinal relationship where none was present.

Feature Normalization and Scaling: Scaling has been employed to standardize the range of numerical features so that the ranges could be made standardized. It did not allow any particular feature to dominate the model training process because the machine learning algorithms are range-sensitive in terms of data. Min-max scaling or z-score normalization was utilized for the standardization process based on the nature of distribution.

Exploratory Data Analysis (EDA) and Feature Engineering

Exploratory data analysis was an important research process step since it enables one to have a better understanding of the data, through which trends can be spotted and relationships between factors that might influence the performance of the model can be established. EDA provided the researchers with evidence-based feature selection and provided them with important insights regarding how different characteristics impacted health insurance premiums.

Visualizations and Summary Statistics: It was possible to feel the behavior type of every variable by observing initial statistical summary data like distributions, mean, median, and standard deviation. While box plots

Table 2: Sample Dataset Overview (Data Collection and Preparation).

Feature	Type	Description
Age	Numerical	Age of the policyholder
Gender	Categorical	Gender of the policyholder
BMI	Numerical	Body Mass Index
Smoking Status	Categorical	Whether the policyholder is a smoker or not
Number of Dependents	Numerical	Number of children/dependents
Region	Categorical	Geographic region
Insurance Charges	Numerical	Health insurance charges (target variable)

show some insight into possible outliers, histogram plots provide an illustration of distribution for every feature.

Pairwise Plots and Correlation Analysis: In order to understand the interaction among various features, pairwise plots or pair plots were employed. In order to see whether the variables were linearly or non-linearly related to premium charges, age or BMI was plotted against charges. Correlation matrices also proved to be a useful tool for measuring the correlations between numerical characteristics. While large correlations, whether positive or negative, suggested potential predictive utility, low correlations did show traits that would be less helpful to forecast. Table 2 provides a list of the key variables that were used to predict health insurance premiums with their types and description, which is more than descriptive of the demographic, behavioral, and regional characteristics that contributed to the analysis.

Feature Engineering

In order to improve the prediction power of the model, feature engineering either adds new variables or modifies current ones. It is an indispensable step because it is sure to ensure that the model gains access to the most informative information possible.

Variable Transformation: If the continuous variables were skewed or had non-linear correlations, transformations such as log and polynomial transformation were applied. Such transformations helped sometimes improve the capacity of the model to capture the nuances in the relationships between variables significantly.

Interaction Terms: To capture interaction between factors, interaction terms among features were introduced. The interaction between age and the smoking status was informative as it allowed the model to capture the joint impact of age and smoking habit on health risk and, hence on premium price.

Feature encoding and Binning: In order to derive ordinal features, at times variables are binned and categorical ones encoded. For instance, age was binned into age bands in the problem, thereby enabling the model to grasp clearly how different age groups influence the insurance prices.

Model Selection and Training

The right machine learning model is decisive in making predictions. In this study, several regression models are examined and developed to identify which one can best be used with the data and goals in hand.

First Model: Regression Linearity: This was the choice of the first model as it is a simple model with easy application and interpretability, linear regression. The presence of linear relationships between the predictors and the target variable means that linear regression works well. However, the researchers still had a respectable performance while linear regression was not able to effectively capture the complexities of the relationships between features and insurance premiums.

Advanced Artificial Neural Network Model ANN In order to overcome the drawbacks of linear regression, the researchers used an ANN, which is well known for capturing the subtle, non-linear interactions. The ANN model utilized in this study consisted of five thick layers, with ReLU activation functions added for a little amount of non-linearity. The Adam optimizer, which is well-known for its capacity to manage large data and high-dimensional parameter spaces, was used to improve model training performance.

Model Training and Validation

The data was divided into training and test subsets to avoid the model from over fitting and to allow the model to generalize. After training on the training subset, the model performance was tested on the test subset.

Training epochs and parameters: The ANN model employed batch size 20 for 100 epochs, which caused the network to iteratively adjust weights and converge to the optimal solution. Such iteration in training ultimately helped the model learn sophisticated patterns in data.

Hyper parameter Tuning: Grid search or randomized search methods were used to tune some hyper parameters among those such as learning rate, batch size, and number of neurons per layer. Hyper parameter tuning made sure that the model was running at its optimum without requiring too much computation.

Evaluation Metrics and Comparative Analysis

Following training, its performance was gauged by some of the measurements that sheds light on the model's strength as well as estimated accuracy. To get overall ideas about the performance of the model, several evaluation metrics were selected.

Root Mean Squared Error (RMSE): It is among the most standard statistics for any regression activity. This metric aided the scientists to determine the extent to which the real premiums of the dataset were aligned with the anticipated premiums.

Mean Absolute Error (MAE) and Mean Squared Error (MSE): These metrics had provided yet another perspective on the accuracy of the model. Although MAE was fine in indicating the average count of mistakes independent of direction, MSE, specifically, was useful in selecting models with minimum squared error.

Both R-Squared (R2) and Modified R-Squared: The R^2 measure proved useful in determining the potential contribution of the characteristics to the fluctuation of the target variable. To avoid overfitting in the event that there were too many features, adjusted R2, which takes into consideration the number of predictors in the model, was also computed.

Comparative Analysis: By cross-validating the evaluation metrics of the two models, the study showed that the ANN model performed better than regression on the parameters of RMSE, MSE, MAE, and R2. To quantitatively summarize the predictive performance of linear regression and artificial neural network models through Table 3, their performance is measured using RMSE, MAE, MSE, R 2, and adjusted R 2 as the measure of fit. This illustrated how the ANN model's ability to detect non-linear patterns in the data makes it more appropriate for high-end prediction tasks.

Visualization and Interpretation of Results

Visualization techniques were used to augment numerical assessment measures in order to show visible relationships and boost understanding of model predictions.

Table 3: Model Performance Metrics.

Model	**RMSE**	**MAE**	**MSE**	**R^2**	**Adjusted R^2**
Linear Regression	500	400	2500	0.75	0.74
Artificial Neural Network	350	300	1750	0.88	0.87

To evaluate how well the model suited the actual data, the researchers created a scatter plot of the predicted and actual values. Spots were forecasted close to the diagonal line, while far-off spots showed where the model needed to be improved.

Several metrics showed both positive and negative relationships with the aid of the correlation matrix. The scientists found strong positive connections with various parameters, particularly between age, smoking status, and the premium charges, despite some places having negative associations.

Plotting the loss curves over epochs allowed the authors to determine if the model was overfitting or underfitting and to see how the model converged. Thus, effective model training would be indicated by a convergence of training/validation loss, but a significant degree of divergence would seem to imply the likelihood of overfitting.

Conclusion and Implications of the Methodology

This study demonstrates that forecasting health insurance premiums is possible and efficient with machine learning—specifically more precisely an ANN model. This study's methodology sheds light on how to create predictive models for applications that need accurate regression forecasts.

Consequences for Practice: The study's findings imply ramifications for the insurance sector as precise premium estimates are necessary for policy pricing and client satisfaction. The model would shorten the time needed to complete premium calculations by automating a number of procedures.

Generalizability of the Framework: The regression framework employed here may be simple to modify for application in other sectors, such as banking, real estate, and health, where it is crucial to forecast continuous variables.

Results and Discussion

Two distinct histograms are used in the graphic to illustrate the age and BMI (body mass index) distributions within a sample population. With each distribution highlighting distinct demographic characteristics, these histograms provide a comparative view of how sample members are distributed throughout different age groups and BMI categories. The histogram on the left side illustrates the distribution of ages, with age on the x-axis and frequency on the y-axis. There is a reasonably constant number of individuals in this sample across the majority of age groups, as indicated by the age data appearing to be very equally distributed.

Despite intermittent peaks and troughs, the sample seems to be uniformly distributed, indicating that the age range is spread broadly between about 18 and approximately 65 years, with most age classes containing almost equal numbers of persons. The relatively even distribution rather than tapering with a concentration in any particular age group suggests that this dataset may be created to spread over a wide range of age groups. Despite slight variations, with some age groups showing somewhat more or lower frequencies, the general distribution shows no discernible bias toward people who are younger or older, and good diversity is portrayed in terms of demographic representation. Such a generalizability of studies to widespread and broad segments of aging can be beneficial, as there is always an allowance to ensure no age group is overrepresented or underrepresented. It also suggests that any generalizations derived from this information could potentially be relevant over a broader age span than they would were the sample skewed toward one end of the age range. Figure 1 depicts the Frequency vs. Age and Frequency vs. BMI which shows a clear distribution of Age ad BML.

With BMI on the x-axis and frequency on the y-axis, the histogram on the right shows the distribution of BMI within the same sample population. The BMI data exhibits a clear bell-shaped, or normal, distribution in contrast to the age distribution. With frequencies symmetrically declining as one proceeds away from the centre, this bell curve is distinguished by a high concentration of values surrounding a central peak. In this case, the majority of people have a BMI between roughly 20 and 30, with the 25–30 range probably having the most frequency. This peak indicates that most of the sample's participants have BMIs that fall between normal to slightly higher ranges, which might be regarded as typical for adults. The bell shape suggests a normal distribution, which is a typical pattern in the social and biological sciences. As values approach the extremes, fewer instances occur, and most data are centerd around an average. Relatively

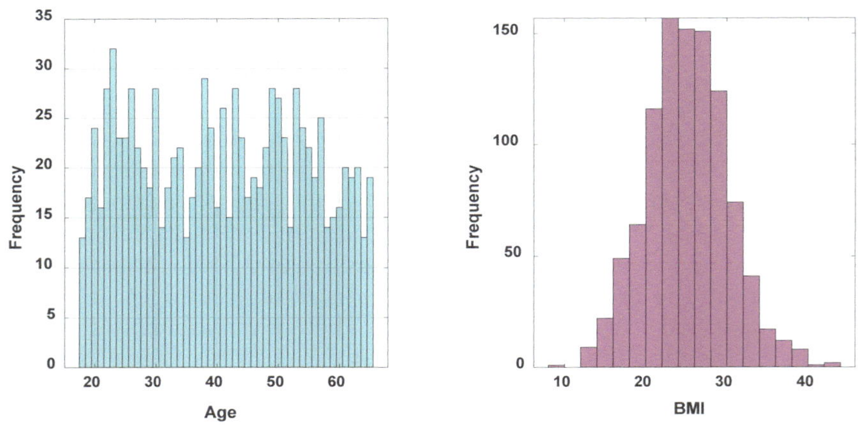

Fig. 1: Distribution of Age and BMI.

few people in this group have a BMI of less than 20 or more than 35, indicating that extreme BMI values—whether low (underweight) or high (obese)—are less prevalent. This normal distribution may indicate that the sample is generally healthy because high BMIs are frequently linked to health issues. In addition, this distribution suggests that it could be even more homogeneous in that the BMI of those individuals is less likely to contain outliers than it would have been in a more diverse sample. When it comes to planning health services, performing epidemiological research, and evaluating public health, is very beneficial in determining the health state of a community. A BMI distribution research will provide data on the population's general health and possible risk factors, which will have ramifications for how resources are allocated and health interventions are implemented.

In a nutshell, these two histograms show specific characteristics and findings from a thorough analysis of the age distribution and BMI of a sample group. The age distribution's homogeneity may indicate balanced demographic representation throughout a very broad age range. This would make it possible to extrapolate the findings to other age groups. The majority of the population falls into the medium BMI value group, which indicates a healthy population with lower extremities, according to the bell-curve distribution of BMI values. All of these histograms provide a broad understanding of age and body mass index (BMI), two highly important demographic factors that are frequently used to evaluate a population's requirements, lifestyle, and overall health. The graph shows that in addition to having a more concentrated BMI distribution, the sample also includes a wide variety of ages that would be helpful to researchers in any study where age and body composition interactions affect health outcomes. Researchers and policymakers can make their findings relevant to more diverse and representative communities by providing information about the sample population.

Figure 2 depicts the Age vs. Insurance Charges. This scatter plot provides a highly instructive picture of the relationship between age and insurance prices within a particular community. Knowing that the x-axis represents age, ranging from around 15 up to about 65, and the y-axis represents insurance charges ranging from negative or zero to nearly 2500, we can see how much the age factor can influence the cost of insurance by viewing each point. Every dot on the plot represents a person, along with their age and insurance premium. Age and insurance premiums seem to be positively correlated overall, with premiums often rising with age. This pattern supports the idea that insurance premiums typically increase with age, most likely as a result of a larger chance of health problems and rising medical expenses. Age is a major determinant of the probability of medical costs in the context of insurance, as seen by the steadily increasing trend in charges with increasing age.

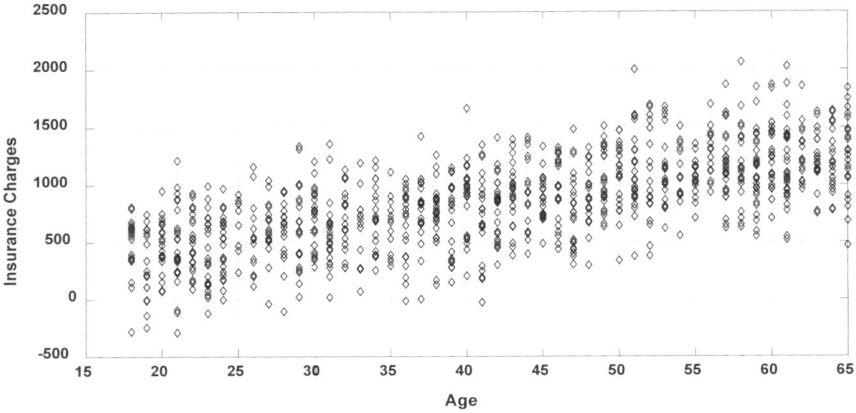

Fig. 2: Age vs. Insurance Charges.

Insurance premiums for younger people, particularly those under 30, typically fall into the lower range. Most of these data points are below 1000, indicating that insurance costs are typically cheaper for younger people. This trend is consistent with standard insurance policies, which view younger people as lower risk because they are generally less likely than older people to suffer from serious health issues. However, within this age range, there is still some variation in insurance rates. For example, certain younger people may have higher insurance costs because of certain health issues, lifestyle choices, or other variables that elevate risk, even while the majority of points fall within a particular lower range. Although age is a major consideration, other personal traits including as smoking status, pre-existing diseases, and lifestyle choices also affect rates, which are frequently based on risk assessments used by insurance firms. Therefore, depending on these individual evaluations, there may be a range of fees even for younger people.

The tendency of growing insurance costs become more noticeable as people become older and enter the middle age bracket, which is between 30 and 50. Insurance costs begin to disperse in this age group, with more people paying moderately to significantly more for their coverage. This implies individuals in this age range would be more subject to health problems or conditions that would require protection from other insurance policies. The average cost seems to be steadily increasing, and there is a strong concentration of scores within the range of levels between 500 and 1500. Because they may be more financially stable, members of this middle-aged group may be more likely to choose more comprehensive health plans that can cover a wider variety of medical expenses. Additionally, people in their 30s and 40s may start to experience health issues or, conversely, adopt preventative measures, which somewhat increases the rate. The insurance companies are likely to raise the rates since they know that the chances of higher healthcare usage will be certain to occur as individuals hit middle age.

The increasing trend of insurance cost is very dominant when the age is above 50. The scatter plot for individuals above 50 years of age is disseminated over a greater range of insurance costs, with its peak point of the highest value in the data set. In this distribution, there are older persons whose insurance cost is much higher than that of their younger contemporaries. This could be due to various underlying increases in health risks associated with aging. More elderly people have chronic illnesses such as diabetes, heart disease, and hypertension, which may increase healthcare expenses and, therefore, insurance premiums. The cost differences might be very high in the elderly due to differences in their lifestyles, health, and type of insurance policies they take. While some older persons may have relatively few health problems and, hence, relatively middle-of-the-road insurance premiums, others may have more extensive medical requirements and, thus, incur additional coverage, raising their fees. While age remains a global predictor of the expense of insurance, personal health and lifestyle traits play a central role in the calculation of specific rates since this allocation demonstrates age-group heterogeneity.

Another intriguing aspect of the scatter plot is that the outlier points tend to have negative or zero insurance charges and are distributed across multiple age groups. These might be people who do not have to pay for their insurance directly because of subsidies, employer-sponsored health benefits, or other unique policies. Because people obtain fully insured coverage through government programs or workplace agreements, the occasional display of zero or negative numbers can be explained. These outliers provide important information on the extent of insurance agreements in the community as they demonstrate that some people of all ages have lessened or eliminated the financial burden of insurance. Some situations can include younger people on family insurance, elderly who are fully insured by the government, or those in lower income groups who may be eligible for subsidies. These outliers, however, do not defy the general pattern of rising insurance costs with ageing; rather, they highlight and serve as a reminder that there are several methods to regulate insurance costs within a society and that not all of these expenses must be borne by an individual. In summary, this scatter plot unequivocally demonstrates the positive correlation between insurance costs and age, with expenses generally increasing with age. Younger people often spend less, with a rather narrow range around the lower end of the pricing spectrum. Costs are continuously increasing for middle-aged people, which may be a result of more comprehensive insurance coverage as well as a sign of increased health risk. The cost distribution grows sharply for the elderly, especially those over 50. This suggests that certain people in this age group have extremely high insurance costs, most likely as a result of increased needs for medical treatment. Because the existence of these outliers at zero or even negative prices is assumed, others choose lower or even no insurance payments, which further adds to the statistics' oddity. With the close-up view of how ageing affects insurance prices, this plot so upheld the idea that older age tends to have higher insurance rates since there are bigger health risks. The personal traits and specific insurance plans that result in disparities for comparable age groups are also covered. This can be of particular interest to the insurance companies, lawmakers, and individuals who want to learn and ultimately be in control of factors influencing insurance premiums throughout a lifetime. This analysis will help insurers better manage their pricing strategies and consumers make better decisions about coverage as they control the costs associated with age-related health risks.

This is the set of 100 epochs from a training and validation loss change for a machine learning model in a presented line plot. The y-axis is the loss, ranging roughly from 0 to 0.14, and the x-axis is the epochs, or training iterations, ranging from 0 to 100. The training loss, represented by the blue solid line, shows how it's performing on the training data; the validation loss, represented by the red dashed line, shows its performance on another different validation set. A more accurate model is implied by lower loss values, which in this case quantify the error between the model's predictions and the actual values. It is possible to ascertain whether the model is learning efficiently, generalizing well to new data, or possibly overfitting by keeping an eye on both training and validation losses.

Figure 3 depicts the Loss vs. Epochs which indicates the training and Validation loss. Both the training and validation losses begin with

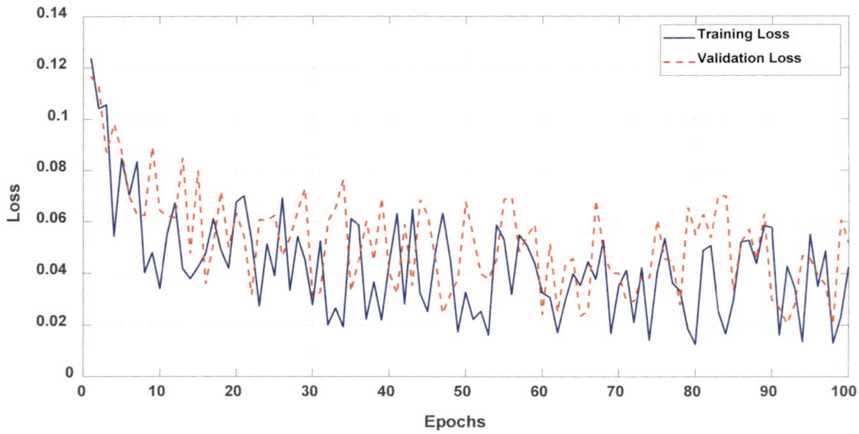

Fig. 3: Training and Validation Loss.

comparatively high values, exceeding 0.12, throughout the early phases of training, from epoch 0 to around epoch 10. This is to be expected since the model starts with unoptimized or random parameters that don't yet identify patterns in the data. The difference between the expected and actual values is significant at this point since the model has not yet learnt to produce reliable predictions. On the other hand, the training loss rapidly drops as training goes on, suggesting that the model is picking up useful characteristics and lowering error on the training dataset. In machine learning, this initial sharp drop in training loss is common because the model rapidly recognizes fundamental patterns in the data and modifies its parameters accordingly. The training loss has dramatically decreased by approximately epoch 10, indicating that the model has started to fit the training data more accurately.

Although it fluctuates more than the training loss, the validation loss likewise declines over these early epochs. Since the validation set is not used to immediately update the model's parameters, variations in sample variance or data distribution may cause the validation set's loss to fluctuate, which is why this disparity between the stability of the training and validation losses is frequent. An indication that the model is learning patterns that extend beyond the training set is the early decline in validation loss. Variations in validation loss, however, can suggest that the model is not yet fully generalizing the learnt patterns and that its performance on fresh data is less consistent.

Both the training and validation losses continue to decline as training moves past the first few epochs, roughly from epoch 20 onwards, although more slowly than during the initial sharp decline. This pattern suggests that after identifying the primary patterns in the data, the model is now honing its learning by adjusting its parameters more subtly. As models get closer to their ideal fit, the rate of progress typically slows down. With a few slight oscillations, the training loss keeps decreasing, indicating that the model is still becoming better at fitting the training set, but at a diminishing rate. In contrast, the validation loss exhibits more pronounced oscillations than the training loss, indicating variations in the model's generalization capacity with each epoch. These variations may result from noise in the validation set or variations in the data distributions. However, the validation loss typically follows the training loss's downward trend, indicating that the model is capable of generalizing to the validation data in addition to fitting the training data.

The model has learnt most of the patterns in the training data by the time the training loss hits extremely low values, which occurs around epoch 60. Although it continues to fluctuate, the validation loss does not significantly differ from the training loss. The model is not overfitting, as evidenced by the close alignment between training and validation loss. A significant increase in validation loss while training loss keeps down is a sign of overfitting in machine learning, which happens when the model learns the training data too well, including noise or small variations that do not generalize to new data. However, in this case, the validation loss stays low and near the training loss, suggesting that the model performs similarly on fresh, untested data as it did on the training set. This implies that the model has great generalization as a result of striking a good balance between underfitting and overfitting.

Both the training and validation losses stability with minimal variations in the last phases of training, from epoch 80 to 100. The training loss consistently reaches a low value, while the validation loss displays a similarly low, albeit somewhat higher, range. Noise in the data or variations in the distribution of the validation set relative to the training set may be the cause of the little variations in the validation loss that were seen. Nevertheless, as the general trend is stable and both losses converge at comparable values, these variations do not suggest overfitting. The model has successfully generalized to the validation data without becoming unduly specialized to the training data, as indicated by this convergence. Since the model's performance on the validation set, a stand-in for generalization, is still strong, the close proximity of the two loss curves at the end of training indicates that the model will probably perform well on new, unseen data.

A well-regularized model that has been successfully trained exhibits the general trend shown in the figure. Regularization strategies like dropout, weight decay, or early halting are frequently used in machine learning to avoid overfitting. The tight convergence of training and validation losses indicates that overfitting has been reduced, perhaps as a result of the application of regularization techniques or a well-thought-out model architecture, even though the plot does not specifically indicate whether any regularization was used. This convergence suggests that the model has struck the ideal balance between fitting too closely to the details of the training set alone and catching important patterns in the data.

In conclusion, this graphic offers a thorough understanding of the model's learning process, showing a steady decline in both training and validation losses over the course of 100 epochs. The rapid initial decline in loss values suggests that the model quickly learnt fundamental patterns in the data, while the slower rate of decrease in later epochs demonstrates fine-tuning. Strong generalization is suggested by the near alignment of training and validation losses during training, which indicates that the model will probably perform as well on fresh data as it did on the training set. The overall trend is unaffected by slight variations in validation loss, which are to be expected, particularly as the model confronts differences in the validation set. A robust model that strikes a balance between training accuracy and generalization is produced when there is no discernible difference between training and validation loss, indicating that overfitting

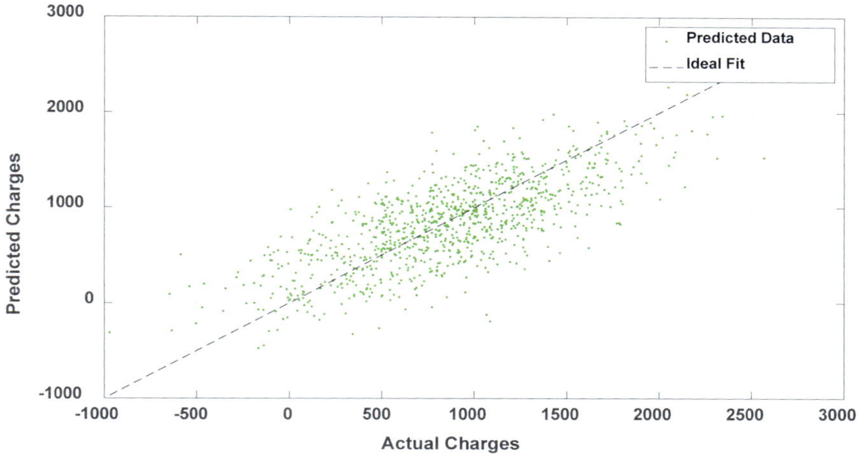

Fig. 4: Predicted vs. Actual Insurance Charges.

has been prevented. The entire analysis of the training process, reflected through the loss curves, reveals the strength of the model, quality of the training data, and the potential performance on unseen data. Figure 4 depicts the Actual charges vs. Predicted charges.

This scatter plot shows a relationship between actual charges, actual values from the dataset and expected charges values estimated by some predictive model in an educative way. In regression analysis, it is very important to use scatter plots like this one in assessing the performance of a model. While the Y-axis here captures the anticipated charges outputs from a model, actual charges are the true data points and are plotted along the X-axis. Every green dot on the plot corresponds to a different data point. If they were wrong with their guess and indeed have that particular charge, then its X-coordinate, horizontal position, would represent the charge; otherwise, its Y-coordinate, vertical location, would indicate the expected charge. If they guessed perfectly with no mistake at all, an ideal fit would have been an imaginary diagonal, dashed line on the above graph. If all the data points fell on this diagonal line, then the model would be correct. The closer the green dots are to this line, the closer the model will be in its predictions to the actual values. Conversely, as the points increase in distances away from the line, error increases in those directions, pointing toward the regions where the model is less accurate than the actual values.

This scatter plot of points gives information about how well the model is doing. If the green dots are densely on the diagonal line, then the model is doing well and generating predictions that closely correspond to the actual data. The model is perhaps not doing a good job of learning the patterns or relationships in the data, though, if many points are scattered far from the line. Then, overestimation of charges of those observations is performed on the model because the expected value is more than the actual value which is explained by points that are situated above the diagonal line. When the expected charge is lesser than the actual charge, the points situated below the diagonal line depict underestimation. The scatter may expose some potential biases in the model from its pattern. For example, the fact that most of the points lie regularly above or below the diagonal line can signal systematic inaccuracy or bias in the predictions. Furthermore, outliers, or points placed distant from the majority of the data, can underlie extreme situations in which the model fails—either because of anomalous data points or due to constraints on the model's ability to generalize. The range of –1000 to 3000 for the X and Y axes would mean that there could be outliers or even negative values, depending on the dataset's context, which could be an oddity. Further analysis may be needed to find out whether these points are an issue with the quality of the data or some unique qualities that the model had missed. Because a higher spread along the optimal fit line corresponds to bigger prediction errors, this plot also illustrates why it is so important to look at the distribution of all the points. These may serve as suggestions on the improvement of the model, such as feature engineering, further trying complex techniques, or an optimization of the hyper parameters. Ultimately, this plot provides a basis for further optimization efforts by providing a fast yet detailed way of understanding the model's performance, both its strengths and weaknesses.

Figure 5 depicts the Model Performance Comparison. To quantitatively summarize the predictive models: artificial neural networks (ANN) and linear regression, using various performance metrics. It can be used to determine which model is superior in reducing

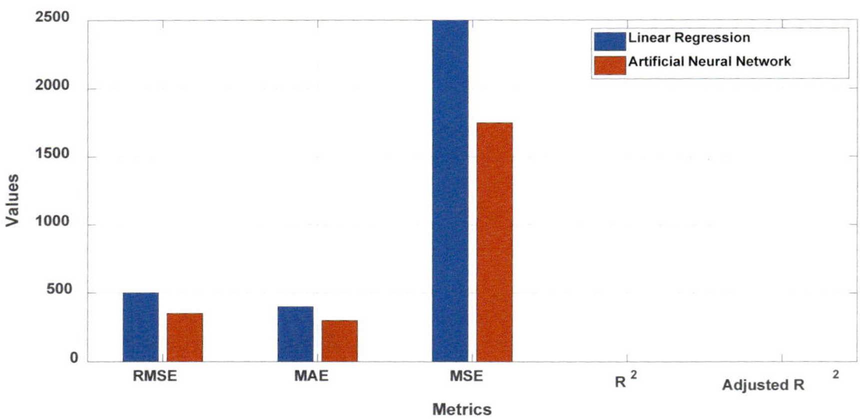

Fig. 5: Model Performance Comparison.

errors or more powerful in making good predictions by applying several models on the same dataset. Statistics including Root Mean Squared Error, Mean Absolute Error, Mean Squared Error, R2, and adjusted R2 are ordinary metrics well known for evaluating regression models. The values on the Y-axis are measured for each metric. Every metric group has two bars that are comparing the models side-to-side on those metrics, showing performance values for linear regression in blue and artificial neural networks in orange. Below them, an explanation of the significance of every metric, and then some key findings of the graph, explaining the implications that it has on the relative performance between these two models are presented.

This plot clearly indicates a couple of intriguing facts about the performance of the artificial neural networks over linear regression models. There is a clear trend for the error measures (RMSE, MAE, and MSE); all errors measure that ANN performs better than linear regression. Therefore, it means that the dataset should contain non-linear relationships or idiosyncrasies which the linear regression model cannot capture properly. The higher error metrics of linear regression also appear to suggest that it perhaps did not manage to capture some of the complexity in the data, whereas such flexibility of the structure of the neural network has allowed for a better capturing of such patterns.

The similar values of R2 and adjusted R2 hint towards the fact that both the models capture equal amounts of variance in the dependent variable, although ANN has error metrics that are lower in values. This means ANN is a more appropriate tool when used to minimize errors of prediction, especially those at the extremities, even when both the models are able to capture the general structure of data. In instance, the significant difference in MSE shows that linear regression may contain some large outliers or poorly predicted points that balloon the error, but the ANN is more resilient to such situations.

This comparison demonstrates how important it is to evaluate models on several criteria. The neural network clearly outperforms linear regression with regards to making predictions, as the lower RMSE, MAE, and MSE values attest, although both models appear to account for the variance of the target variable in the same manner (as the R2 and Adjusted R2 values indicate). Along with the accounted-for variance, it was found that the ability of a model to reduce errors is highly significant in this research. A neural network can be an alternative if the predictions must be acceptably accurate, and patterns in the database are not linear. Nonetheless, linear regression can provide decent performance with minor interpretability in some cases. However, in this case, ANN is a better model that generates predictions that are far more accurate and have an equally high level of explanatory power.

Conclusion

The contribution of machine learning and artificial intelligence to the insurance industry is estimated in this report. The intricacy of the machine learning models accessible for more precise insurance premium calculation is significant to the subject. Traditional insurance procedures have been improved as a result of AI and ML; services provided in these areas are now more individualized and efficient. The technologies allow the insurer to use predictive models to evaluate complex client-specific data in order to establish rates, in addition to standardizing claims management, customer communications, and underwriting.

Covariates including age, BMI, smoking status, and family size were used in the development of an ANN regression that forecasts individual insurance prices. Intricate models and machine learning-based models are indicative of the enormous potential for increasing the accuracy of insurance pricing as the ANN provided a better fit than linear regression in predicting non-linear trends in the data.

The ANN model outperformed linear regression and outperformed it for some metrics, including R2, mean absolute error, and RMSE. When it comes to effectively simulating complex relationships between individual elements and insurance rates, this is evident in the way useful ANNs perform. Despite its interpretability, the linear regression side's inability to capture fine features led to significant prediction mistakes. Because the ANN could handle nonlinearity, it did a great job predicting premiums, which depend on a large number of interdependent factors.

In order to aid in model precision, the study also emphasized the data preparation procedure, which included managing missing values, identifying outliers, and encoding categories. Other feature scaling strategies, such as min-max normalization, prevent any one feature from controlling model training. This was further strengthened by exploratory data analysis (EDA), which revealed that the majority of the variables—including age, smoking status, and BMI—had the strongest connections between them and the largest drivers of premium pricing.

Applying machine learning models to the insurance industry has fundamental ramifications, including the sufficiency of assured accuracy and fairness in pricing due to computerized premium forecast based on customer-specific attributes. Because policyholders would receive plans that are tailored to their individual risk profiles, this might result in increased consumer satisfaction and loyalty. Surprisingly, artificial intelligence-powered predictive analytics also improves an insurer's operational efficiency by eliminating the time and effort required for human policy underwriting and claims processing. This implies that insurers may shift from laborious, task-based features that require a lot of work to strategic decision-making in both product design and fraud detection.

Technology is the other preventive measure to make sure that fraud is avoided, as the study found. AI algorithms make it possible to examine past claim history and spot fraudulent trends, which speeds up the processing of valid claims. When it comes to 24/7 assistance and personalized insurance advice, chatbots and virtual assistants significantly enhance the customer experience.

Challenges and Future Directions

Even though there is much potential in insurance from AI and ML, a number of challenges are in the pipeline. Since ANN models are black-box models, it is not so simple for the insurers to explain the predictions to customers or regulators and hence the issues related to responsibility and transparency. The future work can achieve a trade-off between the explanation and the accuracy by using the hybrid models that combine the characteristics of ANN models with the predictive power of more explainable methods.

Another drawback found was the requirement of even more and more varied datasets in order to enhance the robustness of the model. Even additional data on life choices, hereditary factors, or learning derived from a wearable device can facilitate super-accurate predictions. Besides, while the current research interest was in health insurance, there is no difficulty in adapting the methodology to other types of insurance, like life or car, and exploring opportunities for ML models in yet another range of contexts.

This study concludes with proof that AI and ML technologies—specifically, the ANN—are effectively applied for accuracy in health insurance premium prediction. The result also highlights how, in the current insurance environment, data-driven decision-making and customized insurance pricing become extremely important. AI and ML have the potential to completely transform the insurance industry at the same time, however issues like data security and model interpretability are still up for debate. By using these technologies, insurers may increase customer happiness, reduce operational costs, and become more efficient, opening the door to a more vibrant and long-lasting insurance industry.

References

Anderson, T. 2023. Time-saving technologies in healthcare. HealthTech Mag.
Bhardwaj, N., and R. Anand. 2022. Health insurance premium prediction using machine learning. Comput. Econ.
Brown, R. 2021. Chatbots in online consultations. HealthTech Innov.
Carter, B. 2023. Streamlining healthcare processes with AI. J. Healthc. Oper.
Gonzalez, P. 2022. AI diagnostics and prevention. Med. Innov. Q.
Gupta, P. 2021. Fraud detection in the insurance sector using ML. Insurance Risk Rev.
Gupta, P. 2023. Role of AI in health insurance. Insurance Today.
Johnson, M. 2022. AI in promoting healthy lifestyles. Prev. Health.
Johnson, M. 2022. Data ethics and predictive algorithms in insurance. AI Soc.
Kumar, V. 2023. Customizing insurance plans with AI. Health Econ. Rev.
Kumar, V. 2023. Regression models for health insurance premium forecasting. Mach. Learn. Econ.
Lee, S. 2022. AI in diabetes management. Med. AI Adv.
Morbidity and Mortality Weekly Report. 2021. Morbidity and Mortality Weekly Report.
Park, H. 2023. Early disease detection with AI. AI Med.
Patel, R. 2023. Enhancing risk assessment with predictive analytics. Insurance Technol. Today.
Patel, R. 2023. Wearable tech and AI in underwriting. Digit. Health Rev.
Roy, D. 2023. AI in Indian healthcare. India Tech Rev.
Shah, N. 2022. AI in medication development. Pharm. Insights.
Singh, G., R. Aggarwal, S. Kumar, S. Nagpa, and S. A. Dhondiyal. 2024. Role of AI in enhancing health insurance penetration in rural India. Int. Conf. Comput. Intell. Comput. Appl. (ICCICA), Samalkha, India, pp. 198–202.
Smith, J., and A. Jones. 2022. AI in healthcare. J. Med. AI.
Taylor, L. 2022. Fraud detection in insurance. AI Ethics J.
Taylor, L. 2022. Neural networks for medical claim predictions. AI Healthc. Anal.
Van den Broek-Altenburg, E., and A. Atherly. 2018. Consumer attitudes towards health insurance: a Twitter analysis. J. Soc. Health Anal.
Wilson, D. 2021. Healthcare accessibility with AI. Glob. Health Rep.
Zhang, X. 2022. AI for fraudulent claims detection. Insurance Anal.
Zhang, X. 2023. Predictive analytics in health insurance. J. Healthc. Inform.

Chapter 6

Artificial Intelligence in Insurance

Unlocking Personalized Policies for the Modern Consumer

Puja Mishra[1,*] and *Ashutosh Mishra*[2]

Introduction

Traditionally run on a principle of traditional risk-averseness, the insurance industry now stands at the threshold of significant technological transformation in this very space where adoption of Artificial Intelligence is breaking neck pace. It is no longer just about digitization or workflow improvements but represents the paradigm shift that changes the way insurance products are conceived, delivered, and consumed. Based on this, insurers can definitely switch from one size fits all to highly personalized because AI can process huge volumes of data recognizing and making predictions about the individual behaviors in real time.

The insurance industry, which was always thought to be complex and somewhat ambiguous now uses AI to meet changing expectations in the world of digital advancement. The new world environment demands that even in financial services, such personalization be included in all walks of life. It may also come with promises of more balanced prices and overall customer satisfaction when data is being properly leveraged along with

[1] Sarala Birla University, Faculty of Business Management, Ranchi, India.
[2] Birla Institute of Technology, Department of Business Management, Ranchi, India.
Email: ashutoshmishra@bitmesra.ac.in
* Corresponding author: puja.mishra@sbu.ac.in

DOI: 10.1201/9781003637301-6

AI technologies for the formulation of policies best tailored to individual needs.

We will demonstrate how these innovations in AI-machine learning, predictive analytics, and natural language processing, among others, can empower insurers to transform their customer experience. It will be that much more efficient but now even more value-added and personalized in the automation of underwriting and claims processing and, in fact, customer services itself.

In this way, AI makes it possible to probe customer behavior and preferences for even more responsive and adaptive solutions in insurance. However, at the same time, it brings some problems. Huge stumbling blocks against insurers include data privacy, regulatory complexities, and the ethical impacts of AI on decision-making.

As such, moving further into the topic under discussion, this analysis looks into where AI compels the insurance industry with potential and associated risk. Having all said, this is a conceptual attempt to richness in itself, a conceptual exploration through real-life application of AI within this conceptual framework aimed at putting across all aspects of understanding to changes in an industry for consumer demands being demanded nowadays. This is custom insurance which not only represents the way into operations; but it's a way towards being more customer-centered, innovative with better future. A functional comparison between traditional insurance operations and AI-driven insurance solutions across key operational areas is presented in Table 1.

Table 1: Traditional Insurance Operations vs. AI-Driven Insurance Solutions.

Functional Area	**Traditional Approach**	**AI-Driven Approach**	**Advantages of AI Approach**
Underwriting	Manual assessment, rule-based evaluation	Predictive analytics, machine learning models	Faster risk profiling, improved accuracy
Claims Processing	Paper-based or semi-automated workflows	Automated decision-making, NLP-enabled document reading	Reduced processing time, fewer errors
Fraud Detection	Post-event analysis using historical patterns	Real-time anomaly detection using AI models	Early fraud identification, cost savings
Customer Interaction	Human agents via phone/email	AI chatbots, virtual assistants	24/7 availability, consistent user experience
Risk Management	Statistical models based on historic data	Dynamic data integration and forecasting via AI	Proactive risk mitigation

Literature Review

Quality Customer Experience, here, predictive analytics and machine learning are allowing the insurance companies to automate underwriting as well as analyse humungous volumes of data in real-time by refining the pricing models. The incumbents with new entrants bank on AI for product-process and value chain innovations so as to bolster competitive advantage using the triangle of innovation framework (Christopher and Kavuri, 2023). AI increases the quotient of customer satisfaction through services that are personalized, with cuts on the operational side; in addition, it gives fraud detection of improved types (Giese et al., 2022). Among the critical success factors are strong data integration, innovation culture, and the imposition of legal and ethical standards (Loh and Soo, 2023; Feng, 2024). Overall, these drivers seem to be pointing out the transformative potential concerning the way in which AI changes the landscape of insurance. Big data sets analysis is significantly improved by AI since evidence-based decision-making as well as effective service delivery in one way boost up the personalization much more. Since machine learning algorithms typically detect patterns and trends, large amounts of data can lead an AI to predict what most is likely to occur next and thus strategize on it (Anudeep et al., 2024). Further high-level methodologies include Inverse Propensity Score estimator as well as Doubly Robust methods which evaluate for policymakers personal policies concerning scalability and counterfactual validity (Rafieian and Yoganarasimhan, 2022). However, in order to increase real-time policy evaluation with AI-supported automatic collection and data analysis, governance is increased in a way that greater transparency and accountability are attained (Upreti, et al., 2023). However, the Data Privacy and Algorithmic bias considerations call for such implementation that AI should be put under accountable decision-makers during policymaking (Atan et al., 2019). ML and Predictive analytics are required in this sense to unlock vast reservoirs of customer and insurance information about personalizing insurance products. Random Forest and Gradient Boosting are some of the ML methods through which insurers can differentiate data on insights on customer segmentation and pricing fraud and strategy customization (Jones and Sah, 2023; Vuddanti et al., 2024). MLOps facilitates easy model deployment and boosts productivity in product customization (Rodrigo et al., 2023). Big data processing also enables complex prediction models sensitive to customer needs, which will eventually lead to more competitive premiums (Desai et al., 2022). This is driven by the intent of customers to provide data to get better pricing and, as such, data-driven decisions will remain at the center of insurance (Desai et al., 2022). AI has been somewhat impactful in the terms related to improving accuracy of risk assessment and underwriting with the help of advanced analytics and machine learning methods in use. All this will allow the insurers to scan through the big data, whether it is telematics or customer's behavior; most probably, it then makes the underwriting decision more informed as well as the offers of the policy to the individual (Li et al., 2023). AI-Based RIM that will then come as predictive modeling and scenario analysis so it will unveil how the risk factors can now be appreciated beyond metrics (Anonymous, 2023). Other models for example RBF proved to be highly accurate in the risk prediction whereby one is attaining an up-to 95.2% accuracy in training (Bishop, 2024). Other areas of research would be conducted on continuing the optimization AI's role in the risk management. In general, underwriting practices have witnessed many changes concerning the automated, real-time insight through AI in the mode of enhancing the efficiency and accuracy in assessing risks. AI has created a bouquet of consumer satisfaction about personalization of the experience in insurance services through a bouquet of technological innovation and trends for its bouquet. For instance, an insurer, with NLP and machine learning, through a virtual assistant or chatbot, his interaction can be such that it may make service experience more effective, and it is based on consumer needs for service (Velmurugan et al., 2023; Giese et al., 2022). Moreover, AI-based systems process huge volumes of data that make it possible to automate claims processing, thus allowing for one-click reporting and intelligent claims handling that reduces processing time many times while increasing accuracy multiple times (Chakladar et al., 2024). Furthermore, big data analytics makes it possible for insurers to design customized insurance products, thereby making it possible for insurers to better understand the requirements and preferences of customers and thus increase confidence and engagement (Owolabi et al., 2024). In brief, adding AI enhances the process, while simultaneously gifting an experience to be quite gratifying to the consumer, placing the insurer at market comparison (Kanaparthi, 2024). The ethical issues surrounding the AI adoption are, bias in the algorithm, transparency, accounting of it, and protection of the data. The AI systems automatically perpetuate the biases already ingrained in the historical data and, therefore, inherently possess the potential to continue unfair treatment of specific demographics in insurance. This raises further questions on how light and just insurance practices are (Adeyelu et al., 2024; Yadav et al., 2024; Singh et al., 2024). Besides, opaqueness of AI algorithms further complicates the decision-making processes, which are mostly obscure for the most part to the stakeholders in terms of who made what decisions and even how decisions were reached, for that matter (Morchhale, 2024). Such a lack of transparency lowers public confidence and therefore must have strict ethical frameworks implementing explainability and frequent audits in order to ensure proper alignment of ethics (Thakur and Sharma, 2024; Osasona et al., 2024). This has an implication of adoption into the insurance system that also reaches out to the general public in effects on economic inequality and job replacement, which has led to the multidisciplinary approach in ensuring proper alignment of AI technologies with societal values (Thakur et al., 2024). Data privacy and security issues greatly impact the application of AI in insurance personalization because such issues may deter consumer trust and engagement. AI in personal marketing hugely increases the experiences of the customer, but it gives problems relating to privacy in data collection and profiling and therefore, calls for balance between the benefits achieved and considerations about privacy (Huang and Shen, 2024). The use of encryption and blockchain data technique through usage-based insurance permit securely processed data without being translucently transparent but this makes a confinement in predictive AI model power (Pereira et al., 2023; Szafraniec, 2023). On the negative side, increased use of automation decisions in insurance is likely to raise some ethics as well, such as creating a customer profile without seeking the individual's consent (Lim et al., 2020). Clients fear big data being created from clients. Data hacking may increase a low adoption in insurance organizations of AI-generated products within the insurance field (Deshpande, 2024). Therefore, the solutions of these issues related to privacy and security will ease more trust and easier application of AI in personalized services for insurance. There are multiple regulatory issues that accompany the integration of AI-based technologies in all cases of compliance, risk, and ethical issues. These are data protection, transparency, and accountability that provide the factors to create customer trust and to abide by the legal framework that exists (Fenwick et al., 2024). This means that changing nature of AI post adaptive approaches to regulation as such in the form of regulatory sandboxes allowing innovation while keeping standards for safety. It refers to the point that how AIA slightly complicated risks in terms of plain rights and social values while keeping uncertainty through vague norms (Orwat et al., 2024). This process under question will bring together the different parties, design strong structures that have a balance between innovation and flexibility, in an effort to ensure AI in the insurance organizations is utilized with integrity. AI-Driven Technologies and techniques are used to improve dynamic and real-time insurance adjustments. Automation of processes, Increased risk assessment, Proactively inform the decisions. For example, AI systems would smoothen the underwriting process through predictive analytics for real-time data to be used in quotes, thus making insurers more responsive to change the risk profile. In addition, the massive data quantities, such as real-time market data, boost predictiveness and operational effectiveness, through the machine learning algorithms, with which AI-based financial risk management systems analyse (Zanke, 2024). It further enables the support of assisting insurance in building intelligent adjustment systems that save error instances with labour saved while ensuring to hasten claim handling. A holistic risk intelligence model enables even more to be measured, lifestyle and environmental factors, to further fine-tune optimal effective pricing other than close to custom-made insurance products (Velmurugan et al., 2023). More broadly, these innovations bring AI as a powerful change influencer in the insurance industry and operational transformations encourage agility and responsiveness. AI-based customized models for insurance would transform the entire insurance industry with efficiency, improvement of customer experience, and enabling better risk analysis into its fold. Big data and AI technologies facilitate more customized insurance products and encourage insurers to scan information regarding policyholders for targeted marketing and personalized attention (Jha et al., 2022). This is driven by customer expectations for frictionless experiences similar to what can be found on e-commerce platforms, and they must make the models of distributing and taking risks by insurers evolve to remain competitive (Kanaparthi, 2024). Beyond that, AI promotes trust and a higher level of engagement because it enables institutions to provide relevant products while at the same time improving credit risk management and fraud detection (Loh and Soo, 2023). With the insurers playing the role of wellness partners rather than fulfilling traditional roles, data integration, cultural adaptation, and innovative business models would become important factors beyond legal and ethical considerations for AI implementations to be successful (Lyutova, 2023). In general, the future of insurance is set in for a paradigm shift that makes use of AI in satisfaction of the needs of technology-advanced consumer base. Artificial intelligence represents the highest-level industry disruption possible-the single biggest one-and, additionally, an appropriate mix of these emerging technologies includes shifts in customers' expectations and increasing pressures from competitors.

Research Gaps

Despite the growing wealth of evidence outlining the potential and present applications of Artificial Intelligence (AI) in the insurance sector, there remain various key research gap areas in need of greater study:

1. Lack of Customer Perception Understanding
   The majority of research studies the adoption of AI from a technological or organizational perspective, with minimal concern for consumer attitudes, trust, and behavioural responses to AI-driven insurance offerings. Research in user acceptance and perceived fairness of AI-driven choices is a very under-researched field.

2. Omission of Regulative and Moral Considerations
   Issues of data privacy, bias in algorithms, and compliance are identified, not much academic work is given that offers frameworks or approaches for ethical regulation of AI in insurance. Further research is needed to develop guidelines that align technological advancements with social and legal standards.
3. Failure to Focus on Emerging Markets and Small Businesses
   Existing literature has been concentrated on the use of AI in large, global insurance companies with minimal studies on its viability or performance in emerging economies and small insurers. This gap requires inclusive research studies that examine context-specific challenges and opportunities in lesser-represented geographies and firm sizes.
4. Absence of Standardized Evaluation Measures
   There is no consensus on performance metrics for assessing AI tools in insurance, and it is difficult to compare approaches or replicate results. Common indicators of efficiency, accuracy, customer satisfaction, and compliance need to be established and validated to enhance the field.

The Changing Consumer Expectations

Modern consumers, accustomed to personalization in retail and entertainment, would also want it in financial services. Changes in consumer behavior make insurers more innovative based on a more customer-centric approach for developing their offerings.

- Requirement for Personalization: Customers wish to have policies designed according to their needs, lifestyles, and personal preferences. AI helps this by presenting an opportunity to the insurers to come up with one-to-many, personal, customized products, and services that will be attractive to individual customers to stay long, hence increasing engagement as well as loyalty.
- Seamless digital experiences: The impact of digital platforms has raised new standards for convenience and efficiency. Insurers are using AI to meet these expectations with seamless digital experiences all the way from policy selection to claims handling.

Competitive Pressures and Industry Innovation

The insurance industry, therefore, faces strong competition not only from incumbent operators but also a new wave of players-insurtech start-ups that rely on AI in developing innovative and bespoke solutions. This makes the market intrinsically competitive, which forces incumbents as well as new entrants to invest in AI for both product innovation and process optimization.

- Insurtech Disruption: The companies that are at the very top of the list when it comes to disrupting the traditional insurance models with AI are Insurtech firms. They focus on customer-centric solutions and use AI to analyze data and offer personalized policies in a really quick and efficient manner. This has prompted established insurers to hasten their digital transformation initiatives to stay competitive.
- Product and Process Innovations: AI enables the insurer to innovate through the entire development cycle of products-from underwriting to settling claims. As routine tasks get automated and deliver insights for complex decisions, AI does indeed add to operational efficiency, saving time for insurers to focus more on innovation and interaction with customers.

Opportunities and Challenges

Huge implications of personalizing by AI are there, but those come with them the opportunities and challenges. There's much to be understood for a person to chart through such a course through the AI complexities.

- There emerge new opportunities to exploit data: There now arise new sources of generating value from an enormous amount of data. Insurers have integrated data from various sources providing a holistic view of the customers' needs and risk profiles. These opportunities and challenges are conceptualized through an integrated framework highlighting data, technology, personalization, regulatory, and ethical dimensions, as shown in Figure 1.

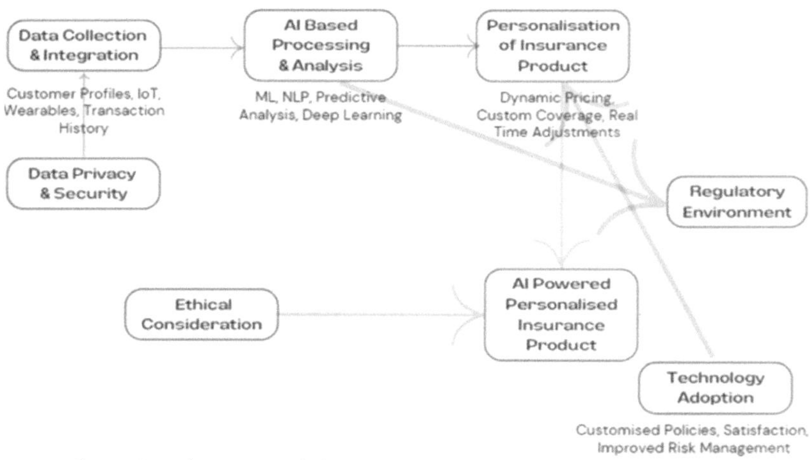

Fig. 1: Key dimensions defining AI being used to transform the industry.

- Data privacy and ethical challenges: The collection of personal data and its analysis by an insurer creates serious issues related to privacy and ethics for an insurer. They need the ability to ensure the data safety of their company while developing transparency in any kind of AI-decision making and reducing the possibilities of algorithmic bias to assure customer trust and win-over regulatory compliance.

The conceptual framework on which integration into personalized insurance occurs through AI is built on a number of key dimensions that define, in aggregate, how AI is being used to transform the industry. This framework will be helpful in systematically analyzing the interplay of technological, operational, regulatory, and ethical aspects of AI within insurance.

Data Integration and Analysis

The core of AI-based insurance personalization is the integration and analysis of vast, varied volumes of data. The insurer therefore collects data from all interaction sources such as interactions with customers, social media, telematics information, wearable devices like fitness bands or smart watches, and transaction records. These data are processed online in real-time using technologies such as machine learning and predictive analytics to produce actionable insights that power personalized insurance products.

- Predictive Analytics: This is the ability to predict what customers need and risk more precisely than most anyone else. Using data history and a pattern in that history, AI models can predict future behaviors or scenarios that would allow them to provide policies tailored to individual profiles of risk.
- Real-time data processing: That allows for time-sensitive responses by the insurance company to emergent needs of a customer that appear and change extenuating conditions. It remains an important component in creating dynamic policy changes and helping improve the risk assessment together with premium-setting accuracy.

Personalization Modes

The application of AI supports personalization through different modes, mainly changing the manner in which insurance companies relate to their clientele.

- Some of the techniques applied allow machine learning algorithms: applied decision trees, neural networks and, finally, support vector machines; which enables insurers to apply relatively subtle criteria for the purpose of segmentation. Insurance products can be highly targeted towards customer groups with first needs, first and foremost, having different requirements and preferences.

- NLP Natural Language Processing Technologies enables personalization of interaction through chatbots and virtual assistants, thus extremely helpful in the development of customer interface. AI-based applications provide instant support for claims and claims processing besides making it extremely easy for customers.

Dynamic Changes and Innovation

Artificial intelligence provides the insurance company with flexibility along with an opportunity to change product lines and innovate dynamically.

- Dynamic Pricing Models: Since actual customer behavior and other relevant factors are assessed in real time, dynamic pricing allows premium adjustment which keeps premiums charged to a customer according to the current risk profile.
- Product Innovation: AI introduces new kinds of insurance products that are more relevant to the behaviour and lifestyle of the modern customer. Such include, among others, usage-based or behaviour-linked insurance that increases the level of customers' satisfaction and assists in getting better engagement and loyalty from them.

Regulatory and Ethical Issues

The integration of AI with the insurance business presents immense regulatory and ethical concerns about proper usage.

- Data privacy and security: Any sensitive information connected to customers should be kept in AI systems with strong data governance. In that sense, Privacy-preserving technologies like encrypting applications and usage of blockchain will become pertinent in that aspect.
- Algorithmic transparency and accountability: Such AI models have to be transparent in their decision-making process so that there is confidence among consumers and the regulators. It develops an explainable AI system manifesting how decisions are made to make it accountable and fair in the process.
- Ethical Issue: The problems with the application of AI-based decision-making systems include issues of biasness, discrimination, and access to personal information. There is also mounting pressure on insurers to extend their ethics frameworks and perform regular systematic audit checks to treat risks emanating from such factors as fairly as possible.

Socioeconomic Impact

Last but not least to consider in integrating AI into an insurance company is this overarching broader social-economic factor: Economic Inclusion-AI may democratize access through cheaper and more personalized products to more-need-of-coverage, yet under-insured or otherwise marginalized groups.

Evolving jobs in Change: Due to the induction of AI, change is naturally going to occur in jobs as well. And in order to create the much-needed influence from it in favour of employment and at the cost of insurers, necessary skills in job and task develop as well.

Advantages of AI in Insurance Personalization

There are many advantages artificial intelligence in insurance has and is constantly changing the way insurers function when it comes to their interface with customers, risk evaluation, and management. The ability to personalize using AI is, of course, fantastic for better customer satisfaction but better operational efficiency and risk management. Now let's unpack each of these advantages as follows:

Level of Customer Satisfaction

Among all these, personalization is one of the most significant factors that lead to customer satisfaction in this domain of insurance. AI highly makes it possible to tailor products and services to closely meet the requirements and preferences of an individual customer.

- Customized Policy Products: This is because AI enables the insurer to make policies uniquely and customarily based on the customer's behaviour, demographic information, and preference. It introduces value and trust since it has customers buy unique products that meet their needs.
- Customer Interactions: It reaches the customer in real time with the help of AI chatbots and virtual assistants. It is only for routine queries that will help the human agent use his time in solving complex issues of the customers. But for this account, the customer enjoys quicker solutions as it is quicker.
- Claims processing streamlined: It automates all the major steps of the claims process, including document verification and fraud detection, so the settlement is quick, thereby, in general improving customer experience, for the policyholders will bother less since usually they get confused when their policies are under claims.

Reasonable Risk Evaluation and Charging

Artificial intelligence enables the processing of vast volumes of data in real-time streams, improving the accuracy of risk assessment and pricing models as complexity grows.

- Dynamic Risk Profiling: This is the profiling method that cannot recognize dynamic behavior in the risk profile of any individual, unlike the static data that is the traditional method of risk profiling. Instead, it utilizes real-time data such as telematics, health records, and social media to build up an accurate and dynamic picture of risk.
- Fair and transparent pricing: AI-based predictive analytics facilitates the building of a pricing model that reflects real risk pertaining to a customer. Instead of average demographic premiums, it provides fair premiums based on the behavior and circumstances of a specific customer. This leads to more transparent and justifiable pricing for the customers.
- Detection of fraud: Artificial intelligence can identify fraudulent activities through pattern and anomaly-based analysis of the claim data. This helps to decrease the loss which an insurer incurs because of fraud and also prevents honest customers from unfair treatment, and hence, fosters higher levels of trust and satisfaction among them.

Operational Efficiency

AI automated complex procedures, which in turn transformed the process of operations since it helps insurers to offer their services at a cheaper cost.

- Automate the repetitive work: AI does the repetitive work otherwise underwriting, claims processing, and customer onboarding. This reduces the number of human employees needed; they can then be put to work on more important strategic initiatives and in engaging with customers. Again, with automation, no human error is possible so accurate and reliable operations are ensured.
- Resource Optimization: AI streamlines processes and accuracy which enable insurers to optimize all their resources by minimizing administrative costs through better balancing human and technological resources and better fulfillment of services. This eventually leads to an organization that is leaner, more agile, more responsive, and more aggressive in changes within the market.
- Proactive Decisions: AI will enable insurers to be far more proactive in taking decisions since it will bring inputs on how customers are acting currently as well as other market information to forecast the

requirements of the customers and shape policies dynamically to respond in real-time to emergent risks as well as opportunities.

Product Development

An opportunity for insurance products, shaped from AI-related insights and developed for emergent needs of customers with passing time.

- Usage-Based Insurance: AI enables the development of usage-based insurance products whose premium would be computed based on actual usage or behavior. For example, vehicle telematics data can be utilized for pay-as-you-drive policies through which customers are given easy and economical options.
- Behavioral-Based Products Over usage: AI enables design of products where the user is compensated for healthy or safe behaviour. Health insurance may turn into rewards of a well-tracked exercise by a wearable device.
- On-Demand Insurance: AI supports new on-demand insurance models of instant consumption where a customer may buy for some special needs for a specific period. This is more convenient and flexible to tech-savvy customers, who would be keen on having a speedy and hassle-free interface in accessing insurance services.

Competitive Advantage

The adoption of AI works both ways, in the best interest of the customer and brings about a fair level of competitive advantage for insurers in this fast-moving market.

- Market Differentiation: AI-based superior personalized services shall help insurers create niches for themselves amidst fierce competition. And the results: attracting and retaining customers in a hyper-competitive marketplace.
- Customer retention: Such close ties of a customer with the insurer through customized services increase the opportunity of retaining the customer and reduce the churn rate. A happy customer will be a loyal customer to the insurance company and even praise the brand, which will grow organically through word of mouth.
- Data-Driven Strategy: Insurers that make the best use of AI can now follow a data-driven approach and will be in a better position to take proper decisions, innovate constantly, and lead in the trend within the industry. In this manner, they emerge as frontrunners in the digital transformation of insurance.

Barrier and Ethical Implications: Applying AI to Insurance Personalization

This means that the implementation of Artificial Intelligence brings with it many benefits but, simultaneously, a number of challenges and ethical dilemmas that should be appropriately addressed and handled in order for its deployment to remain responsible and fair. Those include data privacy, algorithmic bias, transparency, accountability, and regulation. The awareness and mitigation of these challenges can help create trust among insurers, maintain compliance, and allow them to make the most of AI.

Data: The major problem with AI-driven personal insurance is regarding its protection and privacy over the client data. There are huge risks and dangers related to the misuse of data that might arise from mass data collection by the insurers concerning personal and sensitive data.

- Data Handling of Sensitive: Insurance personalization relies on data coming from several sources, like health records, financial transactions, and social media. So, it is a significant concern how data can be protected from unauthorized access through proper usage.
- Compliance with the law: Intricately carved data privacy laws should not frighten an insurer. For example, Europe has the GDPR and the same holds true for other regions too. This sort of compliance is expensive to build and maintain and has to be done with really strong data governance frameworks in place.
- Consumer Trust: There is a potential loss of consumer trust due to data privacy. Insurers should be transparent about how the customer information is collected, stored, and processed. They also owe the consumer some control over their personal data. For some reasons, these technologies seem to represent the future of privacy protecting, encryption, and blockchain. However, they bring in a lot more complexity.

Algorithmic Bias and Fairness

Although the AI systems are pretty powerful, it is no exception that there are biases sometimes resulting in discriminatory practices of some customers.

- Data Bias: AI model will only be good for the data it is being trained with. For example, if the historical data that has been in use contains biases such as racial and gender biases as well as socioeconomic biases, there is a very high probability of perpetuation or even exaggeration by the AI. The outcomes would end up causing some mistreatment of the customers through overcharging them or outright refusal to provide them cover.

One area that would surely raise severe ethical questions in this case would relate to vulnerable sections of society that would probably face more disadvantages from the systemic disadvantage. AI systems need to be developed and monitored with care in a manner to detect and minimize biases so as not to affect the very idea of fair and just insurance services.

- Audits and Controls: Regular access to their AI systems that are regularly audited can solve some of these problems. Such ones include examinations of the data used in training their AI, what logics a given AI uses in its decision-making, and what their outputs are. This would be complemented with third-party review and ethical standards for AI, a shield against bias

Transparency and Explainability

Such complexity in an AI algorithm might virtually make it impossible for stakeholders to trace the systems that come up with a particular decision or degrade transparency and accountability

- Black Box Decisioning: Most AI models and deep learning, in particular, tend to be "black boxes." Hence decisioning is unlikely to be clear. This would likely create confusion and mistrust in the eyes of the customer and regulators who may not even know why premiums for instance have been changed or why claims have been rejected.
- AI Explainability: Of extreme importance for developing an explainable AI; present clear, transparent views regarding a decision-making process. This not only helps the insurance business grow on customer trust but it also provides them with the room to adhere to regulatory requirements related to transparency and accountability.

The insurers must inform the customer how AI works regarding policies, pricing, or claims. How the technology impacts policies, prices, and claims may clear the mystic surrounding AI and bring about much acceptance.

Regulatory and Legal Challenges

The changing nature of AI-related technologies makes it prone to significant regulatory difficulties; in fact, most current legal frameworks are not complete enough to account for the complexity of AI-related deployment in insurance.

- Emerging Regulation: "Proper rules and standards by the regulators are not in place for the financial service usage of AI", leaving behind a sort of uncertainty. Therefore, the question to insurers is whether their self-regulation and keeping track of changing regulatory requirement compliances is at risks.

- Regulatory Sandboxes: In some countries, regulatory sandboxes are being adopted in which insurers are allowed to test their AI-driven products in a controlled environment. This encourages innovation but simultaneously makes the regulators ask insurers to balance experimenting with the need to maintain robust risk management and compliance.
- Cross-Border Problems: Insurance businesses are, per se, cross-border enterprises where the operations of insurers are usually diversified across countries with different conditions under which regulatory matters may differ as well.

Ethical Issues in Automating Decisions

It is very seriously raising an ethical issue involving AI for determining the insurance policies.

- Liability for Decisions: Determining the liability of an AI system for decisions taken involving coverage, claims, or pricing is extremely difficult. The role of the insurer should clearly describe lines of responsibility in and around decisions made by AI in order that customers can avail themselves of redress through error or dispute.
- Impact on Employment: There will be loss of job opportunity in the insurance business. As much as AI might go on to become an efficient tool for the business, social and economic costs have to be addressed when removing people from business processes and core activities within which they have been deployed to get re-skilled and re-employed in new activities.
- Social Equity: Consideration must be made for further implications of AI deployments that would bring more economic inequality or a new form of discrimination. Insurers have a social responsibility to ensure that their use of AI is consonant with and supportive of more universal values, such as equity and inclusiveness.

Comparison of Existing Policies For Modern Consumers

In the background of shifting customer aspirations and advances in technology, various new-age insurance plans have come forth that attempt to provide more tailor-made, adaptable, and technologically facilitated offerings. Of these, usage-based insurance (UBI) has gained significant pace, particularly within the motor vehicle insurance sector. UBI policies leverage telematics units and AI-driven algorithms to score driving behavior in real-time, allowing insurers to offer premiums that reflect observed usage. The most important advantage of this model is its customization; good drivers get lower premiums, generating a sense of fairness and transparency. But concerns over data privacy, surveillance, and the risk of algorithmic bias are significant negatives, especially when consumers are not as fully aware as they might be of how their data are being used or interpreted.

Another intriguing innovation is on-demand insurance, which allows customers to activate protection for specific items or experiences only when needed, typically through mobile phone apps. This model of business is most favored by millennials and gig economy workers and comes with cost savings and convenience. The advantage of such policies is that they are flexible to fit into modern lifestyles that prioritize flexibility and punctuality. The disadvantage of such products is that they are typically brought in with caps in terms of comprehensiveness of coverage and may offer less protection than traditional, continuous policies. In addition, consumers may get confused with the exact terms and exclusions that may lead to disputes at the time of claims settlement.

The peer-to-peer (P2P) model is another option where groups of people pool premiums to cover one another, with unclaimed funds potentially being repaid to contributors. This model aims to instill trust and reduce administrative expenses, appealing to digitally savvy consumers who prefer community-based solutions. The power of P2P insurance lies in its possibility of transparency and expense reduction. Scalability is, however, a problem and long-term demonstration of financial solidity in such models still needs to be proved in the event of high or large numbers of claims.

Such new policy forms reflect the larger change in the consumer demand for bespoke, open, and technology-led insurance products. However, whether these will thrive and endure is contingent on attention to their ethical, legal, and operating dimensions, which justify further research and regulation.

Conclusion

This integration will promote the paradigm shift of the insurance industry toward the most customized and efficient in the near future. Through the AI-driven innovation machine learning capability, predictive analytics, and natural language processing technologies, the insurance firm is able to offer bespoke policies corresponding to the needs of individual clients. This has led further to increased productivity in assessing and managing risks, service operations, and product design, other than improved customer satisfaction.

Nevertheless, AI insurance is not going to be barrier-free. Few challenges include those of data security and private data, algorithm biased, low transparency, all leading up to full-spectrum requirement in terms of comprehensive regulations involved. Today, the whole challenge is, in the same breath as ethicality, data management, and innovation.

In short words, AI Insurance wins when and only the marriage of techno-responsibility with responsibility is sealed. Insurers can, through trustfulness, fairness, and transparency, unchain the power of AI to reform the industry and realize more tailored and inclusive solutions responsive to the innovative needs of modern consumers. This chapter provides a comprehensive overview of these dynamics by describing opportunities and challenges arising from AI-driven personalization in insurance, laying grounds for how technology and human values can peacefully coexist into the future.

References

Abiagom, C. N., and T. I. Ijomah. 2024. Enhancing customer experience through AI-driven language processing in service interactions. Open Access Res. J. Eng. Technol. doi:10.53022/oarjet.2024.7.1.0027

Adeyelu, O. O., C. E. U. Shonibare, and M. A. Shonibare. 2024. Ethical implications of AI in financial decision–making: a review with real world applications. Int. J. Appl. Res. Soc. Sci. doi:10.51594/ijarss.v6i4.1033

Anonymous. 2023. Impact of AI in the General Insurance underwriting factors. Cent. Eur. Manag. J. Influential Scholarly Research Publication. https://doi.org/10.57030/23364890.cemj.31.2.72

Anudeep, A., M. Gupta, S. Mehmi, T. Khanna, G. Chopra, R. Kaur et al. 2024. Towards Intelligent Governance: The Role of AI in Policymaking and Decision Support for E-Governance. https://doi.org/10.1007/978-981-99-8612-5_19

Atan, O., W. R. Zame, Q. Feng, and M. van der Schaar. 2019. Constructing effective personalized policies using counterfactual inference from biased data sets with many features. Mach. Learn. doi:10.1007/S10994-018-5768-3

Bishop, N. T. 2024. Application of machine learning techniques in insurance underwriting. J. Actuarial Res. doi:10.47941/jar.1756

Chakladar, R. D. 2022. Improve CX in insurance. J. Econ. Manag. Res. doi:10.47363/jesmr/2022(3)e102

Christopher, P. H., and A. Kavuri. 2023. Artificial Intelligence (AI) and Business Innovation in Insurance: A comparison of incumbent firms versus new entrants. Proc. Hawaii Int. Conf. Syst. Sci. doi:10.24251/hicss.2023.466

Desai, A., M. Mathkar, M. Nisar, and G. T. Thampi. 2022. Customizing Insurance Product Based on Customer Data Leveraging Learning Algorithms. doi:10.1109/ICAECC54045.2022.9716594

Desai, A., M. Mathkar, M. Nisar, and G. T. Thampi. 2022. Customizing insurance product based on customer data leveraging learning algorithms. Proc. IEEE 4th Int. Conf. Adv. Electron. Comput. Commun. (ICAECC). 8: 1–7. IEEE. https://doi.org/10.1109/icaecc54045.2022.9716594

Deshpande, A. 2024. Regulatory Compliance and AI: Navigating the Legal and Regulatory Challenges of AI in Finance. doi:10.1109/ickecs61492.2024.10616752

Feng, S. 2024. Integrating artificial intelligence in financial services: Enhancements, applications, and future directions. Appl. Comput. Eng. doi:10.54254/2755-2721/69/20241455

Fenwick, M., J. A. McCahery, and M. C. Compagnucci. 2024. Business and Regulatory Responses to Artificial Intelligence: Dynamic Regulation, Innovation Ecosystems and the Strategic Management of Disruptive Technology. doi:10.48550/arxiv.2407.19439

Giese, J., D. Platz, M. Peisker, V. Illguth, and G. Hausmann. 2022. AI in Insurance – More Satisfied Customers, Less Fraud, Better Processes. In AI Changes the Rules of the Game, pp. 140–160. Carl Hanser Verlag GmbH & Co. KG. https://doi.org/10.3139/9783446471825.007

Giese, J., D. Platz, M. Peisker, V. Illguth, and G. Hausmann. 2022. AI in insurance – more satisfied customers, less fraud, better processes. In AI Changes the Rules of the Game, pp. 140–160. Carl Hanser Verlag GmbH & Co. KG. https://doi.org/10.3139/9783446471825.007

Huang, C., and X. Shen. 2024. Privacy-Preserving Data Analytics in Usage-Based Insurance. Wireless Netw. doi:10.1007/978-3-031-54075-2_5

Jha, R. S., and P. R. Sahoo. 2022. Technology Shaping Models of "Personalization" in Insurance. Lect. Notes Netw. Syst. 237–246. Springer Nature Singapore. https://doi.org/10.1007/978-981-19-5221-0_23

Jones, K. I., and S. Sah. 2023. The Implementation of Machine Learning in The Insurance Industry with Big Data Analytics. Int. J. Data Inform. Intell. Comput. 2(2): 21–38. Prisma Publications. https://doi.org/10.59461/ijdiic.v2i2.47

Kanaparthi, V. 2024. AI-based Personalization and Trust in Digital Finance. arXiv.org. doi:10.48550/arxiv.2401.15700

Kanaparthi, V. 2024. AI-based Personalization and Trust in Digital Finance. arXiv.org. doi:10.48550/arxiv.2401.15700

Li, C.-J. 2024. Research on Risk Warning System for Insurance Company Based on Neural Network. doi:10.1109/iccect60629.2024.10546075

Lim, S., J. Suk, H. Ra, X. Song, and Y. Z. Deng. 2020. Consumer's Information Privacy and Security Concerns and Use of Intelligent Technology. doi:10.1007/978-3-030-39512-4_180

Loh, M., and T. Soo. 2023. Opportunities and use cases of AI in the insurance industry. In Artificial Intelligence in Finance, pp. 244–270. Edward Elgar Publishing. https://doi.org/10.4337/9781803926179.00021

Lyutova, O. I. 2023. Insurance premiums and artificial intelligence: Ongoing changes and contours of the future. Sibirskij ûridičeskij vestnik. doi:10.26516/2071-8136.2023.4.23

Morchhale, Y. 2024. Ethical considerations in artificial intelligence: Addressing bias and fairness in algorithmic decision-making. Indian Sci. J. Res. Eng. Manag. doi:10.55041/ijsrem31693

Orwat, C., J. Bareis, A. Folberth, J. Jahnel, and C. Wadephul. 2022. Normative challenges of risk regulation of artificial intelligence and automated decision-making. Soc. Sci. Res. Network. doi:10.48550/arXiv.2211.06203

Osasona, F., O. O. A. Amoo, A. A. T. Akoh, O. A. Abrahams, and B. S. A. Farayola. 2024. Reviewing the ethical implications of AI in decision making processes. doi:10.51594/ijmer.v6i2.773

Owolabi, O., P. C. Uche, N. T. Adeniken, C. Ihejirika, R. B. Islam, and B. Chhetri. 2024. Ethical implication of Artificial Intelligence (AI) adoption in financial decision making. Comput. Inf. Sci. doi:10.5539/cis.v17n1p49

Pereira, K., J. Vinagre, A. Nunes, F. Alonso, F. Coelho, and M. Carvalho. 2023. Privacy-preserving machine learning in life insurance risk prediction. Commun. Comput. Inf. Sci. doi:10.1007/978-3-031-23633-4_4

Rafieian, O., and H. Yoganarasimhan. 2022. AI and personalization. Soc. Sci. Res. Network. doi:10.2139/ssrn.4123356

Rodrigo, M. J., M. Brito, and D. N. Duarte. 2023. Machine Learning on Insurance Premium Prediction. doi:10.1145/3605423.3605450

Shen, Q. 2024. AI-driven financial risk management systems: Enhancing predictive capabilities and operational efficiency. Appl. Comput. Eng. doi:10.54254/2755-2721/69/20241494

Singh, G., R. Aggarwal, S. Kumar, S. Nagpa, and S. A. Dhondiyal. 2024. Role of AI in enhancing health insurance penetration in rural India. Int. Conf. Comput. Intell. Comput. Appl. (ICCICA), Samalkha, India, pp. 198–202.

Szafraniec, M. 2023. Profiling and automated decisions concerning consumers in the insurance market and threats to their right to privacy and the right of disposal over their personal data. Wiadom. Ubezpieczeniowe 1(2023/1). The Polish Insurance Association. https://doi.org/10.33995/wu2023.1.2

Tataryntseva, Y., and I. Strokov. 2023. Modern information technologies in insurance: analysis of advantages and disadvantages. Vìsnik Nacìonal'nogo Tehnìčnogo Unìversitetu "Harkìvs'kij Polìtehnìčnij Ìnstitut". doi:10.20998/2519-4461.2023.5.80

Thakur, N., and A. Sharma. 2024. Ethical Considerations in AI-driven Financial Decision Making. doi:10.47914/jmpp.2024.v15i3.003

Upreti, K., A. Verma, S. Mittal, P. Vats, M. Haque, and S. Ali. 2023. A novel framework for harnessing AI for evidence-based policymaking in E-governance using smart contracts. Commun. Comput. Inf. Sci. doi:10.1007/978-3-031-45124-9_18

Velmurugan, K., K. Pazhanivel, R. Divyasree, E. Gowtham, and S. Guruharan. 2023. Data driven analysis of insurance claims using machine learning algorithm. Int. J. Adv. Res. Sci. Commun. Technol. 269–273. Naksh Solutions. https://doi.org/10.48175/ijarsct-9689

Vuddanti, S., J. Kumar, S. Pagadala, and B. Reddy. 2024. Machine Learning Insights into Personalized Insurance Pricing. doi:10.1109/icscss60660.2024.10625562

Yadav, M., A. Kumar, and R. Jha. 2024. The use of AI in personalized marketing: Balancing benefits and privacy concerns. Int. J. Adv. Res. Sci. Commun. Technol. doi:10.48175/ijarsct-17823

Zanke, P. 2024. The transformative impact of AI and ML in the insurance domain. Int. J. Innov. Sci. Res. Technol. doi:10.38124/ijisrt/ijisrt24mar572

Chapter 7

Impact of Artificial Intelligence (AI) Based Personalized Insurance Solutions on Consumer Satisfaction in India

*Kishlay Kumar** and *Puja Mishra*

Introduction

This will be a very significant contributor to the global economy by ensuring persons and corporates protection for those eventual losses not intended, and which in turn translate into a financial loss. With regards to an insurance company, insurance service delivery has changed with time accompanied with several alternatives such as life cover, health cover among others. The insurance industry is fast shifting towards greater innovation and improved client satisfaction due to digital technologies and data-driven solutions (Dia et al., 2021). According to sources both inside and outside the insurance industry (Bauer et al., 2017; Shipton and Vitale, 2024), a third of insurers and their business models are predicted to vanish within ten years. Big data, blockchain, IoT, and AI presents several potential, but they will also present difficulties due to the unpredictability of the weather and intense competition. AI-driven automation assists in reducing many of the difficulties and opening up some of the potential. However, it's not entirely apparent where AI-led automation is headed.

Research Scholar, Sarala Birla University, Ranchi, Jharkhand, India.
Email: puja.mishra@sbu.ac.in
* Corresponding author: kishlay.kumar29@gmail.com

DOI: 10.1201/9781003637301-7

Health and insurance are being disrupted by artificial intelligence, particularly machine learning and deep learning. AI is used extensively in insurance, including for detecting claim fraud and for virtual agents that interact directly with customers (Wang and Xu, 2018). In the medical field, it is employed to reach a diagnosis and treatment decision (He et al., 2019). Through insights and action from insight-creating services across channels and the whole value chain, value creation via AI occurs. Without a question, humans are essential, but they need assistance in order to process vast volumes of information and react quickly. Given how broad and undeveloped AI is in comparison to its potential, it is a difficult field. Beyond just creating the required technology and conducting usability testing, this is an interdisciplinary topic. Its multidisciplinary character is similar to that of other emerging technologies, such as blockchain. There are a lot of unanswered questions, but the current state of technology and its current diffusion have a big impact on these questions. AI's benefits to consumers in the health insurance market include personalized offers and real-time fee adjustments. Personalized policy offerings, perceived relevance, transparency, and customer trust are some of the barriers that currently exist between the consumer buying health insurance and AI.

Personalization has emerged as a key strategy in the insurance sectors to meet the diverse needs and preferences of individual customers. Traditionally, these firms have used a one-size-fits-all approach, in which standardized products and services are offered to their customers. Now, however, with all the technology and customer data in place, insurance and banking organizations can personalize their offerings to meet the exact needs of each customer. For instance, in the case of insurance, personalization is done based on demographics, lifestyle, and risk profile. This will enable the insurers to provide more targeted coverage options and pricing structures for their policyholders. AI-driven personalization helps the insurers tailor insurance products and services to the specific needs, preferences, and risk profiles of individual customers (Ali Albasheir et al., 2023). Data analysis and understanding of customer behavior allow insurers to design coverage plans, pricing models, and policy features that will be appealing to their target market and thus increase satisfaction and retention. AI technologies help insurers better assess risks as it analyzes large amounts of data and identifies relevant risk factors (Śmietanka et al., 2021; Singh et al., 2024).

It should be pertinent in terms of thoroughness, cost, and conciseness; it should be within the decision-maker's sphere of influence and be relevant and helpful to them. It must provide all the information required for the decision-maker to use it to effectively solve the issue at hand. Nothing crucial needs to be omitted. A lot of work must be done to get as much knowledge as possible, even if it will never be completely complete. If the solution is more costly than the issue, information is not advised.

The benefits of using the information should be evaluated against the cost of gathering and organizing the data (Markgraf, 2019; Teru et al., 2017; Shagari et al., 2017).

The emergence of Artificial Intelligence (AI) technologies are bringing a major paradigm shift in the financial world, which has never seen before, ushering an unprecedented era of security and transparency (Dia et al., 2021; Hendershott et al., 2021; An et al., 2021). In this digital world where data move globally at lightning speed, the demand for a robust, secure, and transparent eco system has reached its critical juncture. Another key aspect is the transparency of the insurance sector (Bukhtiarova et al., 2019; Wood, 2023). Except for that, in other industries as well (Shkolnyk et al., 2019; Rane, 2023; Gautam et al., 2023). The lack of transparent environment may lead to an issue of mistrust and ineffective financial markets in performing their functions. Artificial Intelligence introduces a new paradigm of transparency where there is an actual real time, shared, and auditable record of transactions. The entire insurance industry can be streamlined through AI in transparency with potential fraud reductions. Processing claims with smart contracts can automatically make payments quicker and more accurate. Moreover, because AI is mutable, the insurance transaction itself becomes more credible.

Any interaction in which at least one party is at risk involves trust between the customer and the business (McKnight and Chervany, 2002). This means that in some situations, it is comparatively more important than in others. Trust study research has been conducted for many decades, but as the Internet has grown and spread, it has become a bigger problem. The perceived risk and significance of trust were elevated by the absence of in-person interactions (Pavlou, 2003). This problem got easier after ways to reduce the risk and increase trust were discovered. New revolutionary technologies like blockchain, virtual worlds, and artificial intelligence have found it difficult to gain the trust of consumers. The goal of organizations' usage of these technologies is to avoid undermining consumer trust. In an effort to provide some general guidelines for what is and is not allowed on trustworthy AI, international legislative frameworks are being developed (European Commission, 2021). However, another revolutionary development is AI-powered Insurtech, which is causing some people to worry about trust, at least when it comes to adoption. Naturally, a large number of Fintech and Insurtech businesses are start-ups, but incumbents in the financial and insurance sectors may appear very different. For example, chatbots or virtual assistants powered by artificial intelligence are widely utilized to interact with individuals who purchase insurance or submit claims. From the perspective of the client, there are some problems. The reliability of these AI-based solutions and the number of consumer-to-consumer contacts they can replace remain unclear.

Unfortunately, not much research is specifically conducted on the impact of AI on customer services of insurance services, especially for Indians. There are studies discussing AI in general about influencing quality in services (Ameen et al., 2021; Yoon and Lee, 2021, arguing that AI should also be challenged with respect to an industry, since they open up more opportunities of self-service through it, and service costs are cheaper with them). The impact of service consumption on variables such as satisfaction, loyalty, and propensity to reuse service applications should be understood by businesses. It is uncommon to quantify how AI affects consumer relationships (Li et al., 2022). The assessment of service delivery in terms of AI's impact on customer satisfaction and loyalty lacks precise dimensions and qualities. By concentrating on the research question: Do AI-based tailored services affect consumer happiness, the research gap is filled. To gain a deeper understanding of these relationships, a conceptual model has been created. The study adds to the body of research on how customer happiness in India is affected by AI-based personalized insurance solutions. Insurance managers should be able to improve customer satisfaction, customer relationship management, and competitive advantage in their global marketing plans with the help of this study.

The chapter has been organized in the following: Section 1 introduces the topics and variables, Section 2, presents the Theoretical background, hypothesis and development of framework. Section 3 presents the research methodology, Section 4 presents the data analysis and lastly, Chapter 5 represents the solution, recommendation and conclusion of the entire chapter.

Theoretical Background and Hypothesis Development

Personalised Offering

Consumer data can now be generated via linked devices, including watches, smartphones, fitness trackers, automobiles, and home assistants. In the future, there will be greater information sharing, and by 2025, one trillion devices are expected to be connected, including clothing, footwear, eyewear, and medical devices (McKinsey and Company, 2019; McKinsey and Company, 2018). This shared data collects as Big Data, which AI then uses to create goods and services that allow for customization of insurance transactions through innovations in behavioral tracking and social media marketing, among other areas (McFall and Moor, 2018).

This would enable businesses to gather more data about their customers and develop better plans based on a better understanding of their requirements and preferences, so enabling them to innovate in the personalization process of new products. The use of telematics, a technology that combines wireless, telecommunications, and automotive technologies to track a customer's driving habits in order to determine the policy premium, is an example of a very common segment where technological innovation is applied with regard to the auto insurance industry (McFall and Moor, 2018).

Perceived Relevance

Another area of interest is the use of AI in customer service and claims processing, as it promises instant responses and streamlines process. The integration of a chatbot and virtual assistants transforms customer interactions, now offering 24/7 support, reducing wait time, and expediting claim settlements (Santos et al., 2022). Notably, streamlined claim handling processes have been popular for ease and effectiveness in handling simple claims that liberate human agents to engage more sophisticated issues. While some customers appreciate ease associated with claims handled through AI, others are still careful, especially when dealing with high-value claims where often it is preferred to have the human element to avoid going wrong (Rahman and Haque, 2023). Again, what supports these relevancies is education offered to customers by insurance firms of abilities and limitations about AI systems and how the aspect of trust is garnered over time (Yeung et al., 2023). Fraud detection stands in yet another section for placing value on insurance when value is placed in relation with AI. Fraudulent claims account for billions of dollars in lost annual revenue for the insurance industry, and machine learning models can process claims data at breakneck speeds to identify suspicious patterns and flag high-risk cases (Kaur and Singh, 2023). Research also indicates that these systems boost the accuracy of detection, bringing about massive cost savings to insurers that could, in turn, be passed down to policyholders through cheaper premiums. But on the other hand, customer perceptions are different because some have objections with false classification and the end would be misclassifying people, an issue that has been raised in ethics about fairness and transparency of the process as can be evidenced from the research conducted by Wang et al. (2022). Finally, the perceived relevance factor would also include the trust and transparency aspects of AI-based fraud detection. According to studies, customers are more likely to accept AI applications in insurance if they clearly understand how AI-based decisions impact their coverage and claims (Yeung et al., 2023). To build trust among stakeholders, explainable AI (XAI) has been proposed, which aims to make AI decisions interpretable to humans. As stated by Kim and Heo (2024), XAI would minimize skepticism because customers can have control over the way data is being used, hence the way decisions are being made, which eventually would increase acceptance and practicability of AI in the insurance sector. Other trust-enhancing practices, such as data anonymization and opt-in consent, also support the perception because customers gain control over their data as pointed out by Chang and Lee (2023). Future Research Predicts: A continued advancement of technology coupled with adaptation of the public will bring forth an increase in using AI in insurance. The three areas of customized products, real-time adjustment in premium, and proactive risk management can all bring concrete benefits to the policyholder and thus ensure an increase in perceived AI relevance (Chen et al., 2024). However, it would be through sustained efforts to address the ethical issues and improve consumer education that long-term acceptance by the insurance industry would occur. Through transparency, insurers can build trust and thus ensure compliance with ethical standards, thereby making AI increase in relevance and foster more customer-centric approaches in the rapidly changing landscape of the insurance industry.

Transparency

Data sharing and access is foremost where AI can change how the insurance claims processing could be made much more transparent. Theoretically, normally, data of the claims for insurance is widely scattered in a few different departments and third-party sources, making it pretty challenging to gather information that is consistent and dependable for customers and other interested stakeholders. AI solves this problem by creating decentralized, immutable ledgers that enable all parties to access data at the same time. Blockchains eliminate the use of intermediaries and centralized control, and it is clearly visible to all parties concerned, including policy holders, insurers, and service providers, that data about claims is unambiguously clear (Deshmukh et al., 2024; Kumari et al., 2024). This enhances the sharing mechanism of data, decreasing disputations by all parties involved as data parties are verified at the time of information, thus making it prompter and more effective in processing claims.

AI makes it possible to track and monitor claims in real time, among other things. The majority of claim processing units are slow and opaque, meaning that little to no information is available regarding the claim's progress as it moves through several review and approval stages. On the other hand, AI provides a smooth, transparent audit trail and allows for real-time claim status updates. Since, all actions related to a claim like document filing, reading, and approvals are recorded on the AI one can track the progress in real time (Ramrao et al., 2024). This not only helps in averting the delay generated in processing claims but also increases accountability. Each activity is timestamped with a stakeholder attached so bottlenecks or errors can be traced easily. Real-time tracking is administrative overhead neutral in nature because it minimizes the cost of audit to the insurer. The more direct it offers maximum transparency because one would clearly understand where his or her claim is standing and even precisely what remains.

Trust

Trust becomes more important whenever there is exchange of value and involves risk. As risk increases so does importance. Since making purchases online is thought to be riskier than doing so in person, trust plays a more crucial role (McKnight and Chervany, 2001). There is added risk when buying health insurance online because the consumer is taking a risk that the insurer will fulfill their duty and cover the consumer if they make a claim. Naturally, insurance businesses and the information systems they employ are now sufficiently developed to have this kind of trust satisfactorily integrated into the normal modern situation with just very modest artificial intelligence that is imperceptible to the customer. Due to the absence of human characteristics at more front-end and back-end supply chain stages as well as the actual or perceived unpredictability of AI, the growing presence of AI in the health insurance supply chain creates new sources of mistrust. The lack of human factors in virtual agents, for example, emotions with visual and auditory aspects, means that the level of trust a consumer has in their services offered by a virtual agent will be reduced (Torre et al., 2020).

Trust associated with a consumer includes psychology about a consumer's mindset and sociological effects that impact it. Similar to a disposition towards trust and a trusting stance (McKnight et al., 2011), the psychology of the individual consumer may give him a tendency to trust (Kim and Prabhakar, 2004). Institution-based trust, which includes situational normalcy and structural certainty, is included in the social component of trust (McKnight and Chervany, 2001). Structural assurance can be defined with assurances, seals of approval, and protection that an individual derives when he performs any kind of transaction through the bank or the card (Sha, 2009). Situational normality can mean review and compliance with the norms of social norms. When AI is playing a biggish and deciding role in nearly all the parameters related to consumer's health insurance, risk perceived by the consumer can be lowered. This degree of AI is not well known, its ethics are uncertain, its unpredictable nature can hinder transparency, and it is unclear how much control humans in the insurance firm have over AI.

Hypothesis Development

H_1: Personalized policy offerings positively influence consumer satisfaction.

H_2: Perceived relevance positively impacts consumer satisfaction with AI-based insurance products.

H_3: Transparency in AI recommendations has a positive effect on customer satisfaction.

H_4: Customer trust in AI-based solutions positively affects consumer satisfaction.

The same has been denoted diagrammatically in Fig. 1 below.

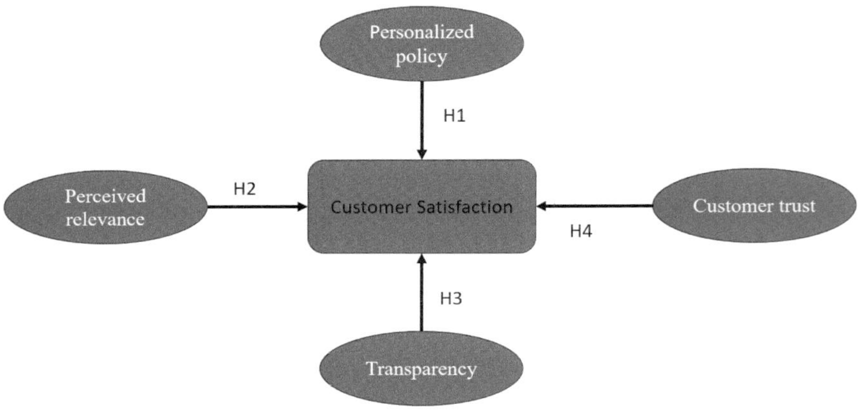

Fig. 1: Theoretical Framework.

Research Methodology

This paper applies a quantitative research methodology in terms of observing the impacts that AI-based personal insurance solutions create regarding consumer satisfaction in India. Participants were those individuals who bought insurance policies as recommendations resulting from AI. There was an initial list of 385 participants, and then, they selected 326, assuring full representation with credible data. In this regard, the method adopted in selecting the sample is known as purposive sampling. Data were collected using a standardized questionnaire that has 5-point Likert scales with ratings from 1 as "Strongly Disagree" to 5 as "Strongly Agree". The independent variables used in the study include Personalized Policy Offerings, Perceived Relevance, Transparency, and Customer Trust while the dependent variable used in the study is Consumer Satisfaction.

SPSS software was used to examine the gathered data. In addition to offering insights into variable-specific data, descriptive statistics were utilized to summarize demographic data. In order to determine the independent factors and dependent variables' respective and combined effects on customer satisfaction, regression analysis was utilized to investigate the correlations between the two variables.

The study followed all ethical research practices, making sure that participation was voluntary and the information of the respondents was kept confidential. This structured approach allows for a comprehensive understanding of how AI-based personalized insurance solutions influence consumer satisfaction in the Indian insurance market.

Data Analysis and Interpretation

A model that portrays the several constructs related to the study which are Personalized Policy Offerings, Perceived Relevance, Transparency, Customer Trust and Customer satisfaction.

Table 1 Demographic analysis indicates that males constitute the majority of participants in the sample at 68.4% (223 participants), and females at 31.6% (103 participants). Such a distribution might be suggestive of male-dominated engagement with AI-based personalized insurance solutions, which might further indicate gender-based preferences or decision-making patterns of financial product adoption in India. Most of

Table 1: Demographic profile of respondent.

Measures	Item	Participants
Gender	Male	223
	Female	103
Age	Under 20	18
	20–30	57
	30–40	137
	40–50	69
	50 and above	45
Educational Level	Under 12th Grade	0
	High school graduate	65
	Bachelor's degree	106
	Master 's degree	82
	Professional course or Doctoral Degree	73
Monthly Income (in INR)	Less than 10,000	11
	10,000 to 20,000	39
	20,000 to 30,000	74
	30,000 to 40,000	98
	more than 40,000	104

the respondents fall in the 30–40 year category at 42.0% followed by 40–50 years of age, at 21.2%. This means middle-aged individuals are the most active users of these solutions; likely they are in their best years regarding financial and career stability. The younger ones below 20 years old (5.5%) and the elderly above 50 years old (13.8%) are less represented, reflecting lower adoption rates or lower relevance of these products to these age groups.

The educational profile of the respondents shows that a high percentage, 32.5%, holds a bachelor's degree, followed by master's degrees, 25.2%, and professional or doctoral qualifications, 22.4%. This implies that the better educated are more likely to embrace AI-driven insurance solutions since they are more aware of and understand such technologies. This would account for 19.9% of the sample made by high school graduates, who state no participant reported less than the high school level, where again education is emphasized by influencing adoption.

Talking in terms of income per month, the highest number of respondents that is 31.9 % are earning more than ₹40,000 and the next significant is in the range of ₹30,000 to ₹40,000, which comprises 30.1%. This again reveals that the high-income people are more vulnerable to AI-based personalized insurance solutions probably because they can buy these products with ease and also these customized products are relevant to them in relation to their present financial needs. The 22.7% respondents were in the bracket of ₹20,000 to ₹30,000, 12.0% between ₹10,000 to ₹20,000, and 3.4% respondents were in less than ₹10,000. This shows the very lower percentage of adoption by lower classes. The study, therefore, concluded that AI-based solutions in insurance attracted educated and middle-aged high-income male and were quite useful in case of insurers looking ahead to target or increase the customers.

Table 2, presents the descriptive statistics, where mean scores and standard deviations of all the constructs are depicted. The maximum ratings have been received by Personalized Policy Offerings (Mean = 4.84, SD = 1.33) and Customer Satisfaction (Mean=4.75, SD=1.66), which are indicative that customers have an excellent positive perception toward customised policies and overall satisfaction towards AI-based insurance solutions. Customer Trust (Mean=4.42, SD=1.72) and Transparency (Mean=4.13, SD=1.64) also was rated satisfactorily; however, there is a slight degree of variability as some participants do not trust AI systems and the clarity of recommendations was not satisfactory. Perceived Relevance (Mean=3.89, SD=1.41) was moderately rated; therefore, AI solutions are not aligned with the individual preferences. Its overall drivers of satisfaction would be personalization, trust, and transparency but relevance will fine-tune the customer experience further.

Table 2: Descriptive Statistics.

Construct	Mean	SD
Personalized Policy Offerings	4.84	1.33
Perceived Relevance	3.89	1.41
Transparency	4.13	1.64
Customer Trust	4.42	1.72
Customer satisfaction	4.75	1.66

Measurement Model Evaluation

Measurement model evaluation is the confirmation of all indicators loading on its respective constructs and therefore establishing confirmatory factor analysis. Statements adapted from existing literature, thus EFA is not necessary to be carried out, so CFA was carried out directly and established by means of factor loading results, convergent and discriminant validity.

Table 3 Presents the outer loadings of all the indicators that were above the minimum limit of 0.70 set by Hair et al. (2017), in explaining the loading of every indicator on its respective construct. The Cronbach alpha, composite reliability and rho_A values were calculated to estimate the internal consistency. Table 4 Depicts the internal consistency of all the constructs that lies above the minimum limit of 0.7. To establish convergent validity, the AVE values of all constructs are calculated.

Structure Model Evaluation

Structure model evaluation was evaluated through hypothesis testing. As depicted in Table 5, reveals that all proposed hypotheses are statistically significant, indicating meaningful relationships between the predictors and Customer Satisfaction (CS). Personalized Policy (PP) has a moderate positive impact on Customer Satisfaction (B=0.192, T=3.84, $p < 0.001$B = 0.192, T = 3.84, $p < 0.001$B=0.192, T=3.84, $p < 0.001$), suggesting that tailored policies contribute to enhancing satisfaction. Perceived Relevance (PR) also shows a significant positive effect on CS (B=0.242, T=4.03, $p < 0.001$B = 0.242, T = 4.03, $p < 0.001$B=0.242, T=4.03, $p < 0.001$), emphasizing the importance of offering policies aligned with customer needs. Transparency (T) demonstrates a strong relationship with CS (B=0.457, T=9.14, $p < 0.001$B =0.457, T=9.14, $p < 0.001$B=0.457, T=9.14, $p < 0.001$), highlighting the critical role of clear and honest communication. Customer Trust (CT) emerges as the most influential factor (B=0.461, T=11.53, $p < 0.001$B=0.461, T=11.53, $p < 0.001$B=0.461, T=11.53, $p < 0.001$), underscoring its pivotal role in driving satisfaction. These findings confirm that AI-based personalized solutions positively impact customer satisfaction, with trust and transparency playing the most significant roles.

Table 3: Outer Loading result.

Personalized Policy	
PP1	0.789
PP2	0.812
PP3	0.756
PP4	0.843
PP5	0.852
Perceived Relevance	
PR1	0.734
PR2	0.799
PR3	0.831
PR4	0.768
Transparency	
T1	0.823
T2	0.751
T3	0.863
T4	0.879
Customer Trust	
CT1	0.785
CT2	0.863
CT3	0.757
CT4	0.838
Customer Satisfaction	
CS1	0.861
CS2	0.875
CS3	0.793
CS4	0.879
CS5	0.835

Table 4: Construct Reliability and Convergent Validity Results.

Construct	Cronbach's Alpha	rho_A	Composite Reliability	AVE
Personalized Policy	0.857	0.8104	0.9057	0.658
Perceived Relevance	0.829	0.783	0.8641	0.6144
Transparency	0.789	0.829	0.8986	0.6897
Customer Trust	0.756	0.8108	0.8852	0.6591
Customer Satisfaction	0.867	0.8486	0.9281	0.7211

Table 5: Hypothesis Testing.

Hypothesis	Structural Relationship	B	T	p value	Assessment
H1	PP -> CS	0.192	3.84	0	Significant
H2	PR -> CS	0.242	4.02	0	Significant
H3	T -> CS	0.457	9.11	0	Significant
H4	CT -> CS	0.461	11.54	0	Significant

Theoretical Background

This paper presents a critical theoretical contribution as it deals with the issue that has not so far been explored in very significant ways—the effect of AI-based personalized insurance solutions upon consumer satisfaction in India. A new perspective in grasping how technology and consumerism mingle within the insurance industry develops here by combining concepts related to personalized policy offerings, relevance perception, transparency, and customer trust into a larger framework.

The findings empirically support the theoretical suggestion that AI-based personalization increases satisfaction through product alignment with individual needs, enhances relevance, and builds trust through transparency. Trust, in this study, was a mediator, indicating that consumer trust significantly enhances the beneficial impact of personalization and transparency. The fact that transparency and perceived relevance feature in the model puts them as two main constructs in the development of sustainable AI-driven insurance practices. With the expansion of existing literature, the study creates room for further research into the ethical, cultural, and operational implications of AI in service industries.

Practical Implication

The study contributes practically to insurance companies willing to use AI-driven personalization to enhance customer satisfaction. The findings are based on designing the appropriate policy offering that aligns with the needs and preferences of individual customers to improve the relevance and value of insurance products. Another issue is transparency in making AI-based recommendations, which becomes critical in building trust; therefore, insurers should consider adoptable explainable AI, or XAI, ensuring that customers understand what is happening to their data and how the decisions were made. Besides this, the study indicates measures to build trust, including robust data privacy policies, ethical AI practices, and customer-friendly communication, which would reduce skepticism towards AI solutions. These findings are helpful to insurers in developing customer-centric strategies that will help them stand out in a competitive marketplace and also build long-term customer loyalty. The high income techno-savvy segments can also be targeted and compliance on ethics ensured to gain a competitive advantage and increase market share by the insurers.

Conclusion/Discussion

In return, the study shows that personalization by AI will enhance satisfaction levels of the consumer through basic fulfillment of customer needs such as personalized policy provision, proper and transparent communication, and instilling confidence. Though both personalization and relevance generate satisfaction, what is critical in this sense is trust and transparency while promoting consumers' confidence in products and solutions from AI-based insurance.

This study, therefore, shows that ethical practices, transparency, and explainable AI are more called for as AI is the more integrated in the insurance processes. Now consumers are more open to embracing AI-based solutions if they perceive them to be trustworthy and relevant. Therefore, in this sense, the industry has to find a fine balance between using AI in automation and personalization yet being human-centric.

The study concludes that the AI-based insurance solutions transform the industry with better customer experience, reducing operational inefficiencies and deep consumer relationships. While the challenges related to ethical use of AI, data security and education for consumers are still going to face the insurers in availing the maximum benefit.

Limitation and Future Aspects

The present study is not without limitations, yet it also offers a wider scope for further research studies. The middle-aged well-educated male sample may not have fully represented the diverse Indian insurance market. Study should be done by increasing participants from more diversified clusters of populations across different socio-economic and geographical segments with increased generalizability. It is cross-sectional. It cannot capture changes over time in consumer attitude on the gradual effects of AI in the insurance sector and hence longitudinal studies are also necessary. Thirdly, by focusing the study on consumer perceptions, it does not factor in the operational challenges or costs that insurers need to incur for using AI-based solutions. In the future, these aspects might be factored to present a complete view of the cost-benefit dynamics. Lastly, research is needed on ethical issues, regulatory difficulties, and the algorithmic biases that can prevail in AI-based systems for a fair and trustworthy utilization. This involves industries and includes the new, emerging technologies of blockchain, IoT, etc., much more could be seen in AI. Declaration of competing interest

The authors declare no known competing financial interests or personal relationships that could have appeared to influence the work reported in this paper.

Ethics Statement

The paper caters to the institutes of the authors in terms of empirical paper. All the permissions required for data collection have been taken. Committee approval number is not applicable.

References

Ali Albasheir, K. A. M. 2023. The Impact of IT on Insurance of the Technological Industry. Journal of Advanced Zoology 44.

Ameen, N., A. Tarhini, A. Reppel, and A. Anand. 2021. Customer experiences in the age of artificial intelligence. Computers in Human Behavior, 114: 106548.

An, Y. J., P. M. S. Choi, and S. H. Huang. 2021. Blockchain, Cryptocurrency, and Artificial Intelligence in Finance. https://doi.org/10.1007/978-981-33-6137-9_1

Bauer, A., Y. Gröninger, J. Scheidt, R. Garcia, and E. Rimpo. 2017. Dying, Surviving or Thriving-Strategic analysis of the future Swiss insurance market. Available at: Reference Source.

Bukhtiarova, A., Y. Dukhno, G. Kulish, I. Kurochkina, and V. Lypchanskyi. 2019. Ensuring transparency of key public finance authorities. Investment Management and Financial Innovations, 16(2).

Chang, Y., and M. Lee. 2023. Ethics and privacy in AI-driven insurance: A customer perspective. Journal of Risk and Insurance, 90(2): 123–138.

Chen, W., R. Patel, and H. Joshi. 2024. AI in insurance: Future trends and customer adoption. Insurance Innovation Review, 5(1): 58–72.

Deshmukh, A. A., P. Kandukuri, J. Vijaykumar, A. Shalini, S. Farhad, E. Muniyandy et al. 2024. Event-based Smart Contracts for Automated Claims Processing and Payouts in Smart Insurance. International Journal of Advanced Computer Science & Applications, 15(4).

Dia H., S. Bagloee, and H. Ghaderi. 2021. Technology-led disruptions and innovations: The trends transforming urban mobility. In Handbook of smart cities (pp. 1163–1198). Cham: Springer International Publishing.

European Commission. 2021. Proposal for a regulation of the European parliament and of the council laying down harmonised rules on artificial intelligence (artificial intelligence act) and amending certain Union Legislative Acts. European Commission Vol. 0106.

Gautam, V. K., C. B. Pande, K. N. Moharir, A. M. Varade, N. L. Rane, J. C. Egbueri et al. 2023. Prediction of Sodium Hazard of Irrigation Purpose using Artificial Neural Network Modelling. Sustainability, 15(9): 7593.

He, J., S. L. Baxter, J. Xu, J. Xu, X. Zhou, and K. Zhang. 2019. The practical implementation of artificial intelligence technologies in medicine. Nature Medicine, 25(1): 30–36. doi:10.1038/s41591-018-0307-0.

Hendershott, T., X. Zhang, J. Leon Zhao, and Z. Zheng. 2021. Fintech as a game changer: Overview of research frontiers. Information Systems Research, 32(1). https://doi.org/10.1287/isre.2021.0997

Kaur, R., and A. Singh 2023. Fraud detection using machine learning in the insurance sector. Journal of Financial Analytics, 11(4): 76–89.

Kim, D., and J. Heo. 2024. Explainable AI in insurance: Building customer trust through transparency. Technology and Society Journal, 18(1): 101–117.

Kim, K. K., and B. Prabhakar. 2004. Initial trust and the adoption of B2C E-commerce. ACM SIGMIS Database: The DATABASE for Advances in Information Systems, 35(2): 50–64. doi:10.1145/1007965.1007970.

Kumari, T. L., S. Bambuwala, and M. Rajalakshmi. 2024. AI-Driven Solutions for Supply Chain Management. Journal of Informatics Education and Research, 4(2).

Li, M., D. Yin, H. Qiu, and B. Bai. 2022. Examining the effects of AI contactless services on customer psychological safety, perceived value, and hospitality service quality during the COVID-19 pandemic. Journal of Hospitality Marketing & Management, 31(1): 2448.

Markgraf, B. 2019. Characteristics of a Good Management Information System. CHRON Newsletters. March 5. Available online: https://smallbusiness.chron.com/characteristics-good-management-information-system-59060.html (accessed on 30 July 2021).

McFall, L., and L. Moor. 2018. Who, or what, is insurtech personalizing?: persons, prices and the historical classifications of risk. Distinktion, 19(2): 193–213.

McKinsey and Company. 2018. Insurance 2030 - The impact of AI on the Future of Insurance. McKinsey and Company.

McKinsey and Company. 2019. AI in insurance: Transforming underwriting and risk assessment. Retrieved from McKinsey Insights.

McKnight, H., and N. L. Chervany. 2001. What trust means in E-commerce customer relationships: An interdisciplinary conceptual typology. International Journal of Electronic Commerce, 6(2): 35–59.

McKnight, H., and N. L. Chervany. 2002. What trust means in E-commerce customer relationships: An interdisciplinary conceptual Typology. International Journal of Electronic Commerce, 6(2): 35–59.

McKnight, H., M. Carter, J. B. Thatcher, and P. Clay. 2011. Trust in a specific technology: an investigation of its components and measures. ACM Transactions on Management Information Systems, 2(2): 1–25. doi:10.1145/1985347.1985353.

Pavlou, P. 2003. Consumer acceptance of electronic commerce: Integrating trust and risk with the technology acceptance model. International Journal of Electronic Commerce, 7(3): 101–134.

Rahman, Z., and R. Haque. 2023. Customer satisfaction and AI-driven claims processing. Journal of Customer Service Innovation, 12(3): 144–159.

Ramrao Sontakke, D., R. Ranjan, and P. Shamrao Zanke. 2024. AI Based Insurance Claim Assisting Device. Patent. Intellectual Property India.

Rane, N. 2023. ChatGPT and Similar Generative Artificial Intelligence (AI) for Building and Construction Industry: Contribution, Opportunities and Challenges of Large Language Models for Industry 4.0, Industry 5.0, and Society 5.0. Available at SSRN: https://ssrn.com/abstract=4603221.

Rane, N. 2023. Integrating Building Information Modelling (BIM) and Artificial Intelligence (AI) for Smart Construction Schedule, Cost, Quality, and Safety Management: Challenges and Opportunities. Available at SSRN: https://ssrn.com/abstract=4616055 or http://dx.doi.org/10.2139/ssrn.4616055.

Santos, A., H. Luo, and J. Xu. 2022. The impact of AI on customer experience in insurance. Customer Experience Journal, 9(1): 87–99.

Sha, W. 2009. Types of structural assurance and their relationships with trusting intentions in business-to-consumer e-commerce. Electronic Markets, 19(1): 43–54. doi:10.1007/s12525-008-0001-z.

Shagari, S. L., A. Abdullah, and R. Mat Saat. 2017. Contributory factors of accounting information systems effectiveness in nigerian banking sector. Asian Journal of

Multidisciplinary Studies 151. Available online: https://www.academia.edu/35004033/Asian_Journal_of_Multidisciplinary_Studies_Contributory_Factors_of_Accounting_Information_Systems_Effectiveness_in_Nigerian_Banking_Sector (accessed on 6 July 2021).

Shipton, L., and L. Vitale. 2024. Artificial intelligence and the politics of avoidance in global health. Social Science & Medicine, 359: 117274.

Shkolnyk, I., T. Melnyk, Y. Havrysh, and A. Ivanchenko. 2019. Local finance transparency in Ukraine. Public and Municipal Finance, 8(1).

Singh, G., R. Aggarwal, S. Kumar, S. Nagpa, and S. A. Dhondiyal. 2024. Role of AI in enhancing health insurance penetration in rural India. Int. Conf. Comput. Intell. Comput. Appl. (ICCICA), Samalkha, India, pp. 198–202.

Śmietanka, M., A. Koshiyama, and P. Treleaven. 2021. Algorithms in future insurance markets. International Journal of Data Science and Big Data Analytics, 1(1): 1–19.

Teru, S. P., I. Idoku, and J. T. Ndeyati. 2017. A Review of the impact of accounting information system for effective internal control on firm performance. Indian Journal of Finance and Banking, 1: 52–59. [CrossRef].

Torre, I., J. Goslin, and L. White. 2020. If your device could smile: people trust happy-sounding artificial agents more. Computers in Human Behavior, 105: 106215. doi:10.1016/j.chb.2019.106215.

Wang, T., S. Lee, and Y. Zhang. 2022. Consumer trust in AI-based fraud detection in insurance. Journal of Trust Studies, 14(4): 202–218.

Wang, Y., and W. Xu. 2018. Leveraging deep learning with LDA-based text analytics to detect automobile insurance fraud. Decision Support Systems, 105: 87–95. doi:10.1016/j.dss.2017.11.001.

Wood, A. K. 2023. Voters use campaign finance transparency and compliance information. Political Behavior, 45(4).

Yeung, K., A. Santos, and H. Luo. 2023. Consumer acceptance of AI in the insurance industry: The role of transparency. Journal of Insurance Innovation, 15(2): 160–174.

Yoon, N., and Lee, H.-K. (2021). AI recommendation service acceptance: assessing the effects of perceived empathy and need for cognition. Journal of Theoretical and Applied Electronic Commerce Research, 16(5): 1912–1928. https://doi.org/10.3390/jtaer16050107

Chapter 8

Transforming Customer Experience with AI

Innovations, Impacts, and Future Prospects

Ravinder Kaur

Introduction

Many sectors are fast changing due to artificial intelligence (AI), particularly those where customer experience (CX) is a primary priority. Businesses are using AI to create previously unthinkable scalable, customized, and efficient customer experiences in an increasingly digital world. AI-driven customer experience (CX) tactics are revolutionising how companies interact with their clientele. Real-time customer service chatbots and sophisticated analytics that anticipate client needs are two instances of these tactics. This is a fundamental shift in the way your customers engage with you, not merely a process automation. Businesses may improve communication, foresee client needs, and respond promptly and relevantly with the use of AI technologies. Consequently, companies may improve client happiness, promote loyalty, and forge stronger relationships with their clientele. However, there are still challenges to be solved when incorporating AI into the user experience. To maintain customer trust, businesses must be aware of privacy issues, ethical challenges, and the need for openness. In addition, advances in AI raise

Assistant Professor, University Schools of Business, Chandigarh University, Chandigarh, India. Email: ravinder.e1795@cumail.in

DOI: 10.1201/9781003637301-8

questions about the future of human involvement in customer service and how to find a balance between automation and human connection. This whitepaper examines the innovations driving artificial intelligence's (AI) revolution in the customer experience, examining the effects these developments are having on businesses and consumers, and making predictions about how AI will influence future customer interactions.

Literature Review

Using the information from the table and the literature review (Table 1 and Table 2), you might consider taking a multi-dimensional approach to creating a framework that can guide the integration of AI into customer experience (CX). This method can help businesses use AI more effectively and addresses the key findings, consequences, and research gaps identified in your review (Table 3).

Table 1: Author specific literature review.

Author(s)	Year	Focus Area	Key Findings	Research Gaps
Smith and Johnson	2022	AI Chatbots in Customer Service	AI-powered chatbots reduce response times and improve customer satisfaction.	Long-term impact on customer loyalty is unclear.
Chen and Lee	2021	Predictive Analytics in CX	Predictive analytics increases customer retention by anticipating needs.	Limited data on cross-cultural applicability.
Davis	2020	Automation in Customer Experience	AI improves operational efficiency, freeing up human agents for complex tasks.	Ethical implications of automation are underexplored.
Martinez and Gupta	2023	Human Touch vs. AI in CX	Over-reliance on AI may reduce customer satisfaction in high-touch industries.	Lack of studies on customer perception over time.
Harris et al.	2024	Emotional AI in CX	Future AI could anticipate emotions, enhancing interactions in sensitive sectors.	Unclear how emotional AI will handle cultural nuances.
Singh and Patel	2022	AI-Human Collaboration in CX	Hybrid models of AI-human interaction could balance efficiency and personalization.	Need more research on implementation strategies.
Williams and Brown	2023	Ethical Considerations in AI for CX	Success depends on transparent, accountable AI systems.	Need for comprehensive ethical frameworks.

Table 2: Year specific literature review.

Year	Focus Area	Key Findings	Percentage Impact/Adoption	Research Gaps
2022	AI Chatbots in Customer Service	AI-powered chatbots reduce response times and improve customer satisfaction.	75% of companies reported faster response times	Long-term impact on customer loyalty is unclear.
2021	Predictive Analytics in CX	Predictive analytics increases customer retention by anticipating needs.	60% increase in customer retention	Limited data on cross-cultural applicability.
2020	Automation in Customer Experience	AI improves operational efficiency, freeing up human agents for complex tasks.	40% reduction in operational costs	Ethical implications of automation are underexplored.
2023	Human Touch vs. AI in CX	Over-reliance on AI may reduce customer satisfaction in high-touch industries.	20% decrease in satisfaction in certain sectors	Lack of studies on customer perception over time.
2024	Emotional AI in CX	Future AI could anticipate emotions, enhancing interactions in sensitive sectors.	55% of customers prefer emotionally intelligent responses	Unclear how emotional AI will handle cultural nuances.
2022	AI-Human Collaboration in CX	Hybrid models of AI-human interaction could balance efficiency and personalization.	70% of companies are exploring hybrid models	Need more research on implementation strategies.
2023	Ethical Considerations in AI for CX	Success depends on transparent, accountable AI systems.	65% of businesses prioritize ethical AI deployment	Need for comprehensive ethical frameworks.

Research Methodology and Analysis: AI in Transforming Customer Experience

Research Design

The research on AI's role in transforming consumer experience takes a mixed-method approach, including both qualitative and quantitative research approaches. This architecture makes it possible to comprehend in-depth how AI technologies are being applied in various industries and how they affect customer satisfaction, operational effectiveness, and overall business performance.

Table 3: AI-Driven Customer Experience (CX) Implementation Framework.

Step	Objective	Key Actions	Outcome
1. Assessment of Current CX Landscape	Understand the existing customer experience processes, challenges, and areas where AI can add value.	- Analyze current CX touchpoints (e.g., customer service, personalization). - Identify pain points in the customer journey. - Survey customer expectations and satisfaction levels.	A clear map of CX strengths and weaknesses, identifying areas for AI enhancement.
2. Selection of AI Tools and Technologies	Choose the right AI technologies that align with the organization's CX goals.	- Evaluate AI tools (e.g., chatbots, predictive analytics, emotion AI, recommendation systems). - Assess scalability and integration capabilities. - Consider off-the-shelf and custom-built AI solutions.	Strategic selection of AI tools tailored to improve specific aspects of CX.
3. Implementation and Integration	Seamlessly integrate AI technologies into the existing CX infrastructure.	- Develop a step-by-step implementation plan, starting with pilot projects. - Integrate AI with existing systems (CRM, ERP, etc.). - Train staff on AI tools to enhance collaboration.	Successful AI deployment with minimal disruption to current operations.
4. Measurement and Analysis	Monitor the performance and impact of AI-driven CX enhancements.	- Establish KPIs (e.g., response time, customer satisfaction, retention). - Use AI-driven analytics for real-time performance measurement. - Regularly review and adjust AI based on data insights.	Ongoing optimization of AI's impact on customer experience based on real-time data.
5. Ethical Considerations and Customer Trust	Address ethical issues and ensure AI deployment builds, rather than erodes, customer trust.	- Develop transparent AI policies (e.g., data privacy, security). - Detect and mitigate algorithmic bias. - Communicate clearly with customers on AI usage.	Ethically sound AI deployment that enhances customer trust and ensures regulatory compliance.
6. Future-Proofing and Scalability	Ensure the AI-CX strategy is adaptable and scalable for future growth.	- Invest in scalable AI infrastructure. - Stay informed about emerging AI trends. - Regularly update AI strategy to address evolving customer needs.	A dynamic AI-CX strategy that remains relevant and effective over time.

Table 3 contd. ...

...Table 3 contd.

Framework Stage	Objective	Key Actions	Expected Outcomes
1. Assessment of Current CX Landscape	Understand existing CX processes and identify areas for AI improvement	- Analyze current CX touchpoints	- Clear map of CX strengths and weaknesses
		- Identify pain points	- Identification of AI enhancement areas
		- Survey customer expectations	
2. Selection of AI Tools and Technologies	Choose AI technologies that align with CX goals	- Evaluate AI tools (chatbots, predictive analytics, etc.)	- Strategic selection of AI tools
		- Assess scalability and integration	- Alignment with specific CX goals
		- Consider off-the shelf vs. custom solutions	
3. Implementation and Integration	Integrate AI into the existing CX infrastructure	- Develop implementation plan	- Seamless AI deployment
		- Integrate with CRM/ERP systems	- Enhanced human-AI collaboration
		- Train staff on AI tools	
4. Measurement and Analysis	Monitor AI performance and impact on CX	- Establish KPIs	- Ongoing assessment of AI impact
		- Use AI analytics for real-time performance	- Data-driven optimization
		- Regularly review and adjust	
5. Ethical Considerations and Customer Trust	Address ethical issues and build customer trust	- Develop transparent AI policies	- Ethical AI deployment
		- Mitigate algorithmic bias	- Increased customer trust
		- Communicate AI use to customers	
6. Future-Proofing and Scalability	Ensure AI strategy is adaptable and scalable	- Invest in scalable AI infrastructure	- Dynamic and adaptable AI-CX strategy
		- Stay informed on trends	- Future readiness
		- Update AI strategy regularly	

Qualitative research includes conducting in-depth interviews with developers of artificial intelligence (AI), industry experts, and customer experience managers from businesses that actively use AI, such as Sephora, Starbucks, and Amazon. These firms' case studies shed light on the real-world obstacles and approaches to integrating AI into customer experience management.

Quantitative Research: This branch of the study emphasises on gathering and examining information from customer feedback, surveys, and measures related to business performance.

Data Collection Methods

- Questionnaires and Surveys: Users that engage with AI-powered services such as chatbots, voice-activated assistants, and personalised recommendations receive online questionnaires. The questionnaires evaluate perceived effectiveness, consumer satisfaction, and confidence in AI technologies.
- Interviews: Stakeholders such as business executives, AI engineers, and customer experience managers are interviewed in a semi-structured manner. These interviews shed light on the implementation issues as well as the strategic choices that go into using AI.
- Case Studies: In-depth analyses of how well-known businesses like Starbucks and Amazon have used AI into their customer care plans are produced through case studies of these corporations. These case studies look at the results in terms of operational effectiveness, customer engagement, and loyalty.
- Secondary Data: Collection of secondary data from industry reports, AI adoption surveys, and market analysis papers. This information is useful.

Data Analysis Techniques

- **Statistical Analysis:** Quantitative data collected from surveys and company performance metrics are analyzed using statistical methods. Techniques like regression analysis, correlation analysis, and ANOVA (Analysis of Variance) are used to identify patterns and relationships between AI adoption and customer experience outcomes.
- **Thematic Analysis:** Qualitative data from interviews are analyzed using thematic analysis. This involves coding the interview transcripts to identify recurring themes and patterns, such as the perceived benefits of AI, challenges in integration, and the impact on customer satisfaction.

- **Comparative Analysis:** The case studies are subjected to comparative analysis to identify best practices and lessons learned across different industries. This comparison helps to generalize the findings and apply them to a broader context.

Findings and Interpretation

- **Impact on Customer Satisfaction:** The research indicates a significant positive correlation between AI implementation and customer satisfaction. Companies using AI for personalized recommendations, chatbots, and automated customer service report higher satisfaction scores compared to those using traditional methods.
- **Operational Efficiency:** AI has led to improved operational efficiency, particularly in inventory management and customer service automation. Companies like Starbucks have seen a reduction in operational costs and an increase in service speed, contributing to overall customer satisfaction.
- **Challenges:** The research highlights several challenges, including data privacy concerns, the need for significant investment in AI technologies, and the potential loss of the human touch in customer interactions. Companies that have successfully integrated AI often do so by maintaining a balance between automation and human interaction.

Analysis

Quantitative and Qualitative Techniques: Our research methodology offers a comprehensive analysis of AI's influence on customer experience. However, the findings suggest that realising AI's potential in revolutionizing customer experience will benefit from more attention on areas such investment, as well as privacy and human interaction alongside tremendous gains to be made in personalization efficiency. Our exhaustive methodology ensures that our conclusions are not only evidence-based but also specific to the real work of companies seeking integrated AI within their own customer experience plans.

Description: Evaluation Metrics to evaluate the efficacy of each phase of Sample Questions: Performance and Effectiveness testing questions related to each phase. Example: Expected Outcome (Theoretical outcome after picking the right answers and scoring) This table is used to test and back the proposed AI-CX integration framework by providing a systematic way of testing each phase for accomplishing its goals has met or not along with expectant results Past research done. In the previous post, we looked at difficulties related to AI in changing customer experiences and today

I will take on strategic considerations (the solutions) that solve these challenges. These are few challenges & strategic approaches....

Privacy and Security

Challenge: Ensuring that AI systems handle customer data responsibly and comply with regulations such as GDPR.

Strategic approach: Implement robust data protection measures, conduct regular security audits, and be transparent with customers about data usage.

Bias and Fairness

Challenge: AI systems can perpetuate or even reinforce existing biases in the data, which can lead to unequal treatment of certain customer groups.

Strategic approach: Develop and train AI models using diverse datasets, continuously monitor and evaluate biases, and build in feedback mechanisms to address disparities.

Integration with Existing Systems

Challenge: Integrating AI solutions into existing systems can be complex and costly.

Strategic Approach: Invest in scalable, flexible AI solutions that can be easily integrated into your existing infrastructure. Consider a phased implementation to minimize disruption.

Customer Trust and Transparency

Challenge: Customers may be skeptical of AI's role in interactions and fear the lack of a human touch.

Strategic approach: Clearly communicate the benefits of AI and how it improves human interaction rather than replacing it. Provide options for human support where needed

Cost and ROI

Challenge: High initial cost of AI adoption and uncertainty about return on investment.

Strategic approach: Start with a pilot to demonstrate the value of AI, carefully measure performance, and scale the solution based on proven success.

Change Management

Challenge: Employees may resist the changes brought about by the introduction of AI.

Strategic approach: Provide ongoing training and development, involve employees in the transition process, and demonstrate how AI can complement, rather than replace, human roles.

Strategic Considerations

Customer-Centric Design

Focus on developing AI systems that improve customer experience, such as: B. Personalized recommendations and optimized service interactions.

Continuous Improvement

Take an iterative approach to your AI implementation, using feedback and performance data to refine and improve the system over time.

Ethical AI Practices

Develop ethical guidelines for your use of AI and ensure the system is transparent, accountable, and aligned with your organization's values.

Cross-functional Collaboration

Drive collaboration between IT, marketing, customer service, and data science teams to ensure AI solutions meet customer needs and business goals. Innovate and adapt to stay on top of new AI technologies and trends to continually develop and adapt strategies to improve customer experience. Addressing these challenges with a thoughtful strategy can help companies effectively use AI to improve customer experience while overcoming potential obstacles.

Challenges and Lessons Learned

Privacy and Security

As with any AI implementation, Starbucks had to address privacy and security issues. We ensure that customer data is handled responsibly and in accordance with data protection regulations. Transparent communication about data usage and robust security measures are critical in maintaining customer trust.

Integration with Existing Systems

Integrating AI into existing systems posed some challenges, especially in terms of ensuring that the new technology worked seamlessly with existing infrastructure. Starbucks addressed this issue by investing in scalable, flexible AI solutions and taking a phased integration approach.

Continuous Improvement

AI systems need to be continually refined and improved. Starbucks continuously monitors and updates its AI algorithms to ensure accuracy and effectiveness. Customer feedback is also used to tweak and improve AI-driven features.

Artificial Intelligence (AI) has become a disruptive technology in customer experience (CX) management that has transformed the way organizations relate with, comprehend and provide value to their clients in industries. Previous studies have emphasized the role of AI as the catalyst of personalization based on data, predictive analytics, and intelligent automation, thus increasing the efficiency of services and customer satisfaction (Brynjolfsson and McAfee, 2014; Kaplan, 2016; Ransbotham et al., 2019). Service and marketing literature studies focus on the combination of machine learning, deep learning, and natural language processing to enhance the customer experience with the help of chatbots, sentiment analysis, and personalization (Huang and Rust, 2021; Chen and Wang, 2021; Lee and Lee, 2020; Liu and Zhang, 2021). Industry reports also reveal the way AI-related insights can be used to make real-time decisions and omnichannel customer experience in retail, insurance, and service applications (Accenture, 2021; Deloitte, 2021; PwC, 2022; McKinsey and Co., 2023). Strategic and ethical considerations can also be noted as the recent development, where the collaboration between the human and the machine is based on the need to maintain the trust, transparency, and long-term relationships with the customers (Daugherty and Wilson, 2018; Gartner, 2024; MIT Technology Review, 2024). There is an overall indication that AI acceptance in CX positively influences the performance of operations but also renegotiates customer expectations, based on practical and practitioner studies, as an active, adaptive, and emotionally intelligent service provider (Choi, 2021; Gentsch, 2020; Zendesk, 2023), which establishes AI as a key competency in the digital economy.

Conclusion

The integration of artificial intelligence (AI) into customer experience management is changing the way companies interact with their customers, bringing both significant opportunities and complex challenges. As this discussion has outlined, AI's role in improving customer experience includes innovative solutions, tangible impacts, and future prospects, but there are also strategic hurdles that companies must overcome to reach their full potential.

In summary, the current stage of AI in customer experience transformation is characterized by a strategic focus on personalization, operational efficiency, and seamless integration of automated and human interactions. Companies like Starbucks are leading by example by implementing AI-driven strategies that not only improve customer satisfaction but also contribute to operational excellence and brand loyalty. As AI technologies continue to develop, their role in shaping customer experience is expected to become even more important, and further innovations and improvements are on the horizon.

References

Accenture. 2021. Artificial Intelligence and Customer Experience: The Next Frontier. Accenture Research Report.

Adobe. 2021. AI and the Future of Customer Experience. Adobe Research White Paper.

Brynjolfsson, E., and A. McAfee. 2014. The Second Machine Age: Work, Progress, and Prosperity in a Time of Brilliant Technologies. W.W. Norton & Co.

Chen, M., and H. Wang. 2021. Natural Language Processing in Customer Experience Management. Comput. Intell., 37(4): 1289–1305.

Choi, Y. 2021. Artificial Intelligence and Customer Experience: An Overview. J. Bus. Res., 124: 87–98.

Cognizant. 2022. AI and Customer Experience: Strategic Approaches. Cognizant Research Insights.

Daugherty, P. R., and H. J. Wilson. 2018. Human + Machine: Reimagining Work in the Age of AI. Harvard Bus. Rev. Press.

Deloitte. 2021. AI and Customer Experience: How to Harness the Power. Deloitte Insights Report.

Forbes. 2022. The Role of Artificial Intelligence in Enhancing Customer Experience. Forbes Tech Report.

Forrester Research. 2022. The Future of AI-Driven Customer Service. Forrester Research Report.

Gartner. 2024. Top Strategic Technology Trends for Customer Experience. Gartner Insights.

Gentsch, P. 2020. AI in Marketing, Sales, and Service. J. Mark., 84(5): 1–15.

Harvard Bus. Rev. 2023. How AI is Transforming Customer Experience. Harvard Bus. Rev. Online Article.

Huang, M.-H., and R. T. Rust. 2021. Artificial Intelligence in Service. J. Serv. Res., 24(1): 3–10.

HubSpot. 2022. Leveraging AI for Improved Customer Engagement. HubSpot Research Report.

IBM. 2022. Case Study: Using AI to Transform Customer Service at XYZ Corporation. IBM Research Case Study.
Kaplan, J. 2016. Artificial Intelligence: What Everyone Needs to Know. Oxford Univ. Press.
Kumar, V., and A. Gupta. 2022. AI for Customer Experience Enhancement. Proc. Int. Conf. AI Big Data.
Lee, J., and H. Lee. 2020. The Impact of AI on Customer Service: A Study of Chatbots. Serv. Ind. J., 40(5–6): 389–404.
Li, J., and Q. Wang. 2022. Deep Learning Approaches in Customer Service Automation. ACM Trans. Intell. Syst. Technol. 13(2): 45–60.
Li, M., and Y. Xu. 2020. Advances in AI for Customer Experience. Proc. IEEE Int. Conf. AI Data Sci.
Liu, Y., and X. Zhang. 2021. Machine Learning for Personalized Customer Interactions. J. Artif. Intell. Res. 70: 235–254.
McKinsey & Co. 2023. AI in Customer Experience: Trends and Predictions. McKinsey Insights Report.
Microsoft. 2023. AI Innovations in Retail: A Case Study on Customer Experience. Microsoft White Paper.
MIT Technol. Rev. 2024. AI-Powered Customer Service: Opportunities and Challenges. MIT Technol. Rev. Insights.
Nguyen, T. H., and Y. S. Kim. 2020. AI Techniques for Enhancing Customer Experience. IEEE Trans. Neural Netw. Learn. Syst., 31(6): 1884–1895.
Oracle. 2022. Customer Experience Transformation through AI: Insights and Case Studies. Oracle CX Insights Report.
Patel, S., and K. Gupta. 2023. AI Innovations in Customer Experience. Proc. Glob. AI Summit.
PwC. 2022. AI and the Customer Experience: Realizing the Potential. PwC Research Report.
Ransbotham, S., P. Kiron, D. LaFountain, and R. Khodabandeh. 2019. Competing in the Age of AI: Strategy and Leadership When Algorithms and Networks Run the World. Harvard Bus. Rev. Press.
Salesforce. 2021. AI-Driven Customer Success: A Case Study. Salesforce Research Report.
ServiceNow. 2023. AI-Powered Customer Service: Trends and Insights. ServiceNow White Paper.
Shapiro, C., and H. R. Varian. 1998. Information Rules: A Strategic Guide to the Network Economy. Harvard Bus. Rev. Press.
Singh, P., and R. Sharma. 2021. Leveraging AI for Personalized Customer Service. Proc. Annu. Conf. Artif. Intell.
TechCrunch. 2021. Innovations in AI for Customer Experience. TechCrunch Business Report.
Wall Street, J. 2023. How AI is Revolutionizing Customer Interactions. Wall Street J. Feature Article.
Zendesk. 2023. The Impact of AI on Customer Support: Real-World Examples. Zendesk Insights Report.
Zhang, W., and J. Huang. 2022. AI-Driven Customer Insights. Proc. AI Bus. Transform. Conf.
Zhang, X., and Y. Wang. 2019. Personalization in E-commerce: The Role of AI. Electron. Commer. Res. Appl., 34: 100–112.
Zhao, L., and Y. Zhang. 2022. AI Algorithms for Customer Sentiment Analysis. Pattern Recognit., 117: 107800.

Chapter 9

AI's Impact on the Future of Insurance Jobs

Automation vs. Human Expertise

L.G. Honey Singh[1,*] and *Amar Kumar Chaudhary*[2]

Introduction

Artificial Intelligence has turned out to be one of the major disruptors of the current era. With the rapid integration of AI in various fields, the traditional models of transactions in economy have seen a drastic change. Exhibiting the potential of replacing humans in industries, AI has become an integral part of the modern industries, with Insurance and allied sectors being the most intensely transformed sectors in the world economy. In Insurance, the integration of AI has reshaped the operational models of the business, and improved the risk management system as well as claims processing. This integration in the mainstream activities of the business has redefined the role of human expertise and requirement as well as efficiency in unprecedented ways.

Use of data analysis and predictive analysis has improved operational efficiencies and lead to personalised consumer experience for the customers. This transformative potential of AI is often why it is considered as the defining technology of the fourth industrial revolution. Traditionally, insurance industry was heavily reliant on the human

[1] Sarala Birla University, Ranchi, India.
[2] Associate Professor, Ranchi University, India.
* Corresponding author: honysngh23@gmail.com

DOI: 10.1201/9781003637301-9

expertise for risk assessment and nuanced decision making. However, with the shifting paradigm, this sector has adopted machine learning algorithms to assess risk profiles, integrated chatbots in the UI to address customer queries and Robotic Process Automation (RPA) to take over the repetitive tasks for operational efficiency and cost reduction.

Historically, the insurance industry has exhibited a great reliance on the humans due to the need for personal insights during the activities involving human interactions. For instance, underwriting requires assessing an applicant's risk level by examining his lifestyle factors, medical history, and other individual details requiring subjective judgement. Similarly, evaluating damage claims and claimant interactions often require empathy and ethical discretion, unique to humans. However, with the rapid development of AI, automation tools have been developed that have shown remarkable proficiency in performing these tasks. The AI algorithms analyze vast amounts of data quickly and identify patterns that might elude a human worker enabling insurance companies to automate substantial portions of underwriting and claims processes.

As Artificial Intelligence continues to penetrate the insurance industry, there has been an increasing rise in the concerns related to job displacements and unemployment. In studies conducted by World Economic Forum and McKinsey Global Institute, it was revealed that those jobs that had a routine and repetitive nature of work were more prone to be displaced by the automation revolution than others. This means the major threat of job displacement is faced by the entry level jobs in the industry. This displacement has been coined as "Technological Unemployment", and it poses a long term viability question on the jobs involving high-volume of data, including form processing and routine decision making tasks.

According to the 2019 report published by Deloitte, AI systems are capable of streamlining the procedures and minimise the manual intervention requirements. Therefore, insurers can leverage this technology to potentially reduce the labour costs by up to 30% over the next decade. This may result in potential loss of numerous entry-level and mid-level job roles in underwriting and claims processing.

While it is true that AI has the potential of replacing a number of routine jobs, it will not be prudent to erect barriers to its entry in the insurance sector. There is a need for hybrid approach that combines possibilities of AI with the human expertise to ensure the insurance industry sees the growth in the dynamic world. This study identifies the roles that have the potential to be replaced by AI and identifies the new job roles that will be generated due to the presence of this disruptor in the insurance sector.

Literature Review

Globally, artificial intelligence (AI) is changing sectors and becoming a disruptive force. Significant progress has been made in industries including healthcare, banking, and manufacturing as a result of its capacity to evaluate enormous information, spot patterns, and make judgments with little assistance from humans (Brynjolfsson and Mcafee, 2017; Agrawal et al., 2024).

AI enhances data analytics, improves risk assessment, and enables more accurate pricing (Kelley et al., 2018). It automates processes like claims handling, underwriting, and customer service through chatbots (Chaubey and Singh, 2020; Sanwal, 2021). AI technologies, including machine learning and natural language processing, are being applied to policy management, claim prediction, and risk estimation (Kolambe and Kaur, 2023). While AI adoption in insurance has been slower compared to other industries due to regulatory constraints, its potential to disrupt the sector is significant (Sanwal, 2021). AI-driven digital transformation is creating new opportunities for insurers, such as customizable life insurance and on-demand property coverage (Chaubey and Singh, 2020). However, the widespread implementation of AI may also lead to job displacement and potentially exacerbate social inequality, impacting both the insurance industry and its customers (Kelley et al., 2018). Studies prove that algorithms can analyze historical claim data and customer profiles to predict future risks and adjust premiums accordingly (Yang et al., 2023). NLP-powered chatbots and virtual assistants have improved customer engagement by providing instant query resolutions and streamlining onboarding processes (Zhang et al., 2020).

In a study conducted by (Zarifis et al., 2023), four different models were proposed which included outsourcing of AI driven functions to the specialists, integration of AI into existing operations, updating business models to align with AI advancements, finally, AI based firms increasing expansion into this sector. Reinforcement and transfer learning, Deep Learning (DL) and natural language processing, along with strong research skills of professionals in the insurance industry is needed to survive in the changing technology (Singh and Chivukula, 2020).

However, the use of AI is not lauded by all and critics believe that industry should adopt responsible AI and win the trust of customers, only then the changed updated model will be accepted. Study conducted by (Frey and Osborne, 2017) suggests that while automation improves operational efficiency, there is a looming threat of routine tasks jobs. Wilson and Daugherty (2018) believe that automation may be used in the jobs requiring large data processing and repetitive tasks, however, for the areas requiring ethical judgement, empathy, and creativity, human expertise still remains indispensable.

In India, a report of (NASSCOM, 2023) reveals that approximately 20% traditional insurance jobs are expected to be displaced by 2030, while new roles in technology development and AI oversights will be created to adapt to the new technology. Predictive models are developed to analyse historical as well as real time data, thereby identifying high-risk customers, forecast claim frequencies, and optimize resource allocation (Kanchetti, 2021). This frees up the human workforce to be engaged in more complex cases and strategic decision making.

Research by (Petrescu and Krishen, 2023) highlights that the hybrid models that combine human expertise with AI-driven insights are prone to outperform purely automated systems. There is a marked reduction in the demand for the roles of repetitive tasks of data entry clerk and claims adjusters (Chen et al., 2021). At the same time, there is a growing need for the professionals skilled in AI management, data science and digital transformation (World Economic Forum, 2020).

Though predictive analytics can reshape the insurance employment requirements, relying only on it is not recommended. Organizations investing in employee training programs are better equipped to harness the full potential of predictive analytics while mitigating workforce resistance to AI adoption (McKinsey, 2022).

Studies show that AI models trained on the biased datasets may unintentionally discriminate against certain demographics (Ferrara, 2024). This may lead to unfair pricing, and claim denials. This aspect is particularly of concern for countries like India, where socio-economic diversity necessitates inclusive and equitable insurance policies. Regulators and insurers both must give priority to ethical AI development, like algorithmic accountability, fostering transparency in AI decision making, and adhering to data protection laws of the country (Gupta et al., 2022).

Another factor impacting AI adoption in insurance sector is the regional differences. Developed economies like United States and Europe have advanced AI integration, driven by robust infrastructure and regulatory frameworks (BIS, 2024). In contrast, emerging markets like India faces challenges of limited digital infrastructure, limited digital penetration and skill shortages, hindering the widespread AI adoption (McKinsey, 2022). Despite these challenges, companies like Bajaj Allianz and HDFC Life gave implemented AI-powered tools for fraud detection, claims automation and customer personalization (IRDAI, 2021).

All these trends indicate a shift in the skills required for jobs in insurance, with greater emphasis on data literacy and technological proficiency. For adopting these changes, insurers will have to foster a culture of continuous learning and innovation (World Economic Forum, 2020). Analyzing the literature reviewed by the researcher, it is clear that AI has already made significant changes in the workforce of the insurance industry. However, there is limited literature on the transformative role of integrating AI and human expertise in shaping the future insurance jobs. This study aims to cover this gap in literature.

AI's Impact on Job Roles in Insurance

A number of cases of insurance companies were analyzed based on the reports published. They have been summarized below in Table 1. It is clear from analyzing these cases that AI has made an indelible mark on the insurance sector. Sector wide implementation of AI, chatbots and machine learning has made shifting towards technological changes easier and cost effective. As stated earlier, from the secondary data analyzed, the major job roles witnessing AI integration were found to be data heavy and repetitive in nature. This has created a space for insurers to cut the number of employees in the organisation.

In insurance, AI is automating customer facing process, improving claim efficiency and faster claims processing (Sanwal, 2021). The technology is shifting the insurance business model from loss compensation to loss prediction and prevention model, creating a potential for new revenue streams. Its impact is extending to the insurability of risks, potentially reducing asymmetric information problems and altering the risk landscape (Eling et al., 2021). As AI is continuing to evolve, it is very likely that it will affect every aspect of the insurance value chain.

Table 1 below shows the impact of AI on the job roles of Insurance sector, referencing the case studies discussed earlier:

Challenges of AI Driven Job Automation in Insurance

Though AI integration has enhanced the overall efficiency of the insurance sector, there are still a number of challenges that Indian demography and customers present to the Insurance sector. One of the challenges in implementing AI in insurance firms is resistance from the workforce, particularly among mid-career professionals who may lack technical skills. This section is also prone to rigidity where upskilling is concerned, especially in terms of technology. The employers will need comprehensive reskilling initiatives to smoothen the transition. Another challenge is that Indian insurance firms often operate with legacy IT systems that are not fully equipped for implementing advanced AI tools.

AI powered technologies, such as RPA, machine learning algorithms and NLP are automating functions like claims processing, underwriting and customer services. Roles requiring manual data entry or policy renewals may no longer require human intervention, leading to a potential loss of approximately 25% job roles.

Table 1: Impact of AI on Job Roles in Insurance Sector.

Case Study	Traditional Role	AI-Influenced Role	Human Displacement?
Nordic Insurance Company (EY Partnership)	Manual claims processing requiring human assessment of invoices, medical records, and photographs.	AI automates document analysis and anomaly detection, while humans handle exceptions and customer engagement.	No, roles transitioned to exception handling and customer service.
Allianz (Soft Skills Training)	Customer service agents handling all queries, often struggling with high call volumes.	AI chatbots manage routine inquiries, while human agents specialize in complex and emotionally sensitive cases.	No, employees are trained in soft skills to enhance customer interaction.
Liberty Mutual (AI Transition)	Underwriters and claims processors manually assessing large volumes of cases.	AI automates data analysis and anomaly detection; humans transition to AI trainers, data ethics specialists, and AI oversight roles.	No, job roles evolved rather than eliminated.
State Farm (AI Underwriting)	Actuaries and underwriters manually assessing risk and pricing policies based on historical data.	AI-driven risk assessment models automate policy pricing, while humans oversee AI decisions and manage regulatory compliance.	No, employees move into AI compliance and customer engagement roles.
Ping An (China) AI Expansion	Human analysts manually reviewing claims, medical records, and accident reports.	AI automates claims approvals, while employees transition into AI training, compliance, and optimization roles.	No, human expertise is integrated into AI management.
HDFC Ergo (Claims Automation)	Claims assessors manually verifying documentation and fraud detection.	AI analyzes claim submissions and detects fraud; humans intervene in complex or disputed cases.	No, employees shift to fraud investigation and high-value case assessments.
ICICI Lombard (AI-Driven Customer Service)	Customer service representatives handling all policy and claims-related queries.	AI chatbots handle routine queries; human agents manage high-priority and complex cases.	No, workforce redirected to strategic customer service roles.
Future Generali (REVA AI Assistant)	Call center agents manually handling high volumes of customer queries.	AI virtual assistant REVA manages policy renewals and queries, while humans oversee AI integration and escalation handling.	No, employees focus on strategic initiatives.
Tata AIG (AI in Fraud Detection)	Fraud detection teams manually reviewing claims for anomalies.	AI flags suspicious claims in real-time; humans conduct in-depth fraud investigations.	No, AI aids human expertise rather than replacing it.
Policybazaar (Predictive Analytics)	Agents manually assessing customer needs and recommending policies.	AI-driven predictive analytics personalize recommendations, while humans provide advisory and relationship management.	No, employees transition to interpreting AI insights and enhancing customer experience.

Another challenge faced is the integration of AI is generating demand for new skill sets. Employees must now be proficient in data analytics, AI management, and machine learning, along with traditional insurance knowledge. Communication and ethical reasoning skills are also essential, particularly for roles that require customer interaction and regulatory compliance. Actuaries are increasingly expected to possess programming skills in languages like Python and R to utilize AI-driven predictive analytics.

Although a number of institutions are addressing this demand by integrating special certification courses on AI and data analytics, there is still a significant disparity in the availability of such programs across different regions and organizational levels. Smaller insurance firms, especially in rural areas, often lack the resources to provide advanced training, exacerbating the skill gap.

The ethical use of AI in insurance jobs raises several concerns. Bias in AI algorithms can lead to discriminatory practices, such as denying claims or policies based on skewed data. AI systems trained on historical data may perpetuate biases present in previous underwriting decisions, adversely affecting marginalized communities.

Privacy is another critical issue. AI systems often require access to sensitive customer data, such as health records or financial information, to perform predictive analytics. Ensuring the secure handling of this data is paramount to maintaining customer trust.

The regulatory frameworks play a crucial role in seamless integration of AI into an organisation structure. However, in a country like India, this is not without its own set of difficulties. One of the challenges in regulating AI is determining accountability for errors or unethical outcomes. If an AI system denies a claim based on flawed logic, the responsibility for rectifying the error must be clearly defined. Human oversight is essential to ensure that AI systems operate within ethical and regulatory boundaries.

Table 2 summarizes the challenges faced as discussed earlier.

Hybrid Model is the Solution

The debate of Automation vs. Human Expertise is incomplete due to the indispensable role played by the humans and the challenges faced by complete AI integration. This gives rise to the idea of rather than thinking in terms of replacement, AI should be used as a complementary body to the existing employees, enabling them to focus better decision making. Companies looking for cost cutting may select the complete automation as a solution, but it is merely a short run solution. However, in the long run, AI creates a specialised and technologically adept workforce.

Table 2: Challenges in Implementing AI in Indian Insurance Sector.

Category	Challenges	Impact on Insurance Sector
Workforce Resistance	Mid-career professionals struggle with technical skills and resist upskilling in AI-related domains.	Slows AI adoption and creates skill gaps.
Job Displacement	Automation of manual tasks like data entry and policy renewals may lead to job losses, especially in rural areas.	Estimated 25% reduction in administrative roles.
Skill Gap	Employees need expertise in AI, data analytics, machine learning, and programming languages like Python and R.	Shortage of AI-trained professionals in insurance.
Legacy IT Infrastructure	Many Indian insurance firms operate on outdated systems that are incompatible with AI solutions.	Increases costs and delays AI implementation.
Training Disparity	Advanced AI training programs are not equally available across different regions and organizational levels.	Smaller firms, particularly in rural areas, struggle to upskill employees.
Ethical Bias in AI	AI models trained on historical data may reinforce discriminatory practices in underwriting and claims processing.	Risks unfair policy pricing and claim rejections for marginalized communities.
Data Privacy & Security	AI requires access to sensitive customer data (health, finance), increasing privacy and security concerns.	Regulatory non-compliance, risk of data breaches.
Regulatory Challenges	Unclear accountability in AI-driven decisions, such as claim denials due to flawed logic.	Need for stricter AI governance and human oversight.

Hybrid roles will merge the computational roles of AI with human cognitive and emotional strength to ensure that the best of both makes operational optimization possible. Recent research explores hybrid models combining AI and human expertise in insurance. AI/ML hybrid models can enhance fraud detection by integrating supervised and unsupervised learning, deep learning, and natural language processing (Saddi et al., 2023). Explainable AI (XAI) is gaining prominence in insurance, particularly in claims management, underwriting, and actuarial pricing, with simplification methods like knowledge distillation and rule extraction being primary techniques (Owens et al., 2022). The synergy between human and computational forecasts in hybrid predictive ensembles has been analyzed, highlighting the potential benefits of combining big data used by AI with the thick, narrative data used by humans (Hong et al., 2024).

Bork et al. (2023) proposed a hybrid human-AI model driven approach that makes use of DMN models to generate machine learning training data, which in turn will inform the human decision modelers of the important features in the original models. Human-AI combination, when adopted in call center services, proved to generate better results compared to human-only and AI-only models (Kahn et al., 2020). If a customer centric organisation is successful, then adopting this hybrid model in insurance also bodes well for the sector. Among the major roles in AI-Human hybrid models, AI risk analyst has become increasingly popular. Using machine learning models to assess and predict risk enables insurers to offer tailored policies, while human experts use AI generated insights to apply to unique market conditions, making the organization better equipped to tackle changing customer needs. In a study conducted by (Deloitte, 2021), it was found that hybrid roles in risk management improves underwriting accuracy by 25%, combining AI's computational power with human insights.

Another role being rapidly overtaken by these hybrid models are customer engagement. Here, the AI driven chatbots and voice assistants are tasked with handling routine customer enquiries, while the systems are coded to transfer the query in case of complex and emotionally charged interactions requiring human expertise. The use of a combination of technology and traditional human intervention has improved customer satisfaction by balancing between automation and empathy (McKinsey, 2022; Singh et al., 2024).

AI models are not capable of running the entire operations of insurer solely. The mechanical nature of AI algorithms ensures that no decision making is influenced by emotional factors. This necessitates the existence of a compliance officer, who oversees the AI systems, ensuring adherence to ethical and regulatory standards. These roles will require proficiency in both laws and AI system management. Collaborative Human-AI roles have the potential to increase the operational efficiency across the insurance sector to 35% by the year 2030 (Boston Consulting Group, 2022).

Therefore, hybrid roles represent a paradigm shift in the insurance sector, blending the computational prowess of AI with the cognitive and emotional strengths of human workforce. While challenges such as skill gaps and ethical concerns still persists, the benefits derived from these models are enough to underscore the viability of this model. Benefits such as enhanced efficiency, cost reduction, quick claim processing to improved customer experience, human judgement, experience and empathy have popularized the benefits of such hybrid models for insurance sector.

A structured overview of these evolving job roles and necessary skills is provided in Table 3 below. This framework highlights the key competencies required to remain relevant in an AI-driven insurance ecosystem.

Table 3: New Job Roles and Essential Skills in AI-Driven Insurance.

New Job Role	Description	Essential Skills Required
AI-Enabled Underwriters	Use AI-generated risk assessments to finalize complex underwriting decisions.	Data analysis, risk modeling, AI-tool proficiency, ethical decision-making.
AI-Assisted Claims Specialists	Work alongside AI systems to handle disputed claims, fraud detection, and complex cases.	Investigative analysis, legal knowledge, AI fraud-detection tools, empathy.
AI Compliance and Ethics Officers	Ensure AI applications in insurance comply with regulatory and ethical frameworks.	Regulatory compliance, AI governance, bias detection, ethical risk assessment.
AI-Integrated Fraud Analysts	Analyze AI-flagged suspicious activities and verify fraudulent claims.	Pattern recognition, cybersecurity knowledge, forensic accounting, AI fraud detection tools.
AI-Powered Customer Experience Managers	Oversee AI-generated insights to enhance customer engagement and satisfaction.	CRM software expertise, AI-driven sentiment analysis, communication, problem-solving.
Data Science and AI Engineers for Insurance	Develop and refine AI models for risk assessment, fraud detection, and automation.	Machine learning, programming (Python, R), insurance analytics, AI model interpretability.
AI Training and Change Management Specialists	Train employees on AI tools and manage workforce adaptation to AI integration.	Digital transformation strategies, human-AI interaction management, employee training methodologies.

By adopting these roles and developing the required skills, insurance professionals can ensure career resilience in an AI-enhanced industry. Rather than displacing jobs, AI is transforming traditional roles into more strategic and technology-driven functions, emphasizing the need for upskilling and continuous professional development. Organizations that proactively train their workforce for these hybrid roles will gain a competitive advantage in balancing automation with human expertise.

Discussion

The aim of this study was to identify the role AI pays in job displacement in the insurance sector. The secondary literature as well as the successful implementation of these models have proven why this integration is the need of the hour. With the rapidly advancing technology, all the sectors are expected to fulfil the technological and automation needs of the customers. The study proves that AI is a boon for the insurance sector.

However, sole reliance on AI models have seen to erode the trust of the customers, especially in sensitive matters. Hybrid approach leads to proper distribution of tasks, with routine and data heavy tasks, while humans are charged with handling emotionally sensitive matters and decision making.

From analyzing the cases from around the world, it is clear that insurance sector is in the midst of the transition. This transition needs to be adopted in a way that the company does not lose the trust of both customers and more importantly employees. The fear of employee retrenchment and being replaced by AI needs to be addressed by the companies. Insurance companies should focus their efforts to adopt AI in the value chain such that the specialised person is working on the tasks of their expertise, thereby cutting cost and increasing efficiency. This would remove the pressure from the insurance companies of being best in all the operational aspect and free them to focus their efforts in improving their core competencies. Adopting such a hybrid model elevates the fear of displacement from the employees while motivating them to upskill and reskill to adapt to the changing requirements.

Managerial & Theoretical Implications

The findings of this research offer actionable insights for managers and decision-makers in the insurance industry. As insurers integrate AI into their processes, managerial strategies must evolve to address both opportunities and challenges effectively. Managers must proactively design strategies to upskill employees, focusing on areas where human capabilities complement AI. Training programs should be tailored to equip employees with digital literacy, AI management, and interpersonal skills. Open communication channels and participatory decision-making can help employees feel valued and engaged in the transition process.

Theoretically, this study addresses the transformative impact of AI and the findings enrich theoretical frameworks on job redesign, human-AI collaboration, and ethical considerations in technology adoption. Theories of job design must evolve to incorporate this symbiosis, addressing factors such as task delegation, skill augmentation, and human oversight. There is a need for robust theoretical models for the collaborative framework and managing employees in the era of automation. Concepts such as "algorithmic justice" and "ethical AI governance" should be integrated into existing theories, providing a foundation for responsible innovation. Additionally, ethical considerations must extend beyond organizational boundaries, encompassing societal impacts and regulatory implications.

Limitations of the Study

- The study is based on the secondary data. Reliance on secondary sources for case studies may lead to biases.
- Findings may not be universally applicable due to variations in organizational maturity, technological infrastructure, and regulatory environments across regions and firms.
- The research does not account for upcoming AI models and their capabilities, which may alter job dynamics further.

Conclusion

AI has demonstrated remarkable efficiency in automating repetitive and data-intensive tasks such as claims processing, fraud detection, and underwriting. These applications significantly enhance speed, accuracy, and cost-effectiveness, enabling insurers to allocate resources to more strategic areas. However, human expertise remains indispensable in managing complex, judgment-intensive scenarios, building customer relationships, and addressing ethical considerations that require empathy and critical thinking.

The emergence of hybrid roles illustrates the synergy between human and AI capabilities. Employees are increasingly leveraging AI tools to augment decision-making, streamline workflows, and personalize customer interactions. However, trust remains a pivotal factor, emphasizing the need for transparency and accountability in AI-driven processes. Insurers must strike a delicate balance between automation and human intervention to maintain service quality and ethical standards. While AI creates new roles and opportunities, its potential to perpetuate workforce inequalities and widen the skill gap remains a pressing concern. Future research should examine the economic and psychological impacts of automation on employees, particularly in emerging markets where job security is paramount. Moreover, ethical considerations surrounding AI use in insurance merit continuous scrutiny. These include addressing biases in AI algorithms, ensuring data privacy, and defining accountability for AI-driven decisions.

References

Agrawal, A., J. S. Gans, and A. Goldfarb. 2024. Prediction machines, insurance, and protection: An alternative perspective on AI's role in production. J. Jpn. Int. Econ., 72: 101307.

Bork, D., S. J. Ali, and G. M. Dinev. 2023. AI-enhanced hybrid decision management. Bus. Inf. Syst. Eng., 65(2): 179–199.

Brynjolfsson, E., and A. Mcafee. 2017. Artificial intelligence, for real. Harvard Business Review, 1: 1–31.

Chaubey, A., and S. Singh. 2020. AI-enabled digital transformation of insurance industry. Commun. Appl. Electron., 7: 6–9.

Chen, C. L., Y. Y. Deng, W. J. Tsaur, C. T. Li, C. C. Lee, and C. M. Wu. 2021. A traceable online insurance claims system based on blockchain and smart contract technology. Sustainability, 13(16): 9386.

Chui, M., B. Hall, H. Mayhew, A. Singla, and A. Sukharevsky. 2022. The state of AI in 2022—and a half decade in review. McKinsey & Company. https://www.mckinsey.com/capabilities/quantumblack/our-insights/the-state-of-ai-in-2022-and-a-half-decade-in-review

Digitalizing Insurance: Indian End-Consumer Perspective. 2023. Nasscom. https://nasscom.in/knowledge-center/publications/digitalizing-insurance-indian-end-consumer-perspective

Eling, M., D. Nuessle, and J. Staubli. 2021. The impact of artificial intelligence along the insurance value chain and on the insurability of risks. Geneva Pap. Risk Insur., 47: 205–241.

Ferrara, E. 2024. Fairness and bias in artificial intelligence: A brief survey of sources, impacts, and mitigation strategies. Sci., 6(1): 3. https://doi.org/10.3390/sci6010003

Frey, C. B., and M. A. Osborne. 2017. The future of employment: How susceptible are jobs to computerisation? Technol. Forecast. Soc. Change, 114: 254–280.

Gupta, S., W. Ghardallou, D. K. Pandey, and G. P. Sahu. 2022. Artificial intelligence adoption in the insurance industry: Evidence using the technology–organization–environment framework. Res. Int. Bus. Finance, 63: 101757.

Hong, B., P. Lu, H. Xu, J. Lu, K. Lin, and F. Yang. 2024. Health insurance fraud detection based on multi-channel heterogeneous graph structure learning. Heliyon, 10(9).

Insurance Regulatory and Development Authority of India. 2021. Annual Report 2020–21. https://irdai.gov.in/documents/37343/366637/Annual+Report+2020-21.pdf

Kahn, L. H., O. Savas, A. Morrison, K. A. Shaffer, and L. Zapata. 2020. Modelling hybrid human–artificial intelligence cooperation: A call center customer service case study. Proc. IEEE Int. Conf. Big Data (Big Data), 3072–3075.

Kanchetti, D. 2021. Optimization of insurance claims management processes through the integration of predictive modeling and robotic process automation. Int. J. Comput. Appl., 2(2): 1–18.

Kelley, K. H., L. M. Fontanetta, M. Heintzman, and N. Pereira. 2018. Artificial intelligence: Implications for social inflation and insurance. Risk Manag. Insur. Rev., 21(3): 373–387.

Kolambe, S., and P. Kaur. 2023. Survey on insurance claim analysis using natural language processing and machine learning. Int. J. Recent Innov. Trends Comput. Commun., 11: 30–38.

KPMG. 2021. Harvey Nash/KPMG CIO Survey 2020: Insurance Insights. https://assets.kpmg.com/content/dam/kpmg/au/pdf/2021/harvey-nash-kpmg-cio-survey-2020-insurance.pdf

Owens, E., B. Sheehan, M. Mullins, M. Cunneen, J. Ressel, and G. Castignani. 2022. Explainable artificial intelligence (XAI) in insurance. Risks, 10(12): 230.

Petrescu, M., and A. S. Krishen. 2023. Hybrid intelligence: Human–AI collaboration in marketing analytics. J. Mark. Anal., 11(3): 263–274.

PricewaterhouseCoopers. 2023. Bridging gaps in the India insurance sector. PwC. https://www.pwc.in/research-and-insights-hub/bridging-gaps-in-the-india-insurance-sector.html

Saddi, V. R., B. Gnanapa, S. Boddu, and J. Logeshwaran. 2023. The role of natural language processing in detecting insurance fraud. In Proc. 2023 4th Int. Conf. Commun. Comput. Ind., 6.0 (C216), pp. 1–6. IEEE.

Sanwal, R. 2021. Impact of artificial intelligence on the insurance industry. In Applications of Artificial Intelligence in Business and Finance, pp. 203–219. Apple Academic Press.

Singh, G., R. Aggarwal, S. Kumar, S. Nagpa, and S. A. Dhondiyal. 2024. Role of AI in enhancing health insurance penetration in rural India. Int. Conf. Comput. Intell. Comput. Appl. (ICCICA), Samalkha, India, pp. 198–202.

Singh, S. K., and M. Chivukula. 2020. A commentary on the application of artificial intelligence in the insurance industry. Trends Artif. Intell., 4(1): 75–79.

State of the AI in India 2021. 2021. Deloitte India. https://www2.deloitte.com/in/en/pages/about-deloitte/articles/State-of-AI-in-India2021.html

The Future of Jobs Report 2020. 2020. World Economic Forum. https://www.weforum.org/publications/the-future-of-jobs-report-2020/

Wilson, H. J., and P. R. Daugherty. 2018. Collaborative intelligence: Humans and AI are joining forces. Harvard Business Review, 96(4): 114–123.

Yang, J., K. Chen, K. Ding, C. Na, and M. Wang. 2023. Auto insurance fraud detection with multimodal learning. Data Intell., 5(2): 388–412.

Zarifis, A., C. P. Holland, and A. Milne. 2023. Evaluating the impact of AI on insurance: The four emerging AI- and data-driven business models. Emerald Open Res., 1(1).

Zhang, J., Y. J. Oh, P. Lange, Z. Yu, and Y. Fukuoka. 2020. Artificial intelligence chatbot behavior change model for designing artificial intelligence chatbots to promote physical activity and a healthy diet. J. Med. Internet Res., 22(9): e22845.

Chapter 10

AI-powered Insurance

Navigating the Future of Risk Management

Charu Sharma,[1,*] *Isha Kansal*[2] and *Gifty Gupta*[2]

Introduction

The use of AI in insurance industries has become prominent, thus changing the traditional outlook of these businesses and offering possibilities for change in the ways risks are managed or services provided to clientele and ways operations can be improved. The adoption of AI technologies is beginning to redefine the insurance market by equipping firms with the data capabilities and helping these organizations to advance sophisticated systems and especially improve the response to consumer needs. Thus, AI in insurance captures a broad spectrum from machine learning algorithms that parse risk parameters all the way to natural language processing systems that improve client engagement (Ankita et al., 2023; Singh et al., 2024). These technologies are being used at underwriting and claims processing area, fraud detection, and in customer relations. The adoption of AI in insurance is driven by several factors:

- **Increased data availability:** The tremendous numbers of IoT devices together with the social networks and other platforms, generated enormous amounts of data which could be used in insurance.

[1] M.M. Engineering College, Maharishi Markandeshwar (Deemed to be University), Mullana, India.
[2] Chitkara University Institute of Engineering and Technology, Chitkara University, India. Emails: Isha.kansal@chitkara.edu.in; gifty.gupta@chitkara.edu.in
* Corresponding author: er.charusharma@gmail.com

DOI: 10.1201/9781003637301-10

- **Advancements in computing power:** With advancements in computer systems, it became possible to work on large dataset and get response within short span of time.
- **Customer expectations:** Today's consumers demand innovations within their engagements and they want personalized, efficient and digital experiences, all of which AI can provide.
- **Competitive pressures:** The situation where more and more new entrants from the field of insurtech startups and IT-giants appear in the market encourages the traditional insurance companies to develop new strategies to remain competitive.
- **Regulatory changes:** The status of some rules are becoming more liberal and adaptable in order to promote the use of AI in financial sectors, including the insurance business.

AI has diverse effects on the insurance sector that ranges from underwriting to pricing, tailoring customer services and processing of claims. Instruments built with AI can detect risks with better accuracy because of their ability to make sense of complicated patterns within the data to precisely and equitably price their insurance policies. In claims processing, AI can thus replace routine work, speed up evaluations and even better identify dubious claims (Tyagi et al., 2022; Adeyeri, 2024). The evolution of insurance models can be broadly categorized into several phases:

- **Pre-industrial era (before 1800s):** Primitive types of insurance that involved mutual aid societies and simple risk-sharing contracts.
- **Industrial revolution (1800s–1900s):** The evolution of modern insurance companies, the standard forms of insurance contracts, and the discipline of actuarial science.
- **Post-World War II era (1950s–1980s):** Adding new types of insurance, several degrees of regulation, and early computerization of operations insurance.
- **Digital age (1990s–2010s):** Development and implementation of online services, digital files and record keeping as well as early stages of data analysis.
- **AI era (2010s–present):** The adoption of artificial intelligence and machine learning in the insurance value chain.

The use of new-generation solutions instead of classical ones has become the primary shift of the insurance industry. Despite the general concept and purpose of distributed insurances have not changed, the method of evaluating risks, setting premiums, and servicing the customers are undergoing radical change (Tyagi et al., 2022; Zhang et al., 2023; Kasaraneni, 2024).

AI-Enabled Transformation in the Insurance Sector

There is a fast-growing trend of applying AI in the insurance industry that is driving changes in central business processes and generating new models of approaches to risk management, customer servicing, and increasing the rates of business performance. This is not a simple process of 'digitizing' current processes; it is about rethinking the insurance value proposition, delivering greater value to customers and members, and rejuvenating operating models. This section examines how precisely AI is disrupting these main sectors of the insurance market (Gurung, 2024).

AI's Role in Risk Assessment

In the insurance industry, AI is providing a revolutionary advancement in risk assessment process, thus providing new solutions to the insurers through better risk assessment that are more efficient and timelier. AI technologies can help insurers better underwrite risks, to improve claims handling and while providing a nicer touch to customers. Risk assessment is at the heart of the insurance business, and AI is dramatically enhancing insurers' capabilities in this crucial area (Kasaraneni, 2024). Figure 1 shows risk assessment in insurance industry.

- **Advanced Data Analytics:** The capabilities of AI are the ability to work with the creation, storage, processing and analysis of large amounts of structured and unstructured data, received from various sources such as social networks, IoT devices, satellite images and public registers. Such a broad risk evaluation is made possible by the analysis of multiple data sets.

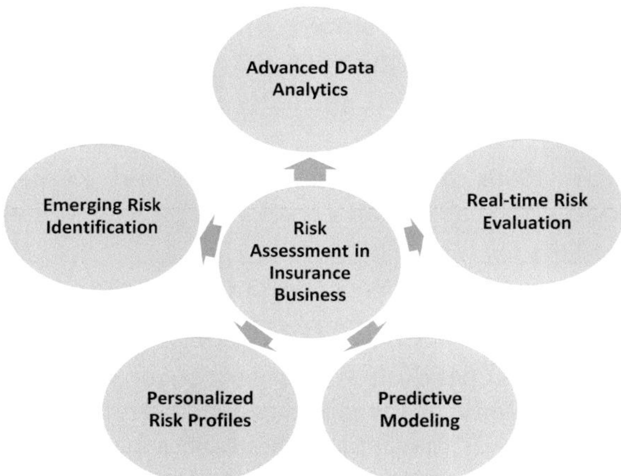

Fig. 1: Risk Assessment in Insurance Industry.

- **Real-time Risk Evaluation:** Real-time risk analysis makes it possible for insurance companies to adjust their risk portfolios and their premiums as per current conditions. For example, in auto insurance, AI can derive risky driving data from telematics and provide a real-time account of risk assessments.
- **Predictive Modeling:** Structured and unstructured data can be analyzed with machine learning algorithms which aim to find out more accurate risks in the future compared with the past patterns. This capability is especially useful in such fields as natural disaster risk assessment, where climate, geographical data and historical event data can be used to predict disasters.
- **Personalized Risk Profiles:** AI enables the design of unique risk personalities because many aspects peculiar to the policyholder are taken into account. This granular approach to risk assessment also affords a much finer degree of pricing and precise policy solutions.
- **Emerging Risk Identification:** AI systems contain the ability to analyze large databases from a diverse variety of sources to detect potential risks that may be missed by conventional techniques. It also makes it possible for insurers to keep up with new threats, and create adequate measures to respond to them.

Customer Service Enhancements

The application of AI in the insurance industry is helpful in changing the traditional methods of customer service delivery in insurance organizations that help policyholders to embrace satisfying experiences while using the insurance services. Here are some of the key ways AI is enhancing customer service in the insurance industry (Perumalsamy et al., 2023):

- **24/7 Availability through Chatbots and Virtual Assistants:** They can easily manage an enormous number of customer inquiries at any one time, answering frequently asked questions, policies and conditions, and claims status. These systems can learn from human and can also imitate natural language and thereby help can assist and get better with time.
- **Personalized Recommendations:** Due to its ability to mine and dissect data, AI can then prescribe the right products for a customer and the right coverage for them.
- **Proactive Customer Engagement:** AI is able to identify and estimate customer requirements, thus the insurance company can contact the customer with information, changes in policies or advice about

potential risks. All these make it possible to proactively approach the customers' needs hence making them happier and loyal.

- **Voice Analytics for Enhanced Support:** Using voice recognition technology, information about consumer feelings and plans based on customer complaints received through phone conversations can be obtained in real time. This technology can assist customer service representatives give more personalized and efficient support.
- **Omnichannel Customer Experience:** AI ensures that the multiple ways customers may engage with firms are consistent and compatible to foster good client experiences of the firms.

Operational Efficiencies

The insurance industry is in a transition era by availing AI technology. Insurers are achieving large process efficiencies by using AI for improving processes, quality of decisions and customer's experiences. AI is contributing to efficient delivery of insurance across multiple value phases. Embracing AI is not just a technological upgrade; it's a strategic imperative for insurers seeking to thrive in an increasingly digital world (Aziz, 2023):

- **Automated Underwriting:** Underwriting applications and other data such as medical history can be input into the system and the AI will use analysis to complete much of the underwriting quickly and accurately. Lender underwriting gets done faster and reduces variability in common-sense decisions.
- **Intelligent Document Processing:** Technology such as OCR and NLP available in AI can identify and interpret information from different documents including applications, claim forms and medical reports. This capability greatly minimizes the time spent to enter and process data manually.
- **Fraud Detection and Prevention**: The commonly used traditional statistical methods can be replaced with machine learning algorithms for precise and faster fraud detection from claims data. The former can alert the insurers to such doubtful claims in order to mitigate the fraud Related losses.
- **Predictive Maintenance:** In property insurance, AI can be of big help in analyzing the data from sensors of IoT and determine when maintenance is required so that costly damages or claims may not occur. The above approach is advantageous to both insurers as well as to the policy holders (Kumar and Kumar, 2024).
- **Resource Allocation Optimization:** With the help of the technology, it is possible to assign employees and resources also, for example,

claims adjuster during natural catastrophes, number of workers, and availability of employees during nights and weekends to service clients when they are more likely to call.

- **Advanced Analytics for Business Intelligence**: One of the major benefits that can result from the implementation of AI-based analytics tools is the ability of the insurer's management to glean as much information on all aspects of the insurer's activities, clients, and the market in general, as possible (La Barbera, 2023; Nukala, 2024).

AI-Powered Tools and Applications in Insurance

Insurance organizations continue to build initiatives using AI technology solutions in business processes and applications. These technologies are disruptive to the conventional insurance value chain whereby insurers are making better decisions, work more effectively, and offer better services to consumers (Aziz, 2023).

Predictive Modeling and Automation

The most predominant use or application of AI in insurance industries is in the areas of predictive modeling and automation (Perumalsamy et al., 2023).

- **Advanced Predictive Analytics:** Those that are implemented through the application of AI are based on machine learning, which helps to predict the outcome from the obtained data.
- **Automated Underwriting Systems:** Fully implemented AI based automated underwriting systems are capable of underwriting applications and sanctions in real-time.
- **Dynamic Pricing Models:** Real-time ability of the AI helps in the creation of premiums which vary with changing risk factors.
- **Chatbots and Virtual Assistants:** In handling of customer relations, AI such as AI chatbots and AI virtual personal assistants respond to inquiries and offer policy details as well as assist the customers walk through processes including claims submission.
- **Robotic Process Automation (RPA):** AI integrated RPA is particularly used to automate complex repetitive tasks in insurance operations.

Risk Identification and Underwriting Improvements

Insurance is all about risk and therefore risk identification and underwriting form the backbone of the insurance business. Over time, and especially with the help of AI and data analysis, these processes are changing in insurers. Risk analysis and underwriting has been virtually reinvented by applying AI, which enables insurers to make more precise assessments of risks and make improved decisions (Kasaraneni, 2024).

- **Advanced Risk Scoring:** Big data, structured and unstructured, is transformed, processed by AI algorithms creating richer risk profiles. This is information from social network accounts, smart appliances, aerial photography, and municipalities.
- **Behavioral Analysis:** Behavioral analytic tools in AI evaluate questionable applicant behavioral patterns and predict risks.
- **Fraud Detection in Underwriting:** Certain features that would indicate that an applicant is likely to defraud the system can also be learned by different machine learning algorithms.
- **Real-time Risk Assessment:** Real-time risk assessment is possible with the help of AI since data from multiple sources is processed regularly.
- **Automated Property Inspections:** Satellite or drone photo data can be analyzed based on using artificial intelligence to know the state of the property and threats.

Claims Processing

Claims processing is a vital area in insurance business, as it influences the company's customers, performance, and financial results. A conventional approach to claims processing as a rule implies a detailed check of documents, paper-based communication, and lengthened reaction time, which creates dissatisfaction among insurance companies and their clients. Specialized AI is redefining the claims processing environment by being able to process more claims, accurately and more quickly (Palakurti, 2024).

- **Automated Claims Intake:** Claim taking could also be done by AI-powered systems with the use of mobile apps, websites, or chatbots for the intake of claims. These systems employ NLP to interpret claim information and sort claims correctly.
- **Intelligent Document Processing:** Similar technologies such as OCR and NLP can not only find but parse through data as found in claims documents, medical reports, and police records. This automation reduces data input loads and increases the flow of the claims process significantly.
- **Fraud Detection in Claims:** Predictive coding techniques used in Mining for patterns that are most likely to point to frauds and scams from the claim data. Such systems can alert auditors when certain claims are made and thus cut losses through fraudulent activities.

- **Automated Damage Assessment:** In auto and property insurance application like computer vision, can help in estimation of repair costs basing on images or videos. This "technological implementation" can within a period of time give estimates, which would help enhance the speed of processing and attendance to claims.
- **Predictive Claims Modeling:** The AI models can identify what the claims end result could be, whether it is likely to go to trial, if it is likely to be subrogated or how much is expected to be paid in a settlement. This information is useful for insurers to better control reserves, and improve the claims administration process.
- **Smart Claims Routing:** By utilizing AI systems, claims can undergo decision making on which adjuster is most suitable to handle specific claim type and workload. This enhances efficiency and the right personnel work on the claims.
- **Virtual Claims Adjusting:** With a virtual adjusting tool, the policyholders can make claims and present evidence through artificial intelligence. These tools can help users to complete the specific documentation on damage, and there is no need for an inspection on site.
- **Sentiment Analysis in Claims Handling:** Through text mining, AI can review the communications of customers during the claims process to determine the level of satisfaction or discontent that a certain policy is causing. This will enable the insurers to have the opportunity of solving customer complaints that may be pending and increase satisfaction (Srabon and Saxena, 2023).

Data-Driven Personalization and Dynamic Pricing Within Insurance Industry

Insurance is a field going through major changes due to the fact that huge volumes of data and superior business analytics can be applied. This section looks at how insurers are capturing data from different sources such as the IoT, social media, and real time monitoring to develop customized insurance products and flexible pricing structures (Kumar and Kumar, 2024).

Use of IoT, Social Media and Real-Time Data

The insurance industry is moving towards a new generation of Insurance 4.0 leveraging IoT devices, social media and real time data analytics.

- **Social Media Data:** Insurance companies follow big data activity tracking in social media platforms to develop an understanding of the lifestyle, which activities are associated with risk taking, and life events that may help to define insurance requirements. Many marketing departments find this data valuable for evaluating risk profiles and tuning marketing messages.

- **IoT Devices:** Telematic devices installed in vehicles capture information on driving habits such as speeds, brake use, and distances. Personal health technologies monitor one's effects and serve as useful information for life and health insurance companies.
- **Real-Time Monitoring Systems:** The weather monitoring system gives current information on the possible dangers in the environment. Traffic surveillance systems provide information on the current state of the traffic and areas that more accidents usually happen.
- **Public Records and Third-Party Data:** Insurance companies then supplement this data by data from public records, credit reports and third-party data sources to gain a better understanding of prospects and clients.
- **Customer Interaction Data:** Sales interactions that occur through internet, mobile application, call centre and other points of contact reveal customer's traits and patterns.

Personalized Insurance Products

Individual insurance solutions are slowly but steadily turning into one of the key drivers of present-day insurance markets. It has become important to cater for these needs because as the consumers become wiser and as technology take its toll on insurers, customized coverage programs have emerged (Althati and Konidena, 2023).

- **Usage-Based Insurance (UBI):** In auto insurance, UBI policies determine the insurance premium based on actual usage of the car instead of demographic details.
- **Behavior-Based Health Insurance:** For this reason, the sequence of health and life insurers is to leverage data from the wearable's to reward good behavior.
- **Micro-Insurance and On-Demand Coverage:** Real-time needs are met using short term, specific coverage options that are provided by the insurers. Such include travel insurance triggered by geographical location or products such as expensive items in the policy, where the coverage is based on the frequency of utilization.
- **Parametric Insurance:** These products release compensation according to specific rules or conditions and not losses, standard examples include; crop insurance that pays out if it rains to a certain level.

- **Lifestyle-Based Packages:** Carriers form packages that reflect lifestyle niches, offering insurance coverage that appeals to buyers as derived from comprehensive information about their customers.
- **Predictive Life Insurance:** This personalization of insurance policies is achieved by undertaking analyses organized from health data, life style and genetic predisposition information to foresee the likelyhood of particular diseases or conditions thereby profiting from tailored premium rates.
- **Cyber Insurance Customization:** Cyber insurance policies are developed unique to an organization's online presence, current security system measures put in place, as well as the susceptibility of the business to cyber risks.

Dynamic Pricing Models

Finally, one of the most crucial strategies in the insurance sector is dynamic pricing which enables insurers to set premiums depending on current information, as well as customer's risk factors (Kuna et al., 2023; Madasamy, 2022).

- **Real-Time Risk Assessment:** Premiums may fluctuate depending on existing risk factors for instance meteorological conditions for property owners in this line of insurance or traffic density for cars in auto insurance.
- **Behavioral Pricing:** Flowing from this is the fact that the policyholder rates are dynamic in that they go up and down depending on the policyholder's risk profiles; safer activities are therefore encouraged by the insurance pricing mechanism.
- **Demand-Based Pricing:** Automated tools work with received information about the consumers' needs and possible threats from competitors to set appropriate prices.
- **Predictive Pricing:** The risk levels of products and services in the future can be predicted by using machine learning models and prices can be modified accordingly.
- **Personalized Discount Structures:** Dynamic models set up unique discount rates that are determined by the risk levels as well as the tendencies of the specific customer (Layn, 2024).
- **Micro-Duration Pricing:** Even the price can be adjusted for very short durations, so that one can have fully flexible and responsive insurance goods and services.

- **Multi-Factor Dynamic Pricing:** Unlike conventional models, AI models analyze a number of dynamic variables (such as behavior price or market conditions or any other condition that might exist) and come up with the best price that need to be given to the products.

Insurance is in the middle of a revolution which encompasses data driven individualization and flexibility in pricing strategies as a result of technological and analytical developments. Through marketing data, insurers offer suitable products to its policy holders while at the same time adjusting the price structure to fit everyone. Customer appreciates this formulation and on the other hand it facilitates better risk management and higher returns. Figure 2 the key benefits of implementing data-driven personalization and dynamic pricing in insurance are discussed (Madasamy, 2022).

- **Improved Risk Assessment:** Better assessment of the risk presentation of every candidate promotes more objective pricing and improved risk management for insurance companies.
- **Enhanced Customer Experience:** Custom products and services delivery to the customer is likely to improve on customer satisfaction hence the loyalty.
- **Increased Market Penetration:** It is therefore found that the concept of product modification can captivate the otherwise untapped markets.

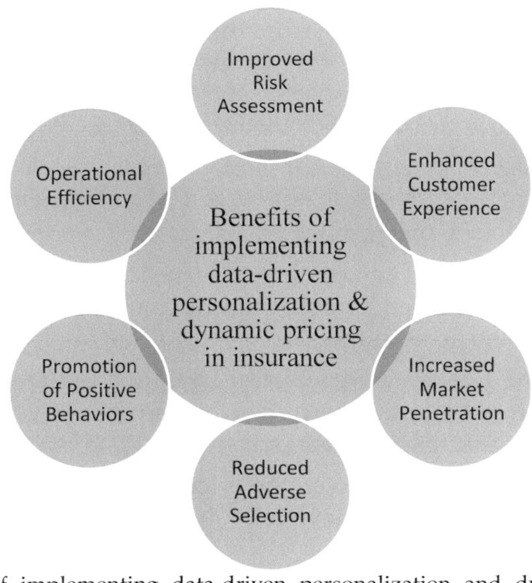

Fig. 2: Benefits of implementing data-driven personalization and dynamic pricing in insurance.

- **Reduced Adverse Selection:** Higher risk differentiation ensures that the insurers do not book disproportionately risky customers.
- **Promotion of Positive Behaviors:** Time varying prices may promote the adoption of the better practices and healthy behaviors.
- **Operational Efficiency:** It also helps to minimize the numerous tasks that are related to the administrative work thus helping in slashing of costs and enhancing the speed at which new products are brought to the market.

It is only a matter of time as the insurance market becomes more complex and the process of risk assessment becomes more accurate and detailed, and the concept of insurance as the sale of individual quotes for an agreed period will gradually turn from a dream into reality. There are possible evolution trends, such as micro-segmentation, expansion into related environments, and reinforcement learning to improve pricing models (Layn, 2024).

Challenges in AI Adoption Within the Insurance Industry

Despite the highly promising prospects AI has when is come to revolutionizing the insurance industry, the technology is far from perfect. This section looks at some of the most appropriate challenges that insurers need to overcome when deploying AI solutions, with an emphasis on data protection issues or privacy, AI accountability, and legal and ethical obstacles (Shasha, 2023).

Data Privacy Concerns

There is a need for insurance industries to ensure their AI systems are security first, follow the law in their country, and regularly check their systems for leaks. As AI systems require vast amounts of data to function effectively, this raises significant privacy concerns:

- **Data Collection and Consent:** Originally, insurers need to admit to obtaining informed consent of the raw data collection and utilization in the frameworks of AI systems.
- **Data Security:** As the collected data become more and more extensive and contain sensitive information, insurers are in greater danger of cyber threats.
- **Data Sharing and Third-Party Access:** AI needs data transfer between different systems or between different organizations making data ownership and control an issue. Insurers must make sure that using data follows laws like GDPR and CCPA.

- **Data Minimization:** AI models are served by more data sometimes, but privacy principles encourage going with the least level of data. Meet the demands of these fairly conflicting requirements properly is not an easy task.
- **Right to be Forgotten:** Upright such as the General Data Protection Regulation or GDPR guarantee a person's right to data erasure that cannot be easily integrated into the learned AI models.
- **Transparency in Data Usage:** This is particularly important because the use of personal data in machine learning and AI systems is not always easy to describe in detailed due to the often-multilayered nature of such systems.

Responsible AI Decision-Making

For the integrity of the AI profession, it is vital that AI is being used responsibly as much as possible. As AI takes on a more significant role in decision-making processes, ensuring these decisions are made responsibly becomes crucial:

- **Algorithmic Bias:** Machine learning algorithms of AI programs can replicate or even magnify prejudice existing in the presented data. It will be crucial for insurers to keep working on bias in their models lest they end up discriminating against some of their customers.
- **Explainability and Interpretability:** Some of the architectures of most current complex AI models especially the deep learning systems are often referred to as 'black boxes', hence their decision-making mechanisms are hard to justify.
- **Human Oversight:** Deciding how much human intervention should be applied to the handling of an autonomous AI system is not easy.
- **Accountability:** With the actual or potential increase in the degree of decision-making left to the application of AI, corresponding concerns arise as to who is accountable for decisions—the AI application, its creators, or the insurer utilizing it.
- **Ethical Decision-Making Frameworks:** It is important to understand that constructing accurate ethical guidelines in regard to AI decision-making process, which would reflect such a company's values and the general population's expectations, is a challenging process.
- **Handling Edge Cases:** AI shall fail to handle some exceptional situations which were never experienced by the AI during the data collection. Insurers definitely require effective guidelines on how to go about the same.

Regulatory and Ethical Hurdles

The insurance industry is heavily regulated, and the adoption of AI introduces new regulatory and ethical challenges:

- **Regulatory Compliance:** AI systems must meet current regulatory requirements of insurance organizations, which often can pose a problem, as these requirements were initially created without taking AI systems into consideration.
- **Ethical Use of AI:** To address the uncertainty problem, insurers need to consider other ethical questions about how to use AI like whether social media data can be used in risk assessment.
- **Model Governance:** Though transparency is now mostly used to talk about the methodology of AI models, there is growing pressure about how these models are built, and how they are verified and maintained as well.
- **Regulatory Uncertainty:** This uncertainty is posed by the fact that there is still relatively much ambiguity regarding regulation of AI in insurance.
- **Liability Issues:** As we see increasing numbers of AI systems used in decision-making processes, we start to consider who is at fault when a mistake occurs. The legal implementation of AI responsibility is not well defined and clear and this causes a lot of concern among insurers (Madasamy, 2022; Kapil and Scholar, 2024; Yu et al., 2024).

Building Trust in AI: Transparency, Fairness, and Innovation With In Insurance Industry

The potential of AI, for risk assessment, claim automation and customized services is almost inexhaustible; however, there must be solutions for the privacy, fairness and creativity issues for trust to prevail. AI transparency is crucial to both regulators and customers of the emerging technology. Insurance firms have to make sure that the results which emanate out of AI are easily understandable by people. The created AI models need to have explainable recommendations in the solutions they offer because customers must have confidence in these processes, while regulators can guarantee ethicality.

Importance of Trust in AI-Powered Systems

One of the critical success factors for the expansion of AI in insurance is trust. Due to the rising centrality of AI in important underwriting, claims, fraud, and customer service, its integrity requires insurer, regulators, or policyholder trust now more than before. Here are several reasons why trust in AI-powered systems is vital for the insurance industry (Madasamy, 2022):

- **Customer Acceptance:** To build that level of confidence, customers have to believe that the AI systems that are being used to make fair decisions about the policies, premiums and claims are being fair.
- **Regulatory Compliance:** There is growing concern for the reliability of the systems in the financial industry especially in insurance where artificial intelligence is now widely adopted.
- **Ethical Considerations:** Engagement with artificial intelligence systems also invites trust in ethical matters, that is, that these systems do not reproduce or even amplify bias or unfairness.
- **Long-term Viability:** However, for AI to operate in insurance in the long run, all stakeholders, from customers to regulators, employees and partners need to trust AI applications.

Transparency in AI Models

A major reason for the need for transparency in models is to develop trust in the insurance market. Despite the fact that more and more applications of AI are used in decision-making processes with regard to underwriting, claims, and fraud recognition, it is crucial for customers and regulators to know how these decisions have been made:

- **Explainable AI (XAI):** Design and proceed with the implementation of models with explainable AI. Employ a technique such as LIME (Local Interpretable Model-agnostic Explanations) or SHAP (SHapley Additive explanations) to get human understandable explanation from black box models.
- **Model Documentation:** Documentation of AI models should involve details such as model's function, data input, training process and used techniques and model constraints.
- **Decision Traceability:** Put into place proper controls that will enable a specific determination of the data and rules by which an AI comes to a certain decision. It is important for audit checks, resolution of disputes, and for improving the AI systems on line.
- **Algorithmic Impact Assessments:** Carry out and report on the feasibility of the effect of the AI systems on the following individuals. These assessments should provide an insight into intended affects as well as possible other effects.

- **Open Communication:** Here, there is a need to inform and engage customers regarding the application of AI hence the call to educate customers on such matters when it comes to their insurance products and service.

Fairness in AI Models

All these aspects raise fairness as a paramount consideration that surrounds the use of AI models in the insurance field. Since there is an ever-growing trend of using AI to make decisions regarding premium pricing, claims estimation and risk estimation, it's crucial to make sure that the model in place is free from bias. By addressing fairness proactively, insurers can build customer trust, ensure regulatory compliance, and foster an ethical AI ecosystem:

- **Bias Detection and Mitigation:** Farther, developing effective methods of recognizing and preventing bias in the algorithms used for creating AI systems. Specific techniques in dealing with biases include; Adversarial debiasing and reweighting.
- **Diverse Training Data:** It is therefore important that the training data used to teach AI models is inclusive of all the population of that model will be serving. Minimally, there should be routinely conducted assessments of the type and nature of the training data with a view of checking its currency and validity.
- **Fairness Metrics:** Explain and track the right metrics of fairness for AI models whether it is demographic parity or equality, equalized odds, or individual fairness. These are the aspects of fairness for which model performance should be assessed on a regular basis.
- **Human Oversight:** Use human supervision for AI decisions especially in critical and/or personal decisions. There should be clear process on when an AI decision will be questioned and who will provide the next level of decision after leaving that decision to AI.
- **Inclusive Design:** Ensure injection in the manner that varies personnel into the design and development of the AI systems. Think about users and their requirements at the time of design.

Balancing Innovation with Accountability

As the insurance industry experiences digital transformation at a high pace, artificial intelligence promises significant innovations including smarter processes, enhanced customer interactions, precise risk evaluation, and effective fraud detection. However, these advantages bring the obligation to ensure responsible implementation. Striking the right balance between innovation and accountability is essential for maintaining trust, ensuring regulatory compliance, and fostering sustainable growth in the insurance sector. This framework should provide clear structure for the development and deployment of AI solutions across the organization. Supporting this, organizations need explicit ethical guidelines that align with contemporary standards and legal provisions. These guidelines create guardrails for AI development while allowing creativity to flourish (Althati and Konidena, 2023; Josyula, 2024).

Continuous learning represents another critical component, as AI systems require ongoing monitoring and refinement. Designing feedback loops enables incremental improvements based on real-world performance data. When ethical considerations and trust-building elements are incorporated into performance metrics, teams naturally prioritize these aspects alongside technical capabilities (Aziz, 2023).

Implementation strategies include:

- Establishing an AI ethics board with diverse representation
- Publishing regular transparency reports
- Developing customer education programs
- Providing comprehensive employee training
- Conducting independent third-party audits
- Creating systematic feedback mechanisms

Several challenges warrant attention during implementation. Finding the right balance between transparency and intellectual property protection requires careful consideration. Regulatory alignment demands vigilance as frameworks for AI governance continue to evolve. The technical complexity of interpreting sophisticated "black box" AI systems presents ongoing research challenges. When insurers truly understand AI's possibilities while acting with transparency and fairness, they can develop systems that deliver business value while building credibility with consumers, regulators, and the broader community. As AI increasingly transforms insurance operations, trust will become an ever more critical differentiator, with forward-thinking insurers setting the standard for the industry's future.

Conclusion

In this chapter, we elaborate how and where AI fits into changing the insurance industry, increasing efficiency and pleasing customers, or even repositioning the concept of risk. A wide set of new software solutions based on AI technologies including predictive analytics, dynamic pricing and automation are building new paradigms in underwriting, claims and fraud detection segments. As for IoT and social media, AI allows insurers to develop a unique product based on customer's risk profile combined with immediate adjustments in pricing, called dynamic pricing. In underwriting, besides improving accuracy in risk prediction also underwriters are able to view risks in a more proactive manner. Paramount to the use of AI systems, future risks like climate change risks or cyber risks can be predicted using patterns derived from real time data. The dynamics in assessments of risk portrayed here are not only enhancing ways in underwriting but also moving insurance quotation and policies towards more precision and differentiation. AI's influence is also inexplicable in customer service where organizations have invested in chats, virtual assistants who offer general service, responding to inquiries and handling claims round the clock. This has enhanced and shortens the response time and save customer's time in the various and upcoming processes to tackle with. Some risks too much attention that needs to be paid include ethical risks, including data privacy, algorithmic bias and model transparency. Insurers need to make AI systems easy to interpret by other people and conforming to equity and regulatory standards to be acceptable to the customer and the authorities. Another issue is the question of how to include AI into pre-existing architectures; another is the problem of the cost of integration and the last the question of how to overcome organizational culture.

References

Adeyeri, T. B. 2024. Economic impacts of AI-driven automation in financial services. 12(07): 6779–6791. doi: 10.18535/ijsrm/v12i07.em07.

Althati, C., and B. K. Konidena. 2023. Enhancing life insurance risk models with AI: Predictive analytics, data integration, and real-world applications. J. Artif. Intell. Res. Appl., 3(2): 448–485.

Ankita, S., I. Mittal, I. Sharma, and A. Kumar. 2023. A report: Machine learning and its applications. Intell. Comput. Control Eng. Bus. Syst. (ICCEBS 2023), pp. 1–6. doi: 10.1109/ICCEBS58601.2023.10448693.

Aziz, L. A. 2023. The role of artificial intelligence in modern banking: An exploration of AI-driven approaches for enhanced fraud prevention, risk management, and regulatory compliance. 6(1): 110–132.

Gurung, A. 2024. Transformative ability of artificial intelligence in risk management.

Josyula, H. P. 2024. The fintech revolution: AI's role in disrupting traditional banking. 8(1): 243–256.

Kapil, D., and G. Scholar. 2024. Advancements in risk management software for dealers and brokers: Latest technologies and methodologies in risk management software development. Preprints, 2024. doi: 10.20944/preprints202404.1872.v1.

Kasaraneni, B. P. 2024. Advanced artificial intelligence techniques for predictive analytics in life insurance: Enhancing risk assessment and pricing accuracy. 5: 547–587.

Kasaraneni, R. K. 2024. AI-enhanced claims processing in insurance: Automation and efficiency. 5: 669–705.

Kumar, A., and L. Kumar. 2024. Navigating the future: The ethical, societal and technological implications of artificial intelligence. Glob. J. Res. Eng. Comput. Sci. 4(2): 83–104. doi: 10.5281/zenodo.10966785.

Kuna, S. S., I. Researcher, and S. Developer. 2023. AI-powered techniques for claims triage in property insurance: Models, tools, and real-world applications. 1(1): 208–243.

La Barbera, S. 2023. Insurtech revolution in the insurance sector: A comprehensive review of the transformational impact and the Lemonade case study. Preprints, 2023. doi: 10.20944/preprints202307.

Layn, B. 2024. Artificial intelligence in finance: Transforming decision-making and risk management for enhanced financial outcomes. Available at: https://scholarworks.uark.edu/finnuht/124.

Madasamy, S. 2022. Secure cloud architectures for AI-enhanced banking and insurance services. Int. Res. J. Mod. Eng. Technol., May 2022. doi: 10.56726/IRJMETS22745.

Nukala, V. 2024. Emerging technologies and their potential impact on Guidewire's. 15(5): 237–248.

Palakurti, N. R. 2024. The intersection of information technology, financial services, and risk management, including AI and ML innovations. ResearchGate.net, August 2024. doi: 10.5281/zenodo.13361616.

Perumalsamy, J., C. Althati, L. Shanmugam, and T. C. Services. 2023. Advanced AI and machine learning techniques for predictive analytics in annuity products: Enhancing risk assessment and pricing accuracy. 2(2): 51–82.

Shasha, Z. 2023. The impact of digital transformation on the insurance business model and innovative opportunities. Financ. Eng. Risk Manag, 6(11): 121–126. doi: 10.23977/ferm.2023.061117.

Singh, G., R. Aggarwal, S. Kumar, S. Nagpa, and S. A. Dhondiyal. 2024. Role of AI in enhancing health insurance penetration in rural India. Int. Conf. Comput. Intell. Comput. Appl. (ICCICA), Samalkha, India, pp. 198–202.

Srabon, S. and C. Saxena. 2023. Artificial intelligence and blockchain technology in insurance business. June 2023. doi: 10.1007/978-981-99-0601-76.

Tyagi, S., T. Jindal, S. H. Krishna, S. M. Hassen, S. K. Shukla, and C. Kaur. 2022. Comparative analysis of artificial intelligence and its powered technologies applications in the finance sector. Proc. 5th Int. Conf. Contemp. Comput. Informatics (IC3I 2022), pp. 260–264. doi: 10.1109/IC3I56241.2022.10073077.

Yu, J., Y. Yu, X. Wang, Y. Lin, M. Yang, Y. Qiao et al. 2024. The Shadow of Fraud: The Emerging Danger of AI-Powered Social Engineering and its Possible Cure. 14(8): 1–22.

Zhang, W., J. Shi, X. Wang, and H. Wynn. 2023. AI-powered decision-making in facilitating insurance claim dispute resolution. Ann. Oper. Res. 2023. doi: 10.1007/s10479-023-05631-9.

Chapter 11

Future Trends and Innovations in AI

Powered Insurance

Reena Thakur,[1,*] *Nischal Puri*[2] and *Pradnya Borkar*[3]

Introduction

The Insurance industry is a very important part of the worldwide economy, as it helps to provide financial protection against any losses due to unforeseen events to individuals and businesses. Insurance industry is constantly striving hard to provide quality services, a variety of products ranging from Health insurance, Life insurance, general insurance and more. As technology is improving day by day for providing an improved customer experience and innovation using data driven solutions.

Recent explosion of data and innovations in Artificial Intelligence (AI) is helping businesses to grow and their engagement with their customers. AI encapsulates various machine learning techniques and advanced algorithms to analyze the data, automate processes and make intelligent predictive decisions. AI has potential from underwriting the policies, customer engagement, claim processing, risk management and its analysis. Using AI, insurance costs can be reduced, operations can be streamlined, and efficiency of insurance companies will be increased (Omotayo et al., 2024; Tereszkiewicz and Południak-Gierz, 2021).

[1] Jhulelal Institute of Technology, Nagpur, India.
[2] Assistant Professor in Dept. of CSE (Data Science), St. Vincent Pallotti College of Engg and Tech., Nagpur, India. Email: nischalspuri@gmail.com
[3] Symbiosis Institute of Technology, Nagpur, India. Email: pradnyaborkar2@gmail.com
* Corresponding author: rina151174@gmail.com

DOI: 10.1201/9781003637301-11

This chapter keeps a bird eye view on how AI and its multifaceted technology helps Insurance industries through designing tailor made products offers, customer engagement, Medical or health Insurance. Also, we discuss other aspects like fraud detections, predicting individual needs, preparing tailor made solutions using customer's data. AI-driven technologies help insurance companies to establish deep connections with the customers. Ultimately this will lead to satisfaction among customers, increased loyalty and finally the success of business. Further chapter discusses challenges, technologies involved in brief, future opportunities. Other aspects will be discussed in next section of chapter (as shown in Fig. 1).

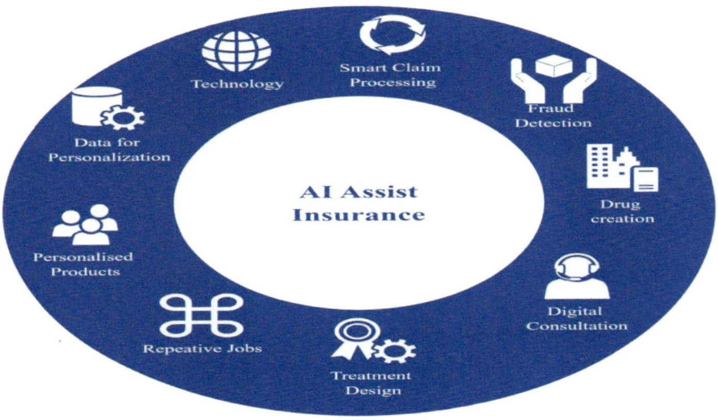

Fig. 1: AI assisting the insurance industry.

Customer Engagement and Designing of Tailor-Made Products

Mostly the insurance industry works on age-wise or group-wise data. So they design the insurance product as per major chunk in population. Traditionally policies are like one-size-fits for all based on factors like lifestyle, past behavioral patterns and preferences. Tailor-made insurance products are more personalized offerings that are prepared to cater to the person-specific needs, risk profiles and individual preferences (Tereszkiewicz and Południak-Gierz, 2021). Such type of engagement will ultimately increase the brand value satisfaction and loyalty among the customer by offering solutions in line with customer's unique requirements.

Machine Learning algorithms help insurance companies to analyze the large volumes of customer data. This will help to detect trends, patterns and correlations compared to traditional one-size-fits for all approaches. Using Historical data ML algorithms can predict more accurately and suggest recommendations. This will allow the companies to design personalized services and products. Based on historical data we can forecast events in the future and its outcome by using predictive analytics and various statistical models. In consideration for the insurance sector using predictive analytics there is a huge scope for detecting losses, claims and assessing customer's usage patterns. Insurers can redefine the offerings in order to mitigate the risks and increase customer satisfaction. NLP, i.e., Natural Language Processing is another dimension of machine learning which can assist the computers to understand the emotions, polarity generated in textual statements for human language. In today's world, people are constantly posting their feedback, viewpoints, reviews and suggestions on Online social networking sites, discussion forums, chats, microblogging websites etc. Due to this there is continuous generation of textual data and to study these data we use NLP. In the context of the insurance industry there is a need of an hour to extract insights from such type of unstructured data. NLP assists systems to detect trends, preferences, customer's sentiment which eventually helps, provide customers personalized offerings and communications accordingly. Further, now-a-days Virtual Assistants and Chatbots are quite robust enough to mimic human conversation to provide automated support and assistance for the customer. This Virtual assistant and chatbots are providing assistance for providing information, answering the queries and guiding them during the digital customer on boarding process, etc., thus ultimately engaging the customer.

By using the NLP and ML capabilities insurance companies offer personalized suggestions, smooth interactions and improve the whole customer experience to the next level. AI driven prediction and analyzing the data, companies can understand their customer behavior in a better way. Using this data companies can prepare the individual's policy plans, their costing plans, model the policy and its features help to target the customer which leads to higher customer satisfaction and retention rate. By using predictive analytics and ML technologies, companies can assist to assess risk profile, underwriting the policy processes and insurance plans costing accordingly. This will ensure faith, transparency and mutual trust among the customers.

By leveraging data-driven customization, companies can offer Personalized offerings and suggestions. Moreover, this will ensure that customers receive correct and timely solutions, This will again boost the business, provide higher levels of customer satisfaction and loyalty (Khatri, 2023; Singh et al., 2024). In short, AI-driven customization will transform the insurance sector by enabling better tailor-made services and products that will cater dynamic needs of customers. And helps ultimately grow the business and provide competitiveness in the market (Ayaz et al., 2023).

Using Data for Customization

Personalization and customization are the words which can be used in place of each other. The Internet of Things (IoT) is also one of the reasons for the explosion of data. Due to various sensors that are available in a variety of devices from home to health wearable devices and automotive devices like dashcam, car driving monitor etc helps assess the customer behavioral patterns. Companies can use this data to mitigate risks, better policy offerings, provide incentive to good behavior and habits. Apart from this, social networking sites also provide insights about their customer's behavior, their visits, life events, preferences and lifestyle etc. (Dian et al., 2020). This will help companies to leverage the data to examine the risks associated, offer personalized insurance, and provide incentive for good behaviors that can mitigate the risk (Khatri, 2023). Historical data regarding the claims contains past information about the insurance claims, which includes the incidents type, amount claims, frequency and outcomes. By analyzing these data, companies can detect patterns, find trends, and factors involved in risk, this allows companies to examine the risk profile of individuals and customize the product offering accordingly. While examining data for customization and offering various benefits, companies have to consider ethical issues involved like data privacy, its usage and customer's consent. Companies must fulfill compliance, provide data protection during the collection of data. Also, companies need to intimate the customers regarding the usage, collection and sharing data transparently (Olukoya, 2022). Moreover, companies need to provide fair and unbiased decision-making in data-driven processes to avoid potential discrimination and help to build trust among consumers.

Enhancing Consumer Engagement through Customization

By analyzing the data of customers and interpreting their preferences, their unique requirements, companies can suggest products relevant to the requirement, policy features and coverage options that cater the specific requisite. Let's discuss some case studies in order to use AI for providing Insurance products. In this first study insurance companies dealing in Health products can create specific products according to the needs of customers. To evaluate this, insurer will analyze their personal data generated from lifestyle information, health devices, EHR (Electronic Health Records), personal preferences and risks. The insurer will gain insights about customers and create plans. Also using such plans, insurers can create plans that provide incentive to healthy behavior like nutritious diet, preventive care and regular exercise. Such wellness plans will not only improve the engagement of customers but also reduce costs related to health risk. Next case study is, insurance for cars, due to advancement in various devices powered with AI technologies attached with cars that can generate data. This data can be leveraged to predict driving behavior, speed braking, acceleration and car's economy. Using this data, companies can assess the driving risks and provide customized suggestions. The customer with good driving habits will get incentive. Such a program will promote safer roads, lower claims and reduced accidents.

Applications of AI in Healthcare

The healthcare industry produces a huge amount of information in terms of patient, disease, new examinations, disclosures, etc. With the help of AI and its data analytics insurance companies can rewrite the policies for a major chunk of the population. Companies can predict the health movement of the population to provide excellent healthcare facilities and services (Ramesh, 2022).

Doing Repetitive Jobs

In the Healthcare sector the jobs are repetitive and can be automated using robots. They can take care of X-rays, MRI's, CT scans and perform test analysis more faster and accurately. This will reduce the burden from radiology and cardiology which required significant time to review the data. Such robots can be helpful for insurance companies for assessing the patient risk profile.

Digital Consultation and Treatment Design

Digital consultation can be very helpful for early detection and early prevention. Nowadays automated health services designed with the help of AI and data driven services can create effective treatment plans. This will organize the treatment and track the effectiveness of therapies. (AI) can assess the early signs of health issues on the basis of symptoms. Additionally AI can use X-rays, MRI's and CT scans. This helps in faster diagnostics, and provides faster treatment design. Such an initiative will improve mortality and help to reduce insurance claims beforehand. Additionally, the information available on public platforms will help many physicians for assessing personalized treatment plans.

Data Ownership Rights

Data ownership and privacy is a big concern in today's world. Nowadays customers are available on multiple apps, services and websites. Personal data ownership is a myth in the growing importance of big data. Data sharing of customer data should be solely the right of the owner. Also companies should reveal the mandatory terms and conditions promptly.

Companies should follow all the compliance and regulation before using the customer data. This will increase the trust and loyalty of customers. There are few challenges in successful implementation of data ownership as many contracts of data exchange are not transparent and do not follow complete privacy regulation for any secondary usage of data. Furthermore, when a service provider holds any data it is their intellectual property rights, so it is difficult to differentiate personal data and company data.

Smart Claim Processing with AI

The usage of artificial intelligence (AI) and machine learning (ML) used to solve how to claim traditional insurance processing in the following manner: The technology has smart analytics, case-specific analytics model which improves correct prediction. This type of technology also reduces the influence of false alerts and, to which the loss results. AI and ML together process several data sets to sense false or ambiguous claims. AI in the security business has improved the claims of the board cycle by making it faster, improved, and less error inclined. AI innovations can be used by Back up plans in the associated ways to more voluntarily oversee claims:

a. Work with a continuous answer-question session administration for a first warning with respect to losing.
b. Pre-survey claims can be done while automating the harm valuation process.
c. Automate claims exaction acknowledgment through rich data examination.
d. Antedate examples of claim volume.
e. Increases misfortune search.

AI-chatbots can be used to work on the running status of claims management that needs different representatives. Artificial intelligence-powered touchless protection claim processing has the potential to eliminate needless human intervention. It is also capable of reporting the claim, detecting damage, updating the framework, and communicating directly with the customer. Customers will be able to submit claims in an issue motorway because of this. Before providing wire instructions to the bank to pay for claim settlement, AI-controlled chatbots used in claim management can audit the claim, verify strategy specifics, and run it through the misrepresentation discovery calculation. As a result, claims with typical paperwork are vulnerable to AI bot audits, which will restrict human efforts.

This will not only reduce the workforce that the insurance company needs, but it will also provide immediate client support. AI-automated protection, claim management can also help organizations avoid fraudulent claims, human error, and serious errors in identifying information designs in claim reports. Even while the digitization of protection necessitates AI-powered customer experience throughout, automating claims can add significant value for executives.

AI automation of decisions that claims controllers often will make increase client loyalty and ensure error-free outcomes. Claims handling done brilliantly using AI can predict the characteristics of claims—AI is capable of inducing attributes of claims that are currently unknown, such as the likelihood of extortion, total loss, or lawsuit. With the latest developments in artificial intelligence (AI) and image recognition, auto insurance companies can continuously assess a car's damage value at First Notice of Loss (FNOL). Advances in AI have been causing a shift in the corporate community's viewpoint. AI is being used in claims management in a number of ways, including as automated self-administration guidance, photo recognition, and harm assessment.

Innovative thinking is enabling organizations to automatically identify extortion and resolve claims efficiently. Ingenious automation of current workflows also seeks to increase process effectiveness, improve customer experience, and reduce the amount of time and resources spent managing or tracking claims. Rapid improvements in AI will bring about unsettling shifts in the security industry. Businesses that embrace cutting-edge technology will flood the market with innovative products, knowledge-boosting bits of information, streamlined procedures, and more.

AI-Powered Fraud Detection

The prevalence of false claims, which have the potential to result in enormous financial losses, is perhaps the hardest thing to deal with in the protection industry as shown in Figure 2. AI is a game-changer when it comes to solving this problem. Using its sophisticated pattern recognition skills, AI quickly sorts through large datasets to find odd or inconsistent patterns in claim submissions. After that, these warning signs are marked for additional examination by human specialists. Insurance businesses may proactively identify and address any fraud by utilizing AI, which guarantees that genuine claims are handled quickly while dubious ones are carefully investigated. This not only protects the company's financial stability but also ensures that actual policyholders won't be inconvenienced by increased premiums as a result of the actions of a couple.

Every nation takes medical insurance fraud seriously, and the patterns of forged behavior differ depending on the circumstances. Every country has several kinds of health insurance frauds, involving several participants. This fraud is primarily being committed by three parties. First, providers of healthcare services, including physicians, hospitals,

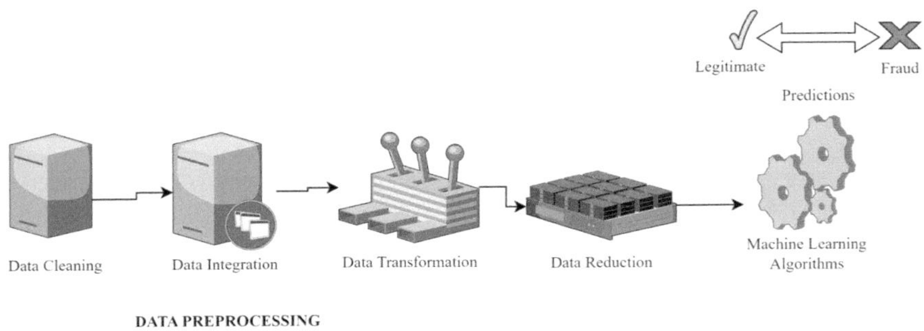

Fig. 2: Fraud Detection at Data Analytical Layer.

ambulance services, and labs. Subscribing patients and their employers is the second. The third is fraud committed by HI providers, which encompasses both the public and private sectors of insurance (Richman, 2021).

Fraud is a serious issue that has plagued every industry for many years. The new method was always utilized by con artists to perpetrate fraud. Healthcare fraud can result in significant losses for people, companies, organizations, and governments. Additionally, it is estimated that frauds within the US Medicare system cost between $600 and $850 billion annually, with faked actions within the system accounting for an additional $125 to $175 billion of the overall loss.

AI methods have shown to be an effective tool for identifying HIC fraud. The HIC fraud detection system is automated by AI. Recent research indicates that the primary application of AI has been in HIC fraud detection, utilizing a variety of ML, deep learning, and data mining algorithms (Khezr et al., 2019). To find abnormalities and identify fraud, behavioral profiling techniques based on machine learning techniques are employed. Each person's behavior pattern is modeled for this reason in order to keep an eye out for any deviations from the norm (Duman and Sagiroglu, 2017). supervised learning, unsupervised learning, and semi-supervised learning are the three types of machine learning approaches utilized in HIC fraud detection (Duman and Sagiroglu, 2017). Using a collection of previously identified fraudulent and authentic records, the supervised learning technique in HIC fraud detection operates.

These documents are used to identify fraud trends and construct the model. The primary advantage of the supervised learning approach is the ease of comprehension of the categorization results it produces. HIC fraud detection employs a variety of classification and supervised learning regression analysis algorithms. Supervised learning techniques such as neural networks, SVM, decision trees, Bayesian approaches, statistical analysis, graph analysis, and rule-based systems are employed to detect HIC frauds (Settipalli and Gangadharan, 2021; Verma et al., 2020). Supervised learning includes numerous disadvantages in addition to advantages. It is difficult to generate and collect data for supervised learning approaches. Data labeling can be challenging if the HIC dataset is quite large. It can be challenging to distinguish between labels in fraud data when they are vague and unclear (Duman and Sagiroglu, 2017).

These limitations can make the deployment of supervised learning difficult in some situations. Unsupervised learning can assist in resolving these supervised learning restrictions. From the unlabeled HIC datasets, unsupervised learning approaches detect the fraudulent behaviors of HIC. One advantage of HIC fraud detection with unsupervised learning is that tagged data is not required (Duman and Sagiroglu, 2017). When tagged data is not available, HIC fraud detection uses unsupervised learning. HIC fraud detection uses a variety of unsupervised learning approaches, including k-means clustering, k-nearest neighbor, data mining, association rules mining, and others. Benefits from both supervised and unsupervised learning can be obtained by semi-supervised learning.

In situations when there are fewer labeled data available than unlabelled data, hybrid semi-supervised learning techniques are employed. In semi-supervised learning, both labeled and unlabeled data are used to build a predictive model (Duman and Sagiroglu, 2017). HIC fraud detection often uses combined clustering and classification as a semi-supervised learning technique.

Blockchain

In Hawaii, security is one of the main issues. To some extent, current centralized systems offer security, but they are vulnerable to malfunctions or malevolent attacks. Blockchain technology, which is a decentralized network, can assist resolve this problem. The concept of blockchain was first identified in Satoshi Nakamoto's proposal for the bitcoin virtual currency. A digital ledger of transactions kept in a series of blocks is called a blockchain (Reebadiya et al., 2021). Each block contains the following information: a timestamp, block header, block number, version, nonce, and transaction data, as well as a cryptographic hash of the preceding block. The format of transaction data is kept as a Merkle tree (Nasir et al., 2022).

If any of the transactions within a block on a blockchain are changed or modified, the hash value of that specific block will vary significantly. It further disrupts the blockchain's block chain, making it easier to identify the altered transaction. Therefore, once a transaction is added to the blockchain, it cannot be removed or changed. Data on the blockchain is therefore unchangeable. To ensure integrity, security, and immutability, each transaction has been digitally signed using a private key and asymmetric cryptography (Nasir et al., 2022). The signing entity can only be authenticated by the owner of the public key.

The transaction data cannot be altered thanks to these signatures (Shah et al., 2021). The single point of failure issue is resolved by the decentralized, peer-to-peer nature of the blockchain communication network. Blockchain resolves disputes between nodes in a distributed application through a consensus procedure as opposed to a central authority (Nasir et al., 2022). Blockchain networks employ a consensus system to guarantee dependability and credibility.

Some of the Key AI Technologies used in the Insurance Industry Include as Shown in Figure 3

Natural Language Processing (NLP)

NLP gives machines the ability to understand and interpret human language. NLP is used in the insurance industry for many tasks, such as analyzing emails, contract reports, claims structures, and consumer demands. It facilitates the automation of procedures linked to sentiment analysis, language translation, and information extraction, which enhances communication and minimizes manual labor.

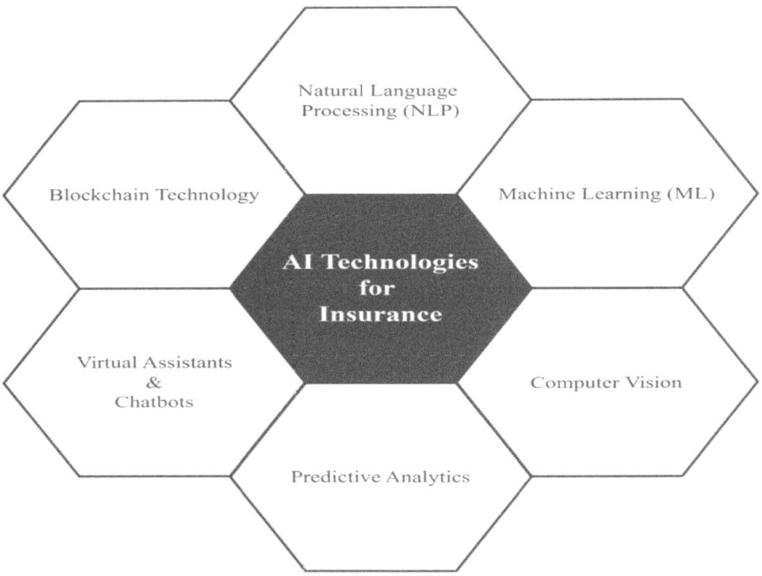

Fig. 3: Enhancing Insurance Operations Through AI Technologies.

Machine Learning (ML)

Machine learning computations enable models to learn from data and make predictions or decisions without explicit programming. Machine learning (ML) is used in the insurance industry for a number of functions, such as underwriting, claims processing, fraud detection, and risk assessment. ML models may identify examples, patterns, and inconsistencies to support dynamic processes by analyzing historical data.

Computer Vision

The development of PC vision technology enables computers to analyze and research visual data from images or videos. Computer vision is used in insurance to perform tasks including damage assessment, automobile appraisal, and property inspection. Insurance companies may evaluate claims more quickly, accurately estimate damages, and expedite the processing of claims with the use of AI-powered conversational specialists who converse or text with customers. They are sent for contract requests, client administration, and claims assistance in the insurance industry. Chatbots enable self-service choices, respond to consumer enquiries right away, and raise customer satisfaction levels all around.

Predictive Analytics

The recent development in algorithms will help predict predictiveness in a more robust way. Data driven technologies help to get more insights from customer data and help to predict behavioral patterns to make policy decisions.

Blockchain Technology

Blockchain technology enables decentralized, changeless records that facilitate simple, safe record-keeping. Blockchain is used in insurance to handle operations including fraud prevention, claims settlement, and policy administration. By creating openness and confidence among stakeholders, it improves data security, lowers the chance of fraud, and expedites cross-border transactions.

Insurance companies may increase policyholder services, streamline decision-making procedures, and modernize their operations by utilizing these AI technologies.

Case Study of Labeled Data for Healthcare Domain

The implementation of a good AI model depends on the quality of labeled data. As per (Label Your Data, 2025) for success of any AI algorithm the data should be properly labeled. To extract the valuable insights from the data, the AI model should be robust and error free. To achieve this, annotation of data must be an important topic. This will upscale the data which will be given as input to the AI model and this will generate precise results which will ultimately improve the operation efficiency of any business. An AI consulting company Mobidev experience this in their real world experience like Hospitality industry, Manufacturing and Healthcare industries. Here we will discuss the Healthcare case where a Welltech startup company is using an AI driven model for a rehabilitation program for their customer. This can be used for the customers of insurance companies as well to apply.

In this human body certain points are landmarks or key points. The goal is to create an AI service for rehabilitation programs by scanning the human image, marking the key points, detect the same with ideal key points and suggest the required measures like exercise, routine, etc. The general open source algorithms that can detect pose are not that efficient as this requires more domain specific information like position of toes or other critical information for suggestion of appropriate theory. For this we need additional labeled data for upskilling the performance of Algorithms which will help in customer satisfaction.

Cytora is an insurtech company for enhancing insurance underwriting with the help of Machine Learning and AI. Cytora created a proprietary algorithm for the identification and detection of risk by analyzing the claim likelihood and its severity (Appinventiv, 2025). Thus, the integration of AI and machine learning into the business will improve the overall competence and success of the insurance underwriting process.

In Asian countries like India, Thailand, Singapore, the drivers, delivery partners, food delivery partners and other freelance roles have seen rapid growth. This combined economy is called the Gig Economy (Twimbit, 2025). There are many challenges in providing financial and insurance services to such workers. So Grab Financial, a subsidiary of Grab, uses the platform data, ride volume, customer rating, activity levels, and transaction histories to provide insurance to gig workers. This data along with Machine learning and AI will help Grab Financial to assess the workers capability and offer them formal insurance and loans. This identification of risk, claim likelihood using machine learning and AI helps Grab Financial to offer financial products like personal loans, microloans, and insurance to its growing base of gig economy workers.

Conclusion

This chapter focuses on AI, ML and its predictive analysis impact on the insurance industry. From the last few decades, a drastic advancement is seen in the world of Artificial Intelligence and Machine Learning not only in a particular field but nearly all the fields. It has fully transformed the world. Thus, it is serving an automated pathway leading to a positive future. But it may be prone to disadvantages if not used correctly. It is costly too, unemployment, difficult to manage, etc. So, along with the advantages of ML and AI, it also can be dangerous if not used properly.

Thus we have tried to touch the multiple dimensions of AI powered insurance. With the ever growing and explosion of data AI powered insurance industry will be a game changer in next decade. So leveraging the technologies is the need of hour. The industry should take advantage of data driven technologies for a competitive environment and amalgamate them with flow. Personalized services and plans will help the insurance industry to build trust and companionship with their customers. This data will also make the customer aware about the risk-reward perspective. Also this will improve their overall health, driving and other behavioral patterns. Due to advancement in image processing the claim processing is becoming contact less and speedup the overall processing. Due to data-driven machine learning algorithms it will become easy for the industry to underwrite policy plans, design products and detect frauds.

Thus the industry should be ready for the challenges and changes. Data ownership is a big concern in this entire process. The customer should not feel cheated and disheartened else this will eventually take the customer away from the current company. The industry should have the ethical and acceptable norms to follow data compliance regulations.

References

Appinventiv. 2025. AI in Insurance. Available at: https://appinventiv.com/blog/ai-in-insurance/.

Ayaz, M., T. Sharma, and S. H. Rao. 2023. Disruptive artificial intelligence (AI) use-cases in insurance. AIP Conf. Proc., 2782(1).

Dian, F. J., R. Vahidnia, and A. Rahmati. 2020. Wearables and the Internet of Things (IoT), applications, opportunities, and challenges: A survey. IEEE Access, 8: 69200–69211.

Duman, E. A., and S. Sagiroglu. 2017. Heath care fraud detection methods and new approaches. Proc. Int. Conf. Comput. Sci. Eng. (UBMK): 839–844.

Khatri, M. R. 2023. Integration of natural language processing, self-service platforms, predictive maintenance, and prescriptive analytics for cost reduction, personalization, and real-time insights customer service and operational efficiency. Int. J. Inf. Cybersecur., 7(9): 1–30.

Khezr, S., A. Yassine, and R. Benlamri. 2019. Blockchain technology in healthcare: A comprehensive review and directions for future research. Appl. Sci., 9(9): 1736.

Label Your Data. 2025. Data labeling use cases. Available at: https://labelyourdata.com/articles/data-labeling-use-cases.

Nasir, M. H., J. Arshad, M. M. Khan, M. Fatima, K. Salah, R. Jayaraman et al. 2022. Scalable blockchains—A systematic review. Future Gener. Comput. Syst., 126: 136–162.

Olukoya, O. 2022. Assessing frameworks for eliciting privacy & security requirements from laws and regulations. Comput. Secur., 117: 102697.

Omotayo, B., C. Chinwe, C. Onyeka, O. Olubusola, A. Wilhelmina, and O. Adeola. 2024. Integrating Artificial Intelligence in Personalized Insurance Products: A pathway to enhanced customer engagement. Int. J. Manag. Entrep. Res., 6(3): 502–511.

Ramesh, C. A. K. 2022. AI Behind The Wheel: Innovations in Auto Insurance and Healthcare. Int. Neurourol. J., 26(4): 30–36.

Reebadiya, D., T. Rathod, R. Gupta, S. Tanwar, N. Kumar. 2021. Blockchain-based secure and intelligent sensing scheme for autonomous vehicles activity tracking beyond 5G networks. Peer Peer Netw. Appl., 14(5): 2757–2774.

Richman, R. 2021. AI in actuarial science – a review of recent advances – part 1. Ann. Actuar. Sci., 15(2): 207–229.

Settipalli, L., and G. R. Gangadharan. 2021. Healthcare fraud detection using primitive sub peer group analysis. Concurrency Comput. Pract. Exper., 33(23): e6275.

Shah, J., S. Agarwal, A. Shukla, S. Tanwar, S. Tyagi, N. Kumar et al. 2021. Blockchain-based scheme for the mobile number portability. J. Inf. Secur. Appl., 58: 102764.

Singh, G., R. Aggarwal, S. Kumar, S. Nagpa, and S. A. Dhondiyal. 2024. Role of AI in enhancing health insurance penetration in rural India. Int. Conf. Comput. Intell. Comput. Appl. (ICCICA), Samalkha, India, pp. 198–202.

Tereszkiewicz, P., and K. Południak-Gierz. 2021. Liability for incorrect client personalization in the distribution of consumer insurance. Risks, 9(5): 83.

Tereszkiewicz, P., and K. Południak-Gierz. 2021. Liability for incorrect client personalization in the distribution of consumer insurance. Risks, 9: 83. https://doi.org/10.3390/risks9050083.

Twimbit. 2025. Reimagining Credit with AI. Available at: https://cdn.twimbit.com/uploads/2025/01/10140233/Reimagining-Credit-with-AI-1.pdf.

Verma, C., V. Stoffova, Z. Illes, S. Tanwar, N. Kumar et al. 2020. Machine learning-based student's native place identification for real-time. IEEE Access, 8: 130840–130854.

Index